FOR NOBLE PURPOSES

The Autobiography of
RICHARD PORTER
Surgeon and Evangelist

Compiled and Edited by
William Porter

MOORLEY'S Print & Publishing

ISBN 0 86071 594 9

© Copyright 2005

British Library Cataloguing in Publication Data.
A catalogue record for this book is available
from the British Library.

MOORLEY'S Print & Publishing
23 Park Rd., Ilkeston, Derbys DE7 5DA
✂⊃   Tel/Fax: (0115) 932 0643   ⊂✂

CONTENTS

FOREWORD

This is the story of a man who was both a skilled orthopaedic surgeon, highly respected in the medical world, and a devout Christian, involved in preaching, evangelism and discipling believers in local churches and through his international travels. He was also a loving husband, father, grandfather and friend.

Richard writes in a very readable style. These memoirs take us through innocent childhood years in the Second World War, travels around the globe, family anecdotes, the development of a medical career and exciting research, a profound spiritual journey, and wonderful stories of people met and lives changed.

Richard was in some ways a quiet man but with great motivation. By his Christian example and visionary outlook on life, he influenced many. He was full of ideas and a heart of love, and tried to faithfully follow His Lord.

Richard was married to Christine for 41 years. Their sons, Daniel, William, Matthew & James, their wives and 11 grandchildren are all testimony to Richard and Christine's loving example and gentle witness to Christ.

This book will make an enjoyable browse for those who knew Richard well, and a fascinating read for those who will know him better through the pages of this autobiography.

William Porter

INTRODUCTION

They say that writing about oneself is not to be recommended. There is usually a bias of which the author is ignorant. On the other hand, it is remembered experience. I was there, and what happened - the facts - should be accurate even if the interpretation is at fault. So here goes. We begin at the beginning.

I was born with a sense of good fortune, surrounded by love – a feeling of belonging, knowing the blessing of many good things, I also knew the source of my good fortune and that I was a debtor to grace. For as long as I can remember, I have wanted to know, worship and serve the God who made the Universe. This has been my lifetime ambition, and I guess it becomes apparent in this book. Whether or not I have been successful, I cannot judge.

BEGINNINGS

1. A winter's Saturday

It was lunchtime on a very cold winter's Saturday, with snow flakes falling in the rain, when I first opened my eyes, took in a deep breath and gave my first raucous cry - 16th of February 1935.

Dr Halcolm was at the bedside, and had been assisted by Dorothy the maid. I was wrapped in a clean towel and placed in my mother's arms. "Sorry it was so difficult, Mary," he said, returning his obstetric instruments to his Gladstone bag, "but this little fellow has such a big head!"

I have had to live with that opinion ever since.

When my father, Luther, heard the first cry of his small son, he was on his knees in the living room below. He was a man of prayer, but he told me later that the delay had made him anxious.

"Thank you Lord," he said.

He knew that his prayers had been answered. He raced up to stairs two at a time, to reach the bedside.

"And thank you Mary". He looked at his son for some time and held Mary's hand. "What shall we call the little man? All right, Richard William it is".

When Luther was asked the same question by the Registrar a few days later, he said, "Richard – that's the name of his paternal great-grandpa, the Rev Richard Brooke, and William – is the name of his grandpa Porter. So it's Richard William, William's first grandson."

2. The Porter roots

I discovered that my genes came from both sides of the Pennines, from the rugged eastern slopes of Yorkshire, where the Porters had their roots, and from the gentler inclines of Lancashire, where the Field family had blossomed. They discovered each other in Luther and Mary.

Seventy years before, in the 1850's, Benjamin Porter (dob 28.04.1822) was a foreman at the Barnsley Gas Works. He married Ann Robinson (dob 13.04.1823) and when still in his 30's he came home from work with some good news.

"Anne, how would you like to move to Skelmanthorpe?"

Benjamin had been offered the manager's post at the new gasworks fifteen miles to the west of Barnsley.

"And there's a house with the job," he said.

A baby was on the way, and Anne knew that her man deserved promotion. Little did she know that their decision would mean a radical change of life, affecting many generations to come.

In the 1850's the wind of the Methodist revival was sweeping like a summer storm down the slopes of the Pennines, and through the rugged Yorkshire valleys. In Skelmanthorpe, Benjamin and Anne were exposed to Primitive Methodist preaching, the like of which they had not heard before, and they became converts.

Their two little boys, George (dob 17.10.1854) and William (dob 02.01.1858), were born into this exciting, dangerous and unpredictable world. There was a high infant mortality rate, and although their brother Joseph (dob 23.11.1861) died in early life, George and William and their young sister Ann (dob 19.06.1860) were survivors.

Their family life was focused on the chapel, with its three Sunday services and Sunday School. There were prayer meetings on Monday and Friday and a class meeting in Anne's home on Thursday. They shared in a pony and trap to visit neighbouring chapels for teas and outings, and from time to time the church gathered by the riverside to pray for the community. They enjoyed the noisy and lively love feasts which rang with testimony, song, prayer and laughter. In addition, their busy year was peppered with a sacred round of baptisms, weddings and funerals. These were heady times, when all the chapels in the valleys experienced conversions and remarkable growth. It did not matter if their windows were sometimes broken and that they were mocked as "ranters."

The three little Porter children developed in the disciplined life of the village school, and in the parochial experience of the village. Their books, which have been passed down the generations, suggest that from an early age they developed a love for literature, poetry and English history and Primitive Methodism.

I was frequently reminded when I was a child, that there had been a near tragedy, when one night George and William had mischievously climbed to the top of the large gas container. The two boys raced round its perimeter walkway, and William's foot slipped and he fell into the water of the float. Had he surfaced into the gas on the wrong side of the water seal, this story would not be written.

However, disaster came to the Porter household when early in life, Anne became a widow. Benjamin died, still a young man, and Anne was left alone to bring up two young boys and her little girl. However, she was a strong and resourceful woman, and she converted her small front room into a shop for the sale of homemade bread.

This was at the height of the Industrial Revolution, and everyone was ambitious. The Methodists also had a strong work ethic.
"What can we boys do Mother?"
George had seen someone in the next village making nails.
"We could make nails. Everyone needs nails - the carpenters and blacksmiths. It's not difficult."
So in the back yard, they started a small home industry and from hard experience, these two boys learnt their manufacturing and business skills.
William had another suggestion.
"Remember that preacher, telling us about Camp meetings at Mow Cop?"
"So?"
"He told us that many of the pottery owners in Burslem have been converted."
"What's on you mind son?"
He shared his idea, that he and George could go to the Potteries. "We'll take the train from Penistone and visit the potteries in Staffordshire." If they met these Pottery owners who were Primitive Methodists, they'd surely sell them a barrel of pots. "Everyone breaks pots, and we could sell some new ones here in Skelmanthorpe. It would save people having to go down to Barnsley."

So whilst still only boys, George and William travelled across the Pennines to Burslem to find a Methodist manufacturer who would sell them a barrel of pots. There was only one problem. They had forgotten to take a reference.

They were promised that a barrel of hardware would be put on the train if their mother sent a letter of recommendation.

In due course, the precious barrel arrived in Skelmanthorpe. Straw was scattered everywhere as the earthenware was unpacked with great excitement. The village had its first china shop!

When the boys were in their twenties, the family returned to Barnsley. George was now a smartly dressed young man, rather small and energetic. They became members of Pitt Street Methodist Church, where Hudson Taylor of China had grown up a generation before. George married the daughter of a wealthy loom manufacturer and besides helping his father in law make looms, he opened a china shop which developed into a high-class general store in Eldon Street. He had a keen eye for business. Later in life, my father-in-law told the tale of his mother entering the Eldon Street store to the sound of George Porter saying "Let Mrs Brown have anything she likes in this shop."

George and his wife Lena had three children, Ossian, Hilda and Marjorie and they owned a rather grand house - Beech Grove. They had come a long way from the front-room village shop at Skelmanthorpe.

William however left Barnsley and pressed on eastwards, for another twenty miles to Doncaster, where he bought a small shop - number 68 French Gate. It had the advantage of being next door to the Guild Hall - the town's police station. William decided to sell china downstairs and live in the rooms above the shop.

Blue-eyed William was 5ft 5inches tall, according to his later passport, and he attended the Primitive Methodist Chapel with its large new congregation in Spring Gardens. Rev Richard Brooke was the minister and William fell in love and won the affection of Arabella Brooke, the minister's daughter. She had been born on June 29th 1859 at Knaresborough. Arabella's mother was Mary Peel, and I still have a tapestry worked in 1852 by Mary Peel when she was a teenager living with her parents in Littletown. And I have two splendid oil portraits of the previous generation - Joseph and Hannah Peel - painted around 1850, and at one time we had some spoons inscribed "J and H P". My own son William - a Methodist minister who is five generations down the family tree, has the Reverend Richard Brooke's mahogany travelling writing case and his preacher's bible.

3. Luther

In the late nineteenth century, Doncaster was a bustling market town, and Porter's China shop in French Gate was a noisy place. Being adjacent to the town's police station, it was on the main thoroughfare which was part of the "Great North Road" - the nation's main artery from London to Edinburgh. The LNER railway station was also only a stone's throw away and the Porter family woke each morning to the whistle of the London train. They learnt to live with the noise of trains, the rattle of trams, the activity of the police next door, and the smell of the stables at the rear. Moreover, their business prospered.

With regularity, little children arrived to enlarge the Porter household - Frank, Florence and Clarence - then Harry who died at birth - and finally my father Luther born on 19th May1904. The little children would run down to the level crossing gates where the North Bridge now stands, and wave to the drivers of the gleaming steam trains travelling to and from Scotland. These were carefree and confident days, before the First World War, days when Britain had an Empire.

William's philosophy was that the china shop existed only to provide enough money to bring up their children and let him support the chapel. Primitive Methodism was his main interest. William was the circuit steward for about 25 churches. He and Arabella entertained visiting preachers, attended Camp Meetings, were delegates to the national Conference. They supported the theological colleges and raised money for overseas missions. They laid foundations stones for new churches, and were proud to belong to a church that was on the move. In 1907, Primitive Methodists made up 2% of the British population. They had 4,905 chapels, 1,153 ministers, 16,209 local preachers, 210,173 members, 607,682 adherents and 477,114 Sunday school children.

My grandfather William bought a magnificent Symphonium which we still treasure. He took a horse and dray to Driffield to bring this wonderful musical box home to Doncaster. You put a penny in the slot and it plays the sweetest of songs as the disk rotated twice. Children find it irresistible. If anyone was late for breakfast, they had to put a penny in the slot and when the box was full, the money was sent to support the missionaries in Africa. A penny was a lot of money when a little boy would receive only one penny and an apple for Christmas, so I guess it was more of a threat than a penalty.

My father writes about his experience in 1911.

"I remember in 1911 my father going to the centenary at 'Mow Cop', with Mr William Huntington and George Simpson who was the Town Crier. I was a boy of seven. When they came back, Simpson said the train was packed at Congleton. A passenger asked what all the crowd was about. Huntingdon said, 'Hundreds called Primitive Methodists have been to a Camp Meeting'. The reply was, 'I never realised there were so many Primitives'. Simpson said it was only a flea bite. "We have foreign missions and hundreds of churches.'"

This must have been the summit of blessing for the Primitive Methodist Church, but from that time and throughout the twentieth century, all the Christian denominations in Britain shared a slow decline in numbers and influence. Darwinism was being embraced by the nation and liberalism invaded the theological Colleges.

In 1938, my father remembered sadly the exciting days of his boyhood as he looked back over twenty years and he wrote - "I went to Mow Cop to see for myself in 1938, with memories of looking over the wall at the Tower. I came to earth quickly when a loud voice swore saying, 'Get out of my way. I want my cows in that field!'"

In 1914, William and Arabella bought a house at 135 Thorne Road. The First World War was beginning, a war which would claim the cream of the nation's youth on the fields of Flanders. The Angel of death would leave few homes untouched, and spiritually the mood of the nation would suffer. "Where was the God who had made Britain great?"

Belatedly in 1918, the Prime Minister called the nation to prayer, uncannily followed eight days later the first British victory in France, and by five months of German retreat, until the Axis finally sued for peace. However, the nation never recovered, especially from the double pain of the influenza epidemic.

In the spring of 1915, my grandparents opened their home to some soldiers who were billeted in tents on the racecourse, and unwittingly they received one young man who carried the dreaded Spanish 'flu. It spread through the family with lightning speed. First, my father Luther who had just entered his teens, became ill and lapsed into unconsciousness. The minister came to pray with the family and as my father lay unconscious, and the minister and Arabella knelt by Luther's sick bed. The minister later recounted my grandmother's sacrificial prayer - "Lord, please spare my little boy Luther and take me in his place". He did this on 6th March 1915. The death certificate says - "Arabella Louisa Porter 55 years of age - Ineffective pneumonia, enteric fever".

Florence at 22 years of age was next to become ill. She was admitted to the Nursing Home in Lawn Road and three days after her mother, she died on March 9th 1915 of enteric fever and intestinal haemorrhage. Frank who was 21 was struck down by the same infection and died in Carr House Hospital on 17th March 1915.

My father Luther, with influenza meningitis, was unconscious, and he hovered between life and death for many days. There was no medical cure. But he described to me on several occasions (although the whole scenario was too awesome to share with many) how in his sleep he had a vision. He was at the gate of heaven and was bathed in a beautiful light. He heard a voice. "Send him back. There is something for him to do. We are not ready for him yet." My father was left in no doubt that he had been given a work to do, and he convinced me that part of this work was to be through me, which was quite daunting!

When Luther regained consciousness, he found that he had lost his brother, his sister and also his mother. His father William was bereft, with his family diminished so quickly, and he was left with only two boys Clarence and Luther. Nevertheless, he came through this fiery furnace of affliction, bruised but faithful. I eventually understood why my Mother and Father chose to include William in my middle name. And I am so pleased that my own son William is a Methodist minister with a burning heart for revival.

Before his meningitis, my father had progressed well from the British School in Chequer Road to win a scholarship to Doncaster Grammar School, but when he returned at twelve years of age he had missed a whole year of schooling. His recovery was slow and incomplete, and thereafter he sometimes had difficulty putting the exact word in its right context. They thought that he was a slow learner at school, but it became obvious he was a little dyslexic. He told me of the shame he felt, having to stand in the corner of the classroom wearing a dunce's cap, but he persevered and with a remarkable sense of contentment. He left school at fourteen, and went into the family retail china business.

On 26th November 1921, my grandfather William and his brother George travelled together through France, Belgium and Holland into "occupied" Germany. They returned expressing some concern about the ferment in Germany with the zeal to rearm, and how vain they believed was the dream that the Great War had been the "war to end all wars". They were to be proved right.

My father told me how one day he sat on the stairs crying and praying for the mother he had lost, when God in a wonderful way answered his prayers.
"Boys, you're going to have a new mother."
William married the matron of Hartley Victoria Theological College and my father saw this as an answer to his prayer - a substitute, although not the real thing - but he knew there was a God who cared about him.
In his late teens after an evening service at Spring Gardens Methodist Chapel, Luther was taken on one side by a lady Deaconess. She asked him he had ever opened his heart to Jesus.
"But my father is the circuit steward," he said.
"That's not my question."
"But I live a decent life. I go to church."
My father responded as this lady gently explained to him what it meant to have a personal faith in Jesus Christ. He always believed that day was an important milestone, and he developed a passionate loving relationship with Jesus which characterised the rest of his life.

Luther enjoyed the friendship of the new minister's son Douglas Simons. They both learnt that God does remarkable things today, and that faith is practical - it has to be used. They decided in the summer of 1927 to set off like the disciples (in Luke chapter 9), on a walk of faith. They would take no money, no extra clothes, make no plans in advance, but just go into Lancashire and preach in the market places, wherever anyone would listen. They bought a railway ticket for as far as their money would take them. Their simple faith was rewarded on the first night when a baker took them to his home, fed them and gave them a bed. Wherever they went they were given food and shelter. They experienced the excitement of discovering that God abundantly provides for anyone who will trust Him completely.

Revd Samuel Chadwick was Principal of the Methodist Cliff College in 1927, and hearing of this faith walk he sent for my father and

Douglas Simons. Samuel Chadwick was one of the greatest Methodist preachers of the day, and it was with trepidation that they knocked on his study door at Cliff College. Chadwick gave them a cup of tea in decorated Doulton china cups, and my father was impressed. He was immediately at home.

"Tell me about your faith walk."

He couldn't stop them.

"I want you to come to Cliff College as students," he said. My father protested that he had had little education, but in 1928 that was no obstacle to Chadwick. Luther Porter was enrolled as a student at Cliff.

He went to Cliff with a youthful passion for evangelism which was enriched during that year as he learnt how to study his Bible, discover the power of prayer, and experience the indwelling power of the Holy Spirit. Cliff College equipped him for a life's mission of introducing others to Jesus.

> *Self-educated, self-supporting, he*
> *Like Saul of Tarsus, labours with his hands*
> *And preaches too. Reliantly he stands*
> *God-called and God-equipped for ministry,*
> *And leads the people's prayers; the liturgy –*
> *His own unlettered dialect, commands*
> *Devotion, as his utterance expands*
> *In glowing admiration. Presently,*
> *He reads the Scripture and the homely voice,*
> *Unspoiled by elocution, tells the news*
> *That once made simple shepherd-folk rejoice,*
> *A message follows such as God can use-*
> *To stimulate devotion and proclaim*
> *The solemn splendour of the Saviour's name.*

"The Lay Preacher," by Douglas A Simons

Cliff used to give each student a "manual" task, and my father was delighted to be the College postman. It meant getting up very early in the morning, going down to Calver Railway Station, picking up the post, and then delivering it to the staff and students. Each morning he would pause outside Samuel Chadwick's study door and hear the great man praying aloud. One morning, my father was kneeling with his ear to the keyhole to listen to Chadwick's prayers when the praying stopped. He listened more intently until the door suddenly opened.

"What are you doing there, Brother Porter?"

Dumbfounded and embarrassed, he rose to his feet.

"Come inside."

There on the desk was a list of the students' names, and Mr Chadwick was praying for each one by name.

"Let's see. Where's your name?"

He ran his finger down the page.

"Right, Brother Porter. I can see we're going to have to pray very hard for you."

Samuel Chadwick was Luther's lifetime hero, and Cliff College to my father was next door to heaven. He made many friends there, he loved the staff, and in later life he supported Cliff as its treasurer for over 25 years. Whit Monday celebrations were the great event of the year, when God answered prayer, kept the rain off the open-air tea tables, and powerful preaching changed the lives of thousands.

He loved to recount the story of the College evangelist, HH Roberts, who was on the staff at Cliff for many years. "This great evangelist was responsible for giving thousands of people tea on Whit Monday," he told me. "It could not rain or all his lovely starched white tablecloths would be ruined. This was always a cause for much prayer. They would lay the tables very lovingly year after year, and pray at the same time. Lord please keep our tables dry. And he did. One year the forecast was for heavy rain and HH Roberts prayed harder. The dark clouds gathered in the afternoon and they could see the rain coming down over the hill. Closer and closer came the storm and the rain began on the west side of the road outside the College. It rained on one side of the road and yet on the other side where the crowds were singing and praying, it remained quite dry. HH Roberts was known as Cliff College's Elijah. I have one of his books today which is a treasure.

When JA Broadbelt was Principal my father became treasurer of Cliff, and he was invited by a succession of College Principals to chair the Whitsuntide meetings. They knew that my father's praying was so powerful. His prayers took you right into the Presence of God. Even in his last years when confined to a wheelchair, the Principal would invite all the speakers of the day to his study at lunchtime and then invite my father to pray for them. They then went out to the various meetings sure that God was about to do great things.

My father wrote to me in 1980 "There is witness of generation after generation. The keeping and saving power of our Lord never changes. When God calls, he expects a reply. I am more convinced of that after 55 years of preaching this gospel of full salvation to all who believe in the power of God's Holy Spirit working in one's own life. Your life can be changed into new creatures for His service. God's divine grace will flow through you more fully to lead you in the paths of righteousness for His name's sake. For since by faith I saw the light, the streams of love supplied, redeeming love has been my theme and shall be till I die. God bless," he wrote "till we meet around His throne in heaven."

Cliff College in 1928 was a time a great preparation for Luther. If he had the opportunity he would have offered himself for the ordained church ministry, but instead he returned to Doncaster to sell glass and china and preach whenever and wherever he could.

The other great event in my father's life also happened in 1928 whilst he was a student at Cliff College. He met Mary.

4. Mary Field

Mary Field was born in Romily on the other side of the Pennines on 20th June 1907. Her father Edward had been a boy in the late nineteenth century, and was part of a Wesleyan Methodist family. He had spent his early years in Doncaster. The Wesleyans tended to look down on the Primitives. They thought they were too noisy, and the Primitives for their part thought the Wesleyans were rather snobby and lacked spiritual zeal. It is not surprising that the "Prims" and the Wesleyans often took different paths. Edward and his two sisters Kate and Emily were teachers at Hyde Park School, and Edward was also the Sunday School superintendent at Priory Place Methodist Church. They were a family versed in the classics, poetry and art. They had a great sense of honest fun.

Edward crossed the Pennines to take up a promising teaching post in Romily, a suburb of Manchester. There, he fell in love with one of his pupils, a beautiful red head and he teased her -
"Bella you've stolen my heart. I shall wait for you if you will marry me one day".

And so at a young age Isabella Walker and Edward Field were married. Isabella's father was a master carpenter who had travelled south from Glasgow. He made the heavy oak doors that still hang in Manchester's Town Hall. The Walkers were quite wealthy landowners in South-east Scotland, and for many years my mother received a small annual income - rather thinly dispersed - from the Walker trust.

Before the days of antibiotics, pneumonia was a deadly disease. Isabella went out in the rain when she should have been at home in bed, and bronchitis turned to pneumonia. Helplessly, the young grief-stricken family watched her slip away.

Mary left home when she was 18 years of age, still suffering from the loss of her mother, and she became a student nurse at Barnsley Beckett Hospital. It was in 1928 that she visited her auntie Kate and her cousin Edward Brooke in Doncaster, and there she met my father. Luther and his friend Edward were sporting their new Harley Davison motor bikes. Mary, and Edward's girlfriend Winnie were invited by the boys for a spin, but only once.

"Hold on tight," said Edward to Mary. "Luther's previous girl-friend was thrown over the handle-bars into a ditch. And once his bike caught fire." My father's motor cycle riding so frightened Mary that it is a wonder their friendship ever progressed.

Not surprisingly Mary failed to share my father's passion for motorbikes. However, each weekend Luther would take his motor cycle over to see Mary in Barnsley and in September 1929, they were married.

The honeymoon was in Bournemouth, with an overnight stop at a five star hotel at the Legion Arms in Broadway. The first night was rather eventful when my father, wanting to put the bedroom light on in the middle of the night, pulled on a sash above the bed, and heard a great bell tolling downstairs. A butler arrived at the door. "You rang sir?"

My grandfather had first moved his China shop from French Gate to a shop in Scott Lane, and then he purchased a new shop at 52 Market Place, Doncaster. He also traded from an open stall in Doncaster Market. My uncle Clarence helped to run the shop, and my father was asked to look after the market trade. It meant standing at a Tuesday and Saturday market in Doncaster, Friday market in Scunthorpe, and in Selby on Mondays.

The two brothers would travel in a big van to the Staffordshire potteries to buy china every Wednesday. It was hard physical work but my father loved it. He bought what he thought his customers needed and sold at as reasonably a price as he could, to ordinary people in the market towns. And he never missed a chance to share his faith with anyone who had an ear to listen. It seemed to me that he gave as much china away to people who came to him with a sad story, as he ever sold.

Luther was the bread-winner, and Mary the home-maker. My sister Isabel was born in 1931. She was a beautiful child with a head of golden curls. They lived in a small semi-detached house in Manor Drive Doncaster, and I arrived into this happy family in 1935.

5. Infancy

Early memories are with me still - the small semi-detached at 58 Manor Drive - days of sunshine and playing in the garden - with lots of little girl-friends of my big sister Isabel - a smart red pedal car smelling of new paint - Mackie the Scottie dog and Tibby the black and white cat - the postman at number 60 who had lost his leg in the first world war and now did his rounds with a peg leg - and the policeman at 56 whose daughter I was told, arrived one Monday in the doctor's black Gladstone bag. There was Dorothy the house maid who cycled from Armthorpe each week day - always against a prevailing wind - the milk man who came with his horse and dray each morning and poured out milk from his aluminium measuring cans into our two pint jug- it amazed me how his horse knew exactly which houses to stop at, without any apparent supervision - and how it kindly deposited a pile of manure at our gate for my father to add to the rose beds - and how the wealthy bountiful relatives from Barnsley would occasionally arrive at our house in an awesome shining Rolls Royce to pay a visit to their poorer relatives.

Sunday afternoon tea each week in Grandpa William's big house was a special occasion. If it was summer time, we would have afternoon tea from a trolley in the garden, the adults would play croquet or bowls, and Grandpa William sat in his deck chair protecting his balding head with a Panama hat. They'd eat cucumber sandwiches and talk about the morning sermon, why the numbers were falling and what should be done about it.

At four years of age I would sit on Grandpa's knee and he'd tell me stories.

"What would you like for your birthday Dicky William?"

I had big ideas.

"A horse and trap please."

Grandpa promised me my own horse, and I know he'd have kept his word had he lived. But William suffered from progressive blindness. The last thing he ever saw, was me running into the room and waking him from his Sunday afternoon sleep.

"I've seen Richard," he exclaimed. Everyone was excited, but the recovery of sight was short-lived.

The regular Sunday afternoon ride in grandpa's Essex saloon was a great adventure for a small boy. My father was always the driver, and three generations of Porters squeezed inside this magnificent black saloon. I remember the concern one day, when this wonderful car gently glided to an unexpected stop, and it stood silently in the middle of the countryside. No one could understand why such a fine handsome car should have suddenly failed.

"You've not touched anything have you Richard?"

I confessed to innocently playing with a tap next to my seat. Somehow this had turned off the source of petrol to the carburettor. Anxiety turned to relief and some laughter, that we didn't have to walk home.

Father and Uncle Clarence would help Grandpa find his way to the toilet at increasingly frequent intervals until one day William took to his bed. Old Dr Hucket visited him. Everyone had a solemn face, and grandpa slipped painfully into a uraemic coma before my fifth birthday. I lost a good friend (and I never got my horse).

6. Family life in the 40's

Home life was reassuringly stable and routine. Monday was wash-day when all the clothes finished up smelling fresh and looking so pristine. It was quite a ritual. My job was to get up early on a Monday and light the gas flame beneath the large copper boiler, and then for the rest of the time it was advisable for small boys to keep out of the way. The dirty clothes would boil away in soapy water for two hours, filling the house with steam. The "whites" would be lifted out of the boiler with a wooden stick and put into an oval aluminium tub for starching. Others would go into a "dolly-tub", and be twisted to get rid of some of the hot water. Sometimes they would be "ponched" or rubbed vigorously on a "rubbing-board". All the clothes would then go through a large "wringer". It was heavy work and I might be invited to turn the handle of this machine.

We prayed that it wouldn't rain on Mondays! When I was old enough I would make sure the washing-line was fixed up in the garden and if it was a dry windy day, the week's washing would soon be blowing briskly in the breeze. It would be collected for ironing in the afternoon, and then be aired by the fire overnight. Monday was never a good day for food. Lunch was always the cold meat left over from the Sunday roast and piping hot semolina pudding. There was a sense of relief in the family when Monday was over.

On Tuesday, Wednesday and Thursday mornings, dust would fly, and there was a strong smell soap and water and polish. These were house-cleaning days. Tuesday afternoon was an interesting time for shopping. I liked to go into town with my mother, especially into the grocers and watch with amazement when she paid for the groceries. After taking the order, the girl would place the money in a small cylinder attached to a wire above her head. She would pull a lever and this cylinder would fly across the shop on the wire to the cashier, who sat in a small glass cubicle. The change would be send back the same way with the receipt. Next day an errand-boy would bring the box of groceries on his bicycle to our back-door.

Friday was a good day. It was baking day, when the house smelled of home-made bread, pastries and all manner of cakes for the week-end. And Saturday was market day when all of us would help my Father in the market.

There was plenty of socialising, especially in the afternoons which were generally more relaxed – a time to visit family and friends. Thursday afternoon was my father's half day, when we were taken out on some excursion in the Rover car.

These were long happy secure days, although in the background there was a sense of foreboding. The adults knew there was a cloud on the horizon.

7. At War

Britain was at war in the Spring of 1940. The nation was expecting a German invasion. Those who had survived the First World War could hardly believe what was happening. Young as I was, I knew our army was trapped on the beaches of Dunkirk, and then the nation prayed, fog came down and the German planes could not attack our men on the beaches. Much of our army was miraculously rescued from defeat and plucked from the beaches of Dunkirk, but what next? The adults looked glum and serious.

I watched Mr Dodd the builder, digging an enormous hole at the bottom of our garden. He covered it with sheets of corrugated iron and then with a mound of earth. It had two pairs of bunk beds and a small table. There was a stove to heat some food and we were prepared for the expected German bombs. In spite of the tension it was something of an adventure for two small children, sleeping in an air-raid shelter under warm blankets and listening to the men talking about war across the garden fence in the darkness of the night.

The two Miss Coultons who were lifelong members at Spring Gardens Methodist Church, had relatives in America. I still have their telegram which says - "Tell them to come". Mother and Father made plans to buy tickets for Isabel and myself on the HMS Mauritania, an evacuee ship about to leave with refugee children for New York. There was much prayer and discussion until finally the plans were cancelled. The family would stay together come what may. The Mauritania was sunk in the Atlantic by a German U boat.

In the 1930's, my father had wrenched his ankle in a rabbit hole on Dartmoor. He was treated by the medical officer in Dartmoor prison - not very effectively I suspect - but even if he was left with a limp, being treated inside Dartmoor prison gave him an excellent story to tell for years to come. In addition my Father's funny feet prevented him joining the army. He walked like a duck, with his feet in external rotation. When he had his medical, the doctors watched him walk across the examination room.

Dr Halcolm said, "I'm afraid I know Luther Porter, and he's not fit for the army".

Uncle Clarence was just too old to be recruited, so the pair of them joined the Police Force as Special Constables, a local force to supplement the regular police. The two brothers ran a china business

26

by day, and on five nights a week they dressed up as policemen and swinging their truncheons, they patrolled the streets of Doncaster. They were Charlie Chaplain look-alikes, and I don't think any serious burglar would have been too concerned about these two new recruits.

They learnt a sober lesson when one of their colleagues ran towards a parachute that was slowly descending onto Doncaster racecourse. Instead of meeting an expected German spy, the constable was killed by a massive explosion from an air born mine.

In the next five years, German bombs dropped onto our town from time to time. We were shaken out of our beds and would scramble quickly to the shelter. One Saturday afternoon the Doncaster railway Plant Works caught fire. It was still blazing at nightfall. There was a fear that the German bombers which flew nightly over the town to drop their loads on Sheffield Steelworks, would think our illuminated town was an easier target. So once the shop and the market were closed, we headed for the country and apart from me falling in a muddy duck pond, we spent an exciting night with friends in an old farmhouse.

There was a little valley close to Pocklington in the Yorkshire Dales where, as a boy, my mother and father used to take us with my cousin John Brooke for a picnic. Millington Springs is a small deep valley cut into the Yorkshire Dales with little hills on the north side. One Thursday we had travelled as a family in the car with a picnic. The children were released to race up the hill with a tablecloth and a picnic basket, and we spread a white tablecloth on the top of the hill to enjoy the sunshine and have a little fun scampering around. Then we heard an aeroplane coming which, as boys, we were convinced must be a German fighter that would either drop a bomb on our white tablecloth or drop a spy in a parachute, thinking we had given the wrong signals. We had vivid imaginations and the fun and incredibility of that day remained in our memories for quite a while.

We learnt how to wear gas masks, and we endured the limitations caused by food and clothes rationing, but we were never hungry. In fact all through the war, we enjoyed fresh butter, cream, eggs and home-rendered bacon from the local farm. However we knew a lot about the lives being lost in the war, when at church there were tears and awkward silences as the names of sons and brothers who would never return home were announced almost weekly to the congregation. I would look at the long roll of honour for the first world war and wonder if it would be matched this second time. German troops were in control of Europe and we were fighting in the Pacific. It seemed to go on for years. Would our troops ever be able to invade the continent, defeat Hitler and bring the men home?

School was an exiting time in spite of the strong discipline. I was part of a class of more than 50 boys and girls. Three things we were taught very well - reading, writing and arithmetic - and I seemed to do quite well in all three. I was selected by the headmaster to record the school's weekly attendance register each Friday afternoon. I learnt a skill which I still retain - the ability to add up a long column of figures by running my finger quickly down the page. I can even read them correctly if they are upside down. I still do not understand the need for calculators.

Some of my friends experienced poverty. Once a boy came to school without shoes. Some were undernourished and for many, awful school lunches were still better than home fare. I must have been fortunate because for me the school meals were awful. They could never match my mother's cooking. I preferred to run home at lunchtime for some real food. As I developed friendships at school I soon realised that I had a unique and special home.

At home there were no arguments and no raised voices. We understood gentle discipline, an occasional smack if we overstepped the boundaries, but lots of kindness and much prayer. I was assured of constant love and was surrounded by security. Most sons will eulogise their mothers, and I am no exception. My Mother was gentle in her speech and manner. She loved us, maybe too much, and she taught us to speak well of everyone. She was blessed with lots of patience and contentment, and absolute honesty. She was always planning something good for her family.

My Father too was always there for us. He was the backbone of the family and the final decision maker. But he was too kind to administer any physical discipline even when it was deserved. When I think of a saint, I picture my Father.

The war dragged on for five years. I recollect that the national atmosphere of gloom and despair slowly turned to cautious optimism. Endless convoys of British and American tanks, lorries and guns passed through the town. Some of the American airmen from the nearby airbases came to church, gave us chewing gum and got girls into trouble. I was old enough to understand the excitement of the invasion of Normandy and study the maps in the Daily Chronicle which recorded the progress of the Allies in North Africa, and across Europe, and finally the fall of Germany in May 1945. The pacific war continued for six more months.

We were having a summer holiday in St Annes on Sea, when on August 10th 1945 I read of the dropping of the Atomic bomb. The atom had been split and the world would never be the same again. So my war ended and the soldiers came home.

In 1945 we moved house from 58 Manor Drive to number 8 Town Moor Avenue. This was a large semi detached Victorian house with cellars and attics. Best of all there was a loft over the garage where I made fireworks and mixed sulphur, Salt Peter and charcoal to make foul smells, and practised chemistry experiments. My memories are of long summer evenings when I played cricket with school friends on the open fields, and of the severe winter of 1947 when snow was waist high and I wrapped up well and sledged until bedtime.

8. Farming

In the war years, we were never short of food. We were especially grateful to the Spittlehouse family - farmers who lived just outside of town - who gave us their produce. I looked forward to Saturday nights when we would motor out to their farm, and whilst my Mother and Father talked to Miss Spittlehouse, in a paraffin lighted kitchen, I would scamper round the farm buildings looking for eggs. I discovered where the hens liked to make nests - in corners of a barn, under a wall, or beneath the eves of an outbuilding - and I returned from each expedition with a collection of several dozen eggs.

There were pigs rooting in the barnyard, and an old sow curled up with a dozen piglets. There were several large work-horses, who looked at me inquisitively over their stable doors, and a herd of black cows. I would roam the pastures and collect field-mushrooms, and return in time to help to churn the milk and pat the butter.

One evening I found Ernest Spittlehouse sitting in a barn in the twilight reading his Bible. I discovered that this simple man had a real faith, and when my father was preaching at his chapel, Ernest would liven up the services. On one hot summer evening, the small congregation was interrupted by a lowing cow pushing its head through the open door. A little later in the service, it knocked over Ernest's bike, and we heard - "Damn it, that's my bike".

One burning August when the sun blazed from the sky every day, my Mother sent me to the farm with a packed lunch to help with the haymaking. The Spittlehouses welcomed even an eleven-year-old novice, because every extra pair of hands was useful. The fields had been cut a few days before and the hay left to dry. Now it had to be loaded onto a cart and taken to the farmyard to make a haystack. It sounded like a great adventure.

The sun shone down powerfully from a clear blue sky and the old cart-horse stood harnessed in the field waiting patiently, swinging its tail from side to side. I was given a large pitchfork and soon learnt by example. I joined the others stabbing into the piles of dry straw and lifting my small effort high towards Ernest who stood on top of the cart. He was placing each offering carefully around the perimeter, gradually building up a large wagon-load of straw.

We worked all morning, stopping for frequent drinks and then we sat under a hedge to enjoy a good lunch that Miss Spittlehouse had prepared for us. It took many cart-loads to clear the field, but we had finished by the time the shadows were lengthening. The best part of the day was sitting on top of the cart-load of hay and holding the horse's rains as it lumbered back to the farm. It was worth the price of a painful sunburn.

GROWING UP

9. New ownership

I was greatly influenced by my father. He was really the one who led me to Christ. He shared with me the adventure stories of his own experience, about the reality and the power of God, and assured me that one day God would speak to me just as He called the little boy Samuel. I loved to go with him to his preaching appointments. He had some remarkable sermons on subjects like "Many are called but few are chosen"; "I will be like the dew unto Israel"; "Can any good thing come out of Nazareth"; "Called to be saints".

The most significant day was Sunday 17th February 1946. I was just 11 years old and the Rev Charles Hulbert was the visiting preacher at Spring Gardens. He stayed at our home for the weekend. After his preaching that Sunday night he invited anyone who wanted to receive Jesus into their hearts to come to the front of the church during the last hymn. I knew the call was to me. My heart was racing and I just knew God was speaking to me. My father had said that one day like Samuel, I would hear God's voice and this was it. I left my seat and went to the front of the church. I wanted to offer my young life to Christ even if I was ignorant of all the implications. I remember wondering why I did not immediately feel much different, but as the days passed, I knew that this had been a pivotal moment in my life. Everything was going to be new from now on. It was more than a contract. It was God's covenant for me. I had a personal friend in Jesus and He would keep His part of the bargain. He loved me and had died for me personally as if I was the only one, and I would live for Him. I remember that a few days later I told a school friend about it, and although I received a blank response, I had made my first attempt to share the news that Jesus is alive and that He can make a difference even in a young life.

I still treasure a red leather Bible I was given by JA Broadbelt, Principal of Cliff College, shortly after I accepted Christ as my saviour. His writing was usually totally illegible, but I could read, "To Richard From JAB your father's friend." I thought God was exceptionally kind that the principal of Cliff Collage should believe in a young boy enough to send him a personal Bible. I later learnt that he always sent Bibles to young people when he heard that they had accepted Christ, because he also gave his heart to Jesus when he was a boy of eleven listening to some Cliff College evangelists preaching in the Yorkshire Dales.

In the middle of the twentieth century Methodism was still suffering decline, but the faithful were trying some strategic planning. The old chapel in Spring Gardens, Doncaster was sold to build a new Chapel in the suburb of Cantley. As a family, we moved our membership to another town church, Priory Place, where there had been a succession of great preachers - Alan Roughley, Harvey Field, Len Barnet, Norman Parsons - men who drew large crowds, and were able to fill the church and balcony with young people every Sunday night. The Chapel was magnificent, with highly polished mahogany pews, a grand towering pulpit which the preacher ascended by a spiral staircase, a large choir above and behind the pulpit with the organist sitting on a throne, looking through his mirror at the assembled congregation. The ground floor would seat 500 and the balcony another 400. A Sunday school of several hundred went to their own classes half way through the morning service, and returned to the chapel again for an hour in the afternoon.

One Sunday morning - my father was preaching somewhere else, and I was sitting in the front pew of the chapel. The preacher, Alderman Jackson, invited us to sign the pledge. My young mind needed no convincing that alcohol was a social evil and I happily promised that in my lifetime I would not drink alcohol.

I felt that by abstaining from alcohol I was making a special covenant with God. Today, when people ask why I do not drink, I have difficulty explaining. There are a hundred social reasons, but really I have made a personal promise, almost like the Rachabites in the Old Testament. It is a promise I have been able to keep apart from drinking some cider at school, tasting the wine of a poor farming family in Italy which was safer than their water, and adding a bit of brandy to the Christmas pudding. I was happy to marry Christine knowing that she shared the same conviction, because I believed that if my family embraced the same promise, they would receive a great blessing. I confess that our pantry looks like a wine shop - with a shelf full of drink, because bottles are often given by patients, and we give them away to friends from time to time.

In the summer of 1946 I passed my 11 plus examination and left Chequer Road School (the old British School that my father had attended thirty years before) and started at the Doncaster Grammar School in September. Life was broadening out. I was learning about Physics, Biology, Latin and French, and sports, music and swimming were exciting challenges. I appreciated the opportunity to use my hands and make things and see how machines worked. And then my mother and father told me that I would be going to a public school the following year - a sacrifice not only in financial terms for them, but an emotional cost both for them and me.

I guess I was a very protected young boy, very family orientated, not very tough when it came to having a fight, and I was completely ignorant about the rigours of a boarding school.

I had a day in London with my mother and father to purchase school uniform. First we bought a large cabin trunk with brass corner pieces to ensure it would last a few lifetimes. Then a wooden tuck box for a few home cooked goodies. We chose a thick woollen dressing gown and a dark green tartan rug to cover the bed on cold winter nights, both of which have survived sixty years - two grey suits, striped shirts with starched white loose collars guaranteed to make the neck of the wearer red and raw within twenty four hours, three pairs of thick wool underpants, grey woollen socks and a school tie. It was with a mixture of interest and apprehension that I packed these things in the cabin trunk and prepared for four or five years of public school life.

In spite of a degree of nervousness, I was optimistic that it must be for the best, and I left home dressed in my new clothes and in good faith to go to Oundle School in Northamptonshire in September 1947. I was very raw and very innocent.

10. Oundle

Oundle was a tough experience. Most of the other boys had already been away from home for a few years. I didn't know the rules of how to survive in a boarding school, and I was quite homesick. In fact over the next five years, I don't think I ever settled down to life at Oundle. My values seemed to be so different from my contemporaries. I didn't excel at sport. I was not physically very tough and was perhaps rather gentle in manner. Looking back, it's not surprising that I had few friends. I didn't fit in. I could never decide whether it was my personality or because I tried to practise a Christian life. It was not for want of trying.

I spent the first year at the Berrystead House, reserved for under 13 year olds, and the housemaster was one of the school chaplains, Rev WC Cole "Willy Boggs". He was not averse to wielding a heavy slipper onto the posterior when things got out of hand.

The Berrystead stands at the far end of the Town's graveyard, and I had to walk 300 yards or so down the narrow church path between the gravestones on the dark winter evenings. The owls hooted and the wind howled, and if I was alone, it was with a pounding heart that I would creep back to the house.

We had a morning run, perhaps half a mile, round the large Berrystead garden and to my surprise, I was often in the lead. Each morning we had to endure a cold bath in a round hip bath that we had filled up the night before. It was meant to "toughen us up".

On a Monday morning, as an incentive to work hard, those who were top of the class had to walk on to the stage in front of the 700 assembled boys to get a certificate from Dr Fisher the headmaster, and I was generally there. I worked hard at everything. I did reasonably well academically, and was advanced a year beyond my age. I also put a lot of effort into sports, spending long hours on the rugby field, playing cricket, rowing and spending many evenings on gymnastics but I never seemed to achieve much. It was a very lonely time at Oundle, and my parents never knew.

We had "chapel" twice on Sunday and on Wednesday mornings, and I got used to the high Anglican form of worship, singing the psalms, learning the collects and sharing in the beauty of the Christian year. However, non-conformism was still in my blood. The chaplain approached me when my friends were being confirmed.
"What about you Porter?"
"No sir, I'm a Methodist. We're converted in Methodism not confirmed!"

I suffered many an unjust beating, once for losing a rugby ball, then for crossing a bathroom floor which was "out of bounds" for all but prefects. I endured being roasted against the prep room fire – held by the fire and then my long trousers wrapped tightly round my legs until the skin burnt.

I lived for the holidays. They were all too brief. We had two weeks at Christmas, two weeks at Easter and eight weeks in the summer. GNER railways had a service called PLA (Passenger Luggage in Advance) which provided free advance transport of a passenger's luggage. A tractor used to arrive at the schoolhouse, and we would load the trunks and tuck boxes on to the trailer. It would trundle off to the station and behold my luggage would be at home waiting for me a few days later. I ran down to the Oundle station to catch the 7.30am school train to Peterborough, and then the 10.30am Edinburgh train that would stop at Doncaster.

I later discovered that if I crept into Oundle market square at 6.20am, I could slip quietly onto the 6.30am Peterborough bus. I noticed that the passengers looked somewhat surprised at their schoolboy companion, but I could reach Peterborough in time for the 9.10am train north, and be in Doncaster a hour earlier than scheduled. I did this for a few years, and my premature escape from school was never discovered.

I endured the long weeks at Oundle, and at the time, I assumed it was good for me. Perhaps it was. Academically I was preparing for a career in medicine. But the lonely years moved round very slowly.

I think I first decided I wanted to be a doctor when I was nine or ten years of age, when I was walking to school along Thorne Road at the top end of the Town Fields. I knew that if I had the ability I would like to follow in the footsteps of our family doctor, Dr Halcolm. He had visited me when I had scarlet fever, and I thought that if I could practise those caring skills, then life would have a purpose. I walked further along the road and stopped to look at the brass plate outside the home of Mr Maitland Smith FRCS – an orthopaedic surgeon. Would I ever become a surgeon? I pictured Jesus as the Great Physician, and had a perfect model. And so throughout my school career, I was looking towards medical school. When I found that I enjoyed biology and had good grades, I believed that was a seal that I probably had an aptitude for medicine.

In 1952 I was accepted at two London Medical Schools, both the University College Hospital and the Middlesex Hospital, provided I had passed four A-level examinations - Physics, Chemistry, Botany and Zoology. My Mother was endowed with a lot of wisdom, and she encouraged me to apply also to Edinburgh University Medical School. They would accept three A levels, whilst London needed four. But when I made an application to Edinburgh, I was told my submission was too late.

Our Zoology teacher was quite eccentric. He used to walk round the classroom and ask questions that I could never understand.
"Porter. What do you know about African bull frogs?"
I knew nothing about them, either before or after the lesson.
"If you lived in Africa, what would you do about mosquitoes?"
It was a sensible question. It made me think, but I was never shown how to gather the essential facts that would be needed by the examiners.
This man never considered the examination syllabus and every one of us failed the exam. So at 17 years of age I left school with only three passes at A-level and not the essential four. I had no university place. I was in the wilderness.
I understood later that God was wanting to show me that our disappointments are His appointments.

11. My sister Isobel
It was August 10th 1952 and Isabel was celebrating both her twenty-first birthday party and her engagement to Ian. My parents had arranged an extravagant celebration in a large marquee in our garden, bedecked with ribbons and flowers. My Mother had prepared the food and I had helped her ice a beautiful two-tiered cake decorated with pink roses. There were about sixty guests and I made my first speech. I was seventeen and sat next to the Methodist minister Harvey Field. I had to explain that I had just left school with no university place, but I knew it would work out all right in the end. He seemed bemused and unconvinced.

Isabel had trained as a nurse at the Middlesex Hospital in London. She had enjoyed the bright lights of the city - going to the theatre and being feasted by eligible young men. One was a guardsman and we knew my parents did not approve. Another was an intellectual student at Durham University, theologically correct but rather dour, and Isabel's interest was short-lived. It was Ian Porter that won her heart - my half cousin from Barnsley - and he showed serious interest. He was Ossian's son, ten years older than Isabel, and he knew the ways of the world. He has a promising career in the family loom making business and Isabel and Ian fell in love.

It was a good match. Ian's father Ossian was a Methodist local preacher who never preached without quoting John Bunyan's Pilgrim's Progress. The Barnsley branch of the Porter family was faithfully Methodist and teetotal. Marrying Ian Porter meant that Isabel would keep her maiden name, and she could expect a life of considerable comfort. Ossian gave them a wedding present of a large plot of land next to the Barnsley family home where they built a grand Georgian mansion ready for the wedding a year later.

I had known from early years that I had a very accomplished sister. As a child she had beautiful curly fair hair, with a natural charm that captivated people's hearts. She was full of fun and laughter. Conversation came easily to her. At twelve years of age she went to the Mount School, York - a Quaker foundation - and Isabel was reprimanded on more than one occasion for breaking the silence of the Sunday morning meeting.

We used to say that Isabel would always "fall on her feet". Once when the London train was moving away from Doncaster station, she pleaded with the stationmaster to stop the train. "I'm a nurse and I have to be on duty," she said, and the train dutifully stopped for her. As I made my speech that hot August afternoon, even if my future was uncertain, I was pleased to see that life was smiling kindly on my sister Isabel.

It was late August 1952, and I went to see our new General Practitioner, Dr Melecka, for some tablets for my mother. He asked me if I had a place at Medical School and I explained the problem. I was in his small consulting room and he picked up the phone. "Maureen, how are you? I have a young man here, quite an exceptional young man who will make a good doctor. He needs a place in Edinburgh. Can you put him on the waiting list?" He was speaking to the Dean's daughter, and within 48 hours I received an offer of a place in Edinburgh to start the following month! I was learning that God frequently turns our plans upside down because He always has something far better for us than we ever imagined. How often in life I was going to find that many times He opens the door only at the last moment.

COMING OF AGE

12. University

I went up to Edinburgh on the train as a boy of seventeen in October 1952. The railway platform was busy with students going north, and the old noisy steam engine whistled and poured out clouds of steam and dirty smoke. I joined three older medical students in a crowed carriage, and was a little over awed by their maturity. At Waverley station I got a taxi to Hanover Street, to some digs that I had seen advertised in the local paper. It was a small dark triangular basement room with a grill window looking up into the street, and it cost £2.17.6 per week. The other residents were commercial travellers and I didn't think much to it. This damp, cramped residence was to be my home for the first few weeks of University life.

The first year Medical School had a massive intake of 200 students studying Physics, Chemistry, Botany and Zoology. We soon realised that only 150 students were expected to reach the second year. If I was going to be in that group I had to work quite hard. In fact, I was relieved to find it remarkably easy. The discipline of public school life stood me in good stead, whilst many others found it difficult to work without close supervision.

I made some good friends in the year group - Graham Barnes who had been to the Methodist public school at Culford - Mike Todd from Kirkaldy, small and cheerful and fond of rugby - Ron Kilgour from Edinburgh who was a little older and wiser than the rest of us. We four, spent a lot of time together over the next six years, and enjoyed many hours playing billiards and snooker at the University Union. For the first time since leaving home at twelve years of age I had some real friends.

I also had another very special group of friends. These were young people in Nicholson Square Methodist Church and I immersed myself in the life of the Youth Fellowship. I joined a crowd of enthusiastic young people for both morning and evening services. We had tea at Miss Nightingale's - lots of sandwiches - and then the Youth Fellowship meeting followed the evening service. There were about thirty folk who met after the evening service. One of us would give a short exposition of a passage from the Bible and we'd divide into two or three small groups to discuss the passage. After 40 minutes or so, we got together again to share what everyone had thought, and then there was a time of open prayer, always singing Wesley's hymn "All praise to our redeeming Lord who joins us by His grace". In the middle of the week we would meet together for an evening in someone's flat, and on Saturday afternoons we usually arranged a walk in the country around Edinburgh. There was a heady exhilaration about a crowd walking in the country and singing hymns in harmony. Life was good in Edinburgh. What a contrast to the years at Oundle. Here I was in a different world. I was surrounded by a crowd of caring people.

13. The beginning of a conversion job

The second term in Edinburgh was momentous. Around that time I had a sense of spiritual dissatisfaction. I was reading Mr Wesley's "A plain account of Christian perfection," and Thomas Cook's "The way of holiness". I discovered Samuel Chadwick's books on "New Testament holiness" and "The way to Pentecost". All these were describing a work of God's grace in the heart at some time after conversion, a second powerful work of the Holy Spirit. Wesley used the term "perfect love" - God's love received in a new way and expressed as outgoing love to one's neighbour. Cook and Chadwick described it as a second blessing, a baptism or in-filling of the Holy Spirit. Whatever language was used, I realised that these saints had experienced and preached about a second work of God in the heart of a believer. I certainly needed more than I had so far encountered, and I was hungry for it.

In January 1953 we had a preacher visiting for the weekend, called Rev Bola. His services were so challenging that a number of people made commitments to Christ. But I wanted something that was not on offer, and I could not define it. I knew I was a Christian believer - with an assurance of being born again - but there was so much more that I needed. Above everything else I wanted to meet with the Lord.

After that Sunday night fellowship in January 1953, I determined not to go to bed until the Lord had showed Himself to me in a new way. So I set about walking the streets of Edinburgh in the dark and into the night, calling upon God. I was somewhere around Toll Cross beseeching God to speak to me, and I put my hand into my raincoat pocket where there was a small Bible that I had bought in a second hand bookshop. I stopped under a street lamp in a quiet square, and this Bible fell open at 2 Chronicles 7 v 12: "The Lord spoke to Solomon a second time by night, and said 'you have not chosen me, but I have chosen this place for me for a house of sacrifice. You will not want for a male child to sit on the throne, if you are willing and obedient.' "

I knew God had spoken out of the night directly to me – a second time. He said that He had chosen me, I had not chosen Him. And He said that He had chosen me to be a place of sacrifice and worship. Personally that was a Damascus Road. I replied to the conditions 'Yes Lord, I am willing, and Yes Lord, I will be obedient in your strength'. I think it was the pivotal point in the whole of my subsequent experience. It was a time when the glory fell to Solomon and I believe also to me as an 18 year old.

My heart was racing as I walked through the night to my digs. I got to bed and I promised that in a few hours' time I would rise early and spend time with God. I asked God to get me up at 6am to pray and read the Bible. Although I had no alarm clock, at exactly 6am I opened my eyes and jumped out of bed. For the rest of my time in Edinburgh, I made a practice of getting up early for an hour of quiet prayer and Bible Study.

I began to live a new kind of Christian life. Miracles began to happen. On the day following that night's encounter with God, on the Monday, it was raining heavily and with hundreds of other students at the University Union I had put my outdoor coat on a peg in the cloak-room before going into lunch. There were hundreds of coats, three or four coats to each peg. After lunch, I went to retrieve my coat and had completely forgotten where I had left it. Aware of God's presence in my life in a new way, I stood in the middle of an aisle and offered a prayer. "Lord will you find my coat for me." I closed my eyes, extended my right hand, grasped the first coat in front of me, and it was mine! I was beginning to learn that the Lord in Heaven is just as interested in the small things of our daily lives as in the great events.

I developed a love for reading the Bible and shared the good news with anyone who would listen. I was sensitive to other people's feelings, and was not intrusive, and I did not lose any friends, though I suspect some thought I was a little unusual. A fellow student Walter Mason, who was later my best man said at our wedding some twelve years later

41

"I was surprised to meet someone at Medical School who believed in the whole of the Bible." I certainly did, and although there is still much that I do not understand, I have never had any reason to change my mind.

I think another challenge that I found when God spoke to me in 2 Chronicles chapter 7 as I re-read the passage, was that God's promise was not to be taken for granted. It was conditional. Verse 17 said, "As for you, if you walk before me as David your father did, and do all I command, and observe all my decrees and laws, I will establish your royal throne, as I covenanted with David your father when I said 'You shall never fail to have a man to rule over Israel'".

14. Basic sciences

The foundations for one's career are so important. If that is wrong the whole edifice will tumble. In 1952 Edinburgh University Medical School took the Basic Sciences very seriously. We were the last intake in Edinburgh to spend a preliminary year studying the Basic Sciences that historically had been considered so important in medicine - physics, chemistry, botany and zoology. It was a repeat of my final year at school but in more depth. It was also more fun, dissecting dogfish, identifying summer flowers in the Botanical garden, understanding for the first time the simplicity of the invariable laws of physics, and the functions of chemistry.

Some argued that these subjects were unnecessary for a medical education, but I never thought so, and I have retained a love for them. How valuable it has proved to be, especially in retirement, to have a re-kindled interest in these subjects - the history of physics from Galileo to Newton and Einstein, Hoyle and Hawkins and now the mystery of quantum physics. And chemistry, discovering again the beauty of the periodic table. And zoology, thinking again about Darwin and encountering Richard Dawkins who promotes atheistic evolution with such fervour, and Leakey with his up-to-date views on the origins of homo sapiens. And botany, the re awakening the wonder of discovering plants in the hedgerow. A new interest in these things is the legacy of that first year in Edinburgh that looking back, I would not have missed.

The next layers of the foundations for becoming a doctor were laid down in the second and third years. An Edinburgh student in the 1950's was expected to know every minute detail of the human anatomy - every muscle of the foot and each tract of the brain. We spent ten hours a week in the dissecting room and were rigorously tested every two weeks. Great friendships were developed between students across the dissecting table, two of us working on the left side and two on the right. Conversations would turn to philosophical subjects like - where is the seat of the soul and what is eternal life? We never discovered the soul of the body we were dissecting. It had flown to a better place.

For several months I earned some extra pocket money by teaching anatomy at the Edinburgh School of osteopathy, until I discovered that the General Medical Council would take a grave view of a potential doctor "associating with unauthorised persons." I was in danger of being struck off before I was even put on, and I quickly decided it was prudent to relinquish this post before anyone complained. However I retained a deep interest in Anatomy, and perhaps this influenced my later decision to become a surgeon. I eventually joined the Society for Clinical Anatomists and at a later date, even when a young surgeon, the Edinburgh Royal College of Surgeons invited me to examine in Anatomy for them. In later life, this privilege was to take me across the world, but that's another story.

Physiology is about how the body works and it is beautiful and straight forward. Biochemistry however seemed much more complicated. I never really grasped how or why chemical reactions take place, but I learned by rote and that satisfied the examiners.

Let me digress a little to explain how I met Daniel Devadah. He was a young boy, dying from Diptheria in the back streets of Bombay. The laryngeal membrane was occluding his airway and his distraught mother ran with him through the muddy streets to the mission hospital. The emergency doctor recognised the emergency and quickly took a scalpel, incised the trachea and the boy breathed fresh air and turned pink again. "I will give this boy to the Lord and to medicine", his mother promised. The family had no money for Daniel Devadah's education, but he was so bright that he won a series of scholarships. In 1953 he had scraped enough money together to travel to Edinburgh to sit the FRCS examination at the Royal College of Surgeons.

Daniel came to Edinburgh in about 1953 and joined our youth fellowship at Nicholson Square. I was eighteen years of age, and he impressed me with his simple faith and his single-minded approach to medicine. He passed the Primary FRCS examination within weeks of arriving in Edinburgh, and received a gold medal as the best student in the final a few months later. He worked for his passage home by taking a locum surgical post at Doncaster Royal Infirmary. He invited me to assist him with a few operations and before we started he knelt down in the surgeon's room and prayed for God's help. "My boss in India taught me to pray before I operate" he said. And when Daniel had asked him why, he had replied, "When you become a surgeon, you will understand why." I decided that I would do the same if ever I became a surgeon. The next time I was to meet Daniel would be thirty years later.

15. Preaching

My father had a unique way of helping me to speak in public at a very young age. He would ask me to stand at the top of the stairs at home and recite some poem or hymn. "Speak slowly and loudly. The deaf people always sit at the back," he said. And I would have to keep reciting my piece until it was perfect.

One of my earliest memories is of Sunday School Anniversaries and reciting a poem on an enormous platform in front of a large congregation. I was pleased to receive some encouragement. "He'll make a preacher one day." Not long afterwards, we were on holiday in Blackpool. I found my way to the empty Winter Garden ballroom, climbed the stage and began to recite my Sunday School piece. Quite a crowd soon gathered and began applauding at the back of the hall which rather embarrassed an over confident young boy.

My father would take me with him when he was preaching in the Methodist churches around Doncaster, and my job was to announce the hymns. When at the age of eleven I started at Doncaster Grammar School I entered the elocution contest for eleven to fifteen year olds and recited Shylock's speech - "The quality of mercy is not strained." I won the first prize, and received a copy of Dickens' Oliver Twist. My mother and I read this classic together, over many long summer evenings.

In September 1946 when I was eleven years of age, I first met the evangelists from Cliff College. It was the St Ledger race-week and my father had invited these evangelists to Doncaster Racecourse to hold an open air meeting. They were such a happy group of young men with radiant faces. I can still see Tom Butler passionately calling people to accept Jesus Christ as their Saviour. They had a couple of accordions. They sang Cliff choruses and gave lots of lively testimonies about their experience of Christ. I was enthralled, and decided I would try to do the same when I was old enough.

I was only seventeen when my father surprised me by saying that he had been booked to preach at two places on the Sunday morning and he wanted me to take one of the services for him. I happily accepted the challenge, and an unsuspecting Methodist congregation at Adwick-Le-Street had to suffer the first stumbling first attempts of a novice preacher. If I was unskilled, at least I had something to say, and I was encouraged that the congregation was appreciative, I guess not because of anything that they found edifying but rather that a mere youth was prepared to stand up and preach.

I was a second year student in Edinburgh and I sensed a great burden to preach. I had something I wanted to share. For a time I considered whether the Lord was calling me to the full time ordained preaching and pastoral ministry, or to missionary work overseas. The first didn't seem right for me, but maybe the second should be kept as an option.

I noticed that a group of Christians had a Saturday night open air meeting half way up Leith Walk. I approached them cautiously and asked if I could preach. To my surprise they agreed, and I spoke rather fearfully to a small crowd about Jesus. It was a start.

I discovered that also on Saturday nights, there was a much larger open-air meeting on the Mound in the centre of Princess Street, and before long I joined this inter-denominational group as a regular preacher. I continued with them every Saturday night for the rest of my six years at medical school. The crowds were often quite large, even in the biting cold of Edinburgh's winter. Numbers swelled when the pubs closed at 11pm. I can say that every time we preached in the open air, it was always followed with some meaningful conversation with at least one troubled or seeking soul.

Many people who listened were just curious. But others were addicts or ex-offenders and in deep need, searching for answers to some of life's problems. After one Saturday night open air meeting, I was invited to have a coffee with one man who had been standing at the back of the crowd and listening intently. He told me he was Professor of Psychology at London University. When I promised to pray for him, he said, "Thanks, I need that more than you can think."

The Methodist Church gave me a "note to preach" in 1954 and I became an accredited preacher in 1957. I decided from the start to preach for a decision, and to assume that there are generally some in the congregation who are open to the challenge of Christ. The first time I preached at my own church - Nicholson Square - a girl called Rita from the Isle of Skye gave her life to Christ. I lived on that 'high' for many days.

My first sermon was on "Come now let us reason together says the Lord, though your sins be as scarlet, they shall be as white as snow." And then "All seek their own, and not the things of Jesus Christ."

16. The 1953 Coronation

Auntie Hilda was my father's cousin. She was the daughter of George Porter in Barnsley. Her flat in London had an ever open door. She had returned from China when it expelled all the missionaries in 1948, and she discovered that there were many overseas students in London in need of accommodation. She opened her flat in Marylebone Road, until the neighbours complained about the smell of curry and the never ending trail of foreigners knocking on her door.

Auntie recruited the help of The Duchess of Gloucester, and they managed to raise enough money to buy a large run-down four story block close to Hyde Park - number four Inverness Terrace. She persuaded the Methodist Conference to adopt this as Methodist International House (MIH) with Auntie as the Warden. It was soon full of grateful students.

At MIH there were prayers every morning, communion once a week and hymn singing on Sunday evenings. It became home to many lonely overseas students. Over the years I developed a friendship with the Mukherjee brothers - Sibu the physicist, Nisu who became a neurosurgeon and Mukuum later to be a professor of Paediatrics. They came to London as Hindus and through auntie's uncompromising witness at MIH, they left as Christians. It was a story oft to be repeated.

Auntie Hilda won the affection of thousands of people by her sacrificial life. I think of the man in the parable in Matthew chapter 25. Auntie had five talents, and she used them with all her might. She gave practical help wherever it was needed. Often when the house was full, she would sleep on a camp bed in the office and vacate her room for a needy student. Her students always came first. When my Uncle Clarence put her on the London train at Doncaster station, he gave her a parcel of fresh bacon - a luxury in those post-war days of austerity. "Thank you she said, it will be such a treat for my students. I've never been able to give them bacon". These were her children.

She would wait for the boat train at Victoria Station and jostle with the communists who were also trying to win overseas students. It was a battle for the minds and hearts of the young people who would return to their countries as leaders, and she wanted to take the ground for Christ.

In June 1953 Auntie Hilda invited me to stay at Methodist International House for the Coronation of Queen Elizabeth the Second. I took the train from Edinburgh to London. There was hardly a spare bed in the city. At MIH many were sleeping on the floor.

The coronation was a tremendous pageant - a time for the nation to celebrate after waking up from the hardship of war. I rose with the dawn at 5.30am and, after a sharp breakfast of corn flakes, I walked to a pre-booked seat on the Mall. Many had slept all night on the pavements and there was a buzz of excitement. I read the morning paper sitting on a damp hard bench. Hillary had conquered Everest. It was a great day to learn that the first man to reach the top of the world was British.

Every space along the Mall was filled with an expectant crowd. They were good humoured and colourful. Re-coated soldiers lined the route. First came the guards on horse back, in colourful tunics and helmets shining, battalion after battalion of the three services, pipers and brass bands and then the coaches of foreign dignitaries. The Queen of Tonga received the loudest cheer, and I was proud to remember she was a Methodist. Finally our own royals, and eventually Prince Philip and Her Majesty Queen Elizabeth. The roar of the crowd was deafening, with flags waving and people cheering. It was great to be a young man of eighteen and to be British.

17. My second visit to London - Harringay

My next visit to London was with my sister Isabel during the Easter holiday in 1954. There was another crowd and another great event. This time it was Billy Graham conducting his first major mission to England and it had caught the media's attention. Joe Blinco – an ex-Cliff College evangelist, - was the Methodist minister at Archway Central Hall, and Isabel and I called at his office in the late morning. "The crowd is so great that we can't get everyone in," he said. He searched in his desk and said, "I have only two tickets left, but you shall have them."

That evening we followed the enormous crowd surging into Harringay indoor stadium and presented our two tickets at the door. To our surprise we were ushered on to the platform! I sat in the row behind Billy and to his right, and I saw this passionate young man with his Bible held high in his right hand. He preached as I've never heard anyone preach before. He delivered short sharp sentences, challenging an enormous crowd of 15,000 which was packed into this great indoor arena. "You don't become a motor car by being born in a garage. Neither are you a Christian by being born into a Christian home". I knew that. There was total silence as we sat spellbound under the authoritative word of God.

With great simplicity, power and authority, Billy just preached the good news from the Bible. "The Bible says," he repeated again and again. "You must be born again." He concluded - "I'm going to invite you to get up out of your seats and come down to the front. Walking down here won't make you a Christian, but it is a sign that you are coming to Jesus Christ. He was not ashamed to die in public for you. Don't be ashamed to come openly to Him." The choir sang, "Just as I am, I come," and there was the awesome sound of hundreds and hundreds of shuffling feet moving down the steps and out to the front of the auditorium. I had never seen anything like it. This was God's offer of grace for England, never seen in this generation before, and I was witnessing it.

Billy was invited to preach before the young Queen at Sandringham. Winston Churchill called him to Downing Street. Billy Graham says in his book "Just as I am", that Churchill said, "Tell me Reverend Graham, what is it that fills Harringay night after night?" "I think it's the Gospel of Christ," said Billy without hesitation. "People are hungry to hear a word straight from the Bible. Almost all the clergy of this country used to preach it faithfully, but I believe they have gotten away from it."

"I'll tell you, I have no hope, I see no hope for the world," said Winston and looking at Billy he said, "Do you have any real hope?" Although the Duke of Windsor had arrived for luncheon, Winston said to his aide, "Let him wait!" and he invited Billy to explain the way of salvation. They prayed and shook hands.

The gospel was hot news across the country in 1954. Billy's final meeting was at Wembley, the nation's main open air stadium filled to its maximum100,000 seating capacity, with 20,000 more standing on the sacred turf.

Not all the clergy were impressed. The President of the Methodist Conference that year was Donald Soper, and his criticism was typical of many Methodist leaders. A few weeks later he stayed the night in our home in Doncaster. I drove him to Retford for an open-air meeting in the market place. A man in the crowd asked him why he was condemning Billy Graham, and when Dr Soper argued that sudden conversions were spurious, the man said, "I've been a Methodist Local preacher for fifteen years. If that is the position of Methodism, I resign now." I knew that this had shaken Dr Soper, and he talked to me about it in the car as we travelled back to Doncaster, I voiced my full support for Billy's message. I fear it had little effect on Dr Soper. I was saddened that this leader in Methodism was preaching against the evangelical gospel. This was the beginning of a pain I would feel for a lifetime – a pluralism in the Methodist Church with many denying the simple truths of the Bible, and scoffing at evangelism.

The ridicule was sometimes painful.

18. Methodist history and tensions
In almost every village in England today, you will find at least 2 chapels, often derelict and falling into disrepair. One would have been a Primitive Methodist Chapel and the other a Wesleyan Methodist

Chapel. There had been a spate of chapel building to accommodate the new believers as the Methodist revival swept the land, but why two parallel chapels?

In the early 1880s, groups of Methodists, particularly in Staffordshire, were convinced that the Wesleyan Methodists were losing the evangelical zeal and they were partly correct. These Methodists in Staffordshire were passionate about evangelism and decided to form camp meetings similar to those occurring in the United States. They would bring their farm wagons together into a large area and have preaching meetings sharing testimony and song. Beneath the wagons would be groups of people praying and they were not disappointed in discovering again the fire of John Wesley and Whitfield. The Wesleyans looked over their shoulder and called them 'ranters'. They were often despised and persecuted, particularly down in Northamptonshire, but they accepted ridicule by their Wesleyan brothers and their numbers grew enormously. Thus, two parallel churches developed in the early 1880s. The Wesleyans made sure that their children were educated and they often became teachers and administrators. The Primitives, on the other hand, frequently encouraged their offspring into becoming merchants.

Both the Primitive Methodists and the Wesleyan Methodists built theological colleges to train their preachers. Wesleyans took pride in teaching the new theology, interpreted by the Primitives as liberalism. So, when I was a boy, my understanding of the difference between Primitives and Wesleyans was that sometimes it was more apparent than real. The Wesleyans seemed more sophisticated and the Primitives more spiritual. It was not highlighted in my family because I knew of sophisticated Primitive Methodists and very spiritual Wesleyans but this simple assessment satisfied me as a boy as I wondered why each village had two Methodist chapels, often with identical structures and usually sharing the same preachers.

In 1935 the Primitive Methodists and the Wesleyan Methodists joined together again as one church, also bringing in the Bible Christians of Devon and Cornwall, forming one Methodist Church, as it exists today.

Throughout the twentieth-century I have witnessed the tension in Methodism, between the evangelical high view of the Bible and the liberal position. Methodism has called itself a pluralistic church, and most congregations have been composed of both evangelicals and liberals, worshipping and working together in mutual love. The evangelicals have been trying to make their voice heard, hoping to change the church. Likewise the liberals have been vocal, endeavouring to convince their brethren of the error of their ways.

In the early part of the twentieth century the polarisation was portrayed in the positions of Samuel Chadwick at Cliff College - a Bible College - compared with the liberal Dr Maltby at Theological College. The evangelicals were distressed when young men left Cliff on fire with evangelical zeal, to be accepted for the Methodist ministry, and the flame was quenched by what they believed was unbalanced teaching and the hurtful withering criticism of the liberal tutors in the Theological Colleges. The evangelicals grieved that a generation of ministers poured out of the colleges and into the circuits, tainted they believed with a biased doctrine of doubt and unbelief.

At grass roots level however, a large number of Methodists remained evangelical. Those who could not accept liberal theology from the pulpits week after week, left Methodism to join the Baptists, Pentecostal or the evangelical Anglicans. Others like our family hung on, bearing witness to what we believed was the truth and praying for better days. We loved the Wesley hymns, believed Wesley's theology, and enjoyed the warmth of Methodist fellowship. In contrast, the liberals were arguing that the theology of the eighteenth century is inadequate for the twentieth.

In 1928 my Father was driving his motor cycle to Cliff College, and passed a stranded motorist. Stopping he found an elderly gentleman looking sadly at a puncture. My Father got on his knees and changed the wheel for him. "To whom am I indebted?" asked the gentleman. "I'm Luther Porter, a student at Cliff College," he said. Next morning Chadwick told the College that he had a phone call from his old adversary Dr Maltby. "He says that he is indebted to Cliff College! When he had a puncture yesterday, one of our students was a Good Samaritan to him, and kindly changed the wheel."

People tried to build bridges but there was also much unkindness. A President of Conference and respected Methodist theologian in the late 1940's wrote witheringly about sharing the platform with a famed evangelical preacher: "He spoke without sense on entire sanctification. He ends up by asking all who want to claim the blessing straight away to come out and line up in front. He dragooned two or three hoary saints out of their seats, including Mrs Rogers who has got it, and lives in Beulah land, two or three trembling girls, and has a high old time procuring the second blessing for these lined up sinners. Grace was given us to stand our ground. Old Dr L has more holiness in his little finger than Y, the Pentecostals, Cliff College and Keswick. The effect on one sinner was to make him execute a Satanic dance round the room." Such was the scorn that may liberals reserved for the evangelical Methodists.

Robert Newton Flew had the nerve to say what many evangelicals would echo, "How long, O Lord, how long? And aren't we ministers the real culprits in the sickness and impotence of Thy church?"

I grew up with this tension, sometimes hurting deeply. I was a delegate to the Methodist Conference in Nottingham in 1964. It took great courage on my part to take the rostrum and speak to 500 or so delegates in the debate about the declining membership of the Methodist Church. I said that my generation wanted answers from the ministers about the reality of God. "If God is real, tell us how to find Him. Too often our congregations ask for bread and they are given the stones of doubts and uncertainty. Can we expect anything other than decline?"

Very quickly Donald Soper, who was now Lord Soper, hurried from the back of the platform and grasped the microphone. He looked directly at me and tried to destroy all that I had said in a few sentences. I felt rather small, but I had said my piece. Don English came to shake my hand afterwards, and said, "Well done Richard".

19. Revival in 1954

I don't know if the Edinburgh Methodist church was witnessing revival, but as we moved into 1954 there were times of tremendous blessing. Revival was in the air in Scotland. Duncan Campbell had returned from the Outer Hebrides with remarkable stories of the work of God. I heard him preach to a packed church on Psalm 24, "They shall receive the blessing". He laboured the point that the definite article was so important - THE blessing. It was for those who had clean hands and a pure heart. It was the blessing that he had witnessed in Uist.

He explained how two old ladies over eighty years of age, had prayed for revival and were guided to invite him to their island of Uist. When he stepped off the small boat on to the shore and knew he was already in revival. "I didn't bring it," he said, "it was already there. Revival was in the atmosphere and hundreds were compelled to yield their lives to Christ. The island was alive with the Presence of God." He gave an example of a crofter who didn't profess faith, and was on the moor cutting peat when he was so overpowered by the Spirit of God that he fell on his face in awe.

At the same time, in our Methodist fellowship at Nicholson Square, we saw God at work in many people's lives. Our youth fellowship steadily grew in numbers and influence. Before the end of 1955 there were more than one hundred converted students meeting every Sunday night, each one sharing a life-changing testimony.

I worked hard at my medical studies during the week and then made sure I had time off from mid-day Saturday until Monday morning. The weekend was very busy. On Saturday afternoon thirty or forty of us would walk in the country, over the hills or along some Border trail, singing the hymns of Wesley. On Saturday night and into the early hours of Sunday, many of us would be on the Mound preaching in the open-air. At midnight, we would often visit the Grass Market to speak to the alcoholics and try to find them a bed for the night. Often I would share in the late night City Mission meetings or the packed Gospel celebration at Carubbas Close Mission on the Royal Mile.

At 8.30am Sunday morning, we would join one of the many groups meeting outside the Royal Infirmary to go onto the wards and take a service. Then for an hour we would find a room at church to read and study a book - for example Cook's "New Testament Holiness" - and then have a time of prayer. Eleven o'clock was the morning service. I had lunch in the digs and spent the afternoon writing letters before having tea at Miss Nightingale's. Their home would be packed with students sitting all over the house eating sandwiches and singing gospel hymns. We had a prayer meeting at 6pm before the evening service at 6.30pm. Then the Youth Fellowship from 8 to 10pm and a walk back to the digs, tired but with so much to think about and be thankful for.

At that time Billy Graham visited Kelvin Hall in Glasgow for the "Tell Scotland" mission. After one anatomy lecture, I was pushed forward by my friends to announce to the 200 strong medical year group, that we had organised a bus to go the Kelvin Hall. It was quite terrifying to stand on the floor of the large Anatomy auditorium with tier upon tier of my curious peers wondering what I was going to say. A few came with us to Glasgow and some were impressed.

John Cash joined the bus party. He was the son of a Methodist minister, and he and some of his friends responded to Billy's appeal. Later that Saturday night, John stood with us on the Mound and witnessed to starting a new life in Christ. In later years John was President of the Royal College of Physicians of Edinburgh, and head of Blood Transfusion in Scotland.

20. Friends
During my first years in Edinburgh I was blessed with a number of very special friends. Jim Gordon was one. I suppose we were joint mentors, helping each other along the Christian way. We learnt a lot about prayer and studying the Bible.

One night Jim and I were so caught up in reading the eighth chapter of Romans that we did not get to bed until 3am. I had just turned out the light at 3am when Ian - a physics student - came knocking on my door. "I want to receive Christ," he said. I found Jim and the three of us knelt by the bed. Ian said a most simple of prayers: "Nothing in my hands I bring, simply to Thy cross I cling." Next day with a radiant face he said, "Last night, I came like Pilgrim to the cross and the burden fell from my back." Ian became a respected physicist in one of the Canadian Universities.

Jim came from a miner's home in Dumfriesshire. His family were Brethren. I spent a night in this home, and remember how the whole family sat around the kitchen fire in the evening as we read and studied the Bible together. I was privileged to be invited to the Brethren meeting hall - they were quite exclusive. And even more, they accepted me into their mission team - a group of young men touring Dumfriesshire for a week in the summer of 1954.

One late July afternoon, in a village tucked away in the Dumfriesshire hills, about six of us stood around a cul-de-sac in a housing estate. We preached and sang the gospel and shared testimony. Many mothers and children came to the garden gates and we talked to them one-to-one. Quite a number those people made a commitment to Christ that afternoon.

At the end of the week's mission, on the Saturday morning bus journey into Dumfries, I suggested to Jim that he go up to the front of the bus and talk to a man sitting by himself. "No, you go," he said "and I will pray for you." I was sitting against the aisle and dutifully moved forward to talk to this man. We arrived at the market place in Dumfries, the three of us stood on the pavement with bowed heads in prayer, and this stranger offered his life to Christ. What can you say when God is at work like that!

Jim convinced me that it was right to be baptised as a believer. We went to Charlotte Square Baptist Church and were baptised, much to the annoyance of our Methodist minister who asked if I wanted to remain a Methodist. I did.

Jim became head of Art for the schools in Angus, and is now a highly respected Scottish artist.

Another great friend was Norman Bromley. He used to be a bookie's runner at Doncaster races, and he was too fond of alcohol. One Sunday night, quite out of character, he walked into Priory Place Methodist Church, when Rev Harvey Field was preaching about the three men who were delivered in the fiery furnace. Norman was challenged and when I spoke to him outside he agreed to come with me the next night to a fellowship meeting in a miner's home in Carcroft. At the close of that little meeting, Norman was on his knees asking the Great Shepherd to accept his wandering sheep. He rose to his feet a new man.

Norman's father told my uncle Clarence that he had a new son. Norman had often come home incapably drunk and would have to be covered with a blanket at the foot of the stairs. Now his boy was radiant with a new faith in Christ. Norman shared with us in preaching in the chapels, and in the open air in many of the villages around Doncaster and Epworth. He went to Cliff College as a student, and for forty years has been pastor of an independent church to the north of Doncaster.

Joe Wells was also a triumph of grace. He had been lost behind enemy lines at Dunkirk, and in desperation had fallen on his knees beside a French road and had asked God to get him to the beaches. There before his eyes was a map and a compass, and he escaped back to England. He got married, had two small sons, but soon forgot the promise he had made to the God who had saved him. He became an alcoholic, broke up the furniture in his home, and left London to join a gang of contracting electricians. In Wolverhampton a girl was visiting the public houses inviting the men to the Saturday night mission meeting at the Central Hall, where Howard Belben - a future Cliff College Principal – was the minister. Joe agreed and heard a man give a testimony that could have been Joe's own story. He left in tears as they were singing "My chains fell off." Next week, Joe's gang moved up to Doncaster and on the Sunday he found his way to Priory Place. I spoke to him after the service and he took a hymn book home and started to read the same hymn again, "My chains fell off, my heart was free." He found me the following evening. "I've been sitting on that seat at the top of the Town Fields," he said, "and a verse has kept going through my mind: 'I will restore unto you the years that the locusts have eaten.' Is that in the Bible?" he said. We found it and I encouraged him. "I think you've been converted." And he had.

Joe stayed with us in Doncaster for about six months, growing in faith and learning about evangelism. He shared in many services, giving testimony and seeing people come to Christ. We eventually persuaded him to return to his wife Doreen in London. She was good enough to take him back. She discovered that she had a new father for her two boys David and Peter. Joe spent all his time witnessing, and he introduced his brother Tom to Christ. When Tom was converted, the publican where he used to drink in London complained that he had to order a barrel of beer less a week.

Many people helped me in those years. We had a vibrant Doncaster Cliff Fellowship that met every Saturday night, and I learnt so much by sharing with these young people during the Christmas, Easter and long summer holidays. There would be about 50-70 of us meeting for a couple of hours using a simple model - hymn, prayer, a number of favourite choruses interspersed with up to date testimonies, a Bible reading, a short address, and a final hymn. These times were really alive with Christian joy and with much expectation. During the week we would go with an accordion in small groups witnessing round Doncaster in pubs, youth clubs and on street corners.

I was able to introduce the Edinburgh people to Cliff College, taking a bus of about 40 young folk down to Cliff each year for the Pentecost anniversary weekend. There were many who discovered faith, and others who experienced a Holy Spirit baptism of love and power. Dr Sangster used to preach in the Big Tent on the Sundays and held us all spell-bound with his powerful word. The climax was when he preached on the 'Paraclete' - The Holy Spirit the Advocate, when scores of people responded in faith and in tears.

Billy Graham agreed to preach at Cliff College on Whit Monday 1955. Fifty of us went down from Edinburgh, full of expectation. The forecast was for rain. At the Sunday morning prayer meeting in the College chapel, we sang - "We shall have a bright tomorrow, all will be well." But it rained all Monday morning. Billy was on the platform in the afternoon in the open-air, and my father was the chairman of the meeting. Before the meeting began, Billy asked Ted Eagles the Principal, "Do you have anyone sick on the campus." They told him about Mrs Bagelly, the wife of the College Administrator, lying bedfast and paralysed. "I must go and see her and pray with her," he said, and he marched up the College lane to her home. "My dear, I've come specially to see you. I want you to do something for me. Will you pray for me whilst I am preaching today?"

The crowd was estimated at 50,000 and it stretched up the hill side almost out of sight. It drizzled a bit, but as Billy made his appeal, and a number of people dropped to their knees, the sun broke through the clouds, and in the breathtaking quietness of the afternoon a small skylark rose from amongst the crowd, soared into the sky and sang the sweetest song imaginable.

Cliff was a source of hope for many Methodist people in those days. Two Cliff men - Tom Butler and Herbert Silverwood, were of an older generation, and I was privileged to count them as personal friends. Tom Butler travelled the country, tirelessly preaching for ten-day missions. He always left a church with new converts and a congregation renewed for evangelism. He went to Jersey in about 1955 and had a wonderful mission at Sion. One lady Mrs Luce had lost her baby that year and when Tom was on mission at Sion, she had a dream and saw her baby in heaven. The next night she responded to

Tom's appeal and accepted Christ. It was the beginning of a great awakening at Sion and the start of a lively Cliff Fellowship there, which I used to attend when in Jersey on holiday.

On a Sunday morning in 1999 I met a man called Mr Luce at Bethlehem chapel in Jersey. He told me that he was the son of the lady blessed by Tom's ministry in the 1950's. He had known the Lord as a child, but has stopped going to church and had drifted for years. Then recently, lying on a hospital trolley with a serious haematemesis, he had prayed and promised that if God restored him he'd return to the fold. And he did. God is faithful down the generations!

Herbert Silverwood was another Cliff evangelist and a Connexional Methodist evangelist. He was a man of God, admired by many. He loved to be in the open air, preaching at the seaside, and several men went into the Methodist ministry who first heard the gospel from Herbert. He was the most entertaining comic, able to keep his congregation laughing throughout his whole sermon. He pretended that he had little education, but he was a wise man. "Richard," he said, "always keep the poker handy. Remember Wesley's hymn - 'Still stir up Thy gift in me.'" He gave me HH Robert's book on Isaac Marsden - inscribed "God works wonders" and this remains a personal treasure.

21. The Cook family
A very formative influence on my life as a student was getting to know the Cook family. The first time I preached at Nicholson Square, an American lady spoke to me at the door after the service. She had come over to Edinburgh for two years to get some good Scottish education for her children - Van Dyke and Celene. This family made our church their home base and I got to love and respect them enormously.

Captain Cook had been born in Islay on the West coast of Scotland. He became a seaman on the Clyde and eventually got his 'ticket' and was a Shanghai River Boat Captain. In the 1930's he married Francis Cook of the China Inland Mission (CIM).

When the Japanese swept down the Chinese mainland in the early 1940's, the three eldest children of the Cook family were interned in Chee Foo camp in the Shandong Province. Mrs Cook and her three smaller children were imprisoned in the infamous Stanley Camp in

Hong Kong, and the Captain was interred in mainland Japan. They shared with me wonderful stories of the faithfulness of God throughout their difficult war years.

The Captain had been on the Yellow Sea in 1941 and heard a distress call from a nearby Japanese ship. He rescued the crew, and generously gave the Japanese captain his cabin and bunk until they could land him in Japan. Then came the war with America in 1942 and Captain Cook found himself under house-arrest in Japan. He could not leave his quarters but learnt that the commandant in charge of him was the very captain he had rescued from the sea a year previously. He somehow found an entrance into the Japanese captain's office and the two friends embraced. The Commandant promised to try to get repatriation for the Captain's three eldest children in Chee Foo, and Mrs Cook and the three little children in Stanley Camp if ever there was an exchange of prisoners. It took a few years, but eventually, undernourished and black with pellagra, Mrs Cook was reunited with her children in Cape Town. There she waited. Each morning she and her children read together from "Daily Light" and then one day said confidently to the six children, "The Captain is coming for us today." She had just read, "The Master has come and is calling for you." This was the voice of God, promising her that her husband would come for her that very day. And he did. I learnt from the Cooks, that God speaks to us directly through the pages of the Bible if we look and listen and believe.

The Captain had been in Glasgow in 1940 and had attended morning service. The text of the sermon was from Jeremiah 32 verse 7 "Buy it for me". A few days earlier, the Captain had been looking at a prefabricated metal hut, wondering whether to buy it and ship it out to Shanghai in order to have somewhere to live when his ship was in port. But it seemed so foolish. The Japanese were swarming down into Shandong, and any property would soon be in enemy hands. But the word of the Lord clearly said "Buy it." So he did. He shipped the metal hut to Shanghai, had it erected on some land he owned and had rented to Mr Willis a Christian book-seller. Immediately the hut was erected, the Japanese came into the city, and the Captain never occupied his little home.

Mr Willis, the Christian book-seller who found himself looking after this little hut in Shanghai, was an unusual missionary. He did not belong to any official organisation, and so in spite of the Japanese invasion, he was able to carry on selling Christian books. His shop and the little hut was a secure haven for many Chinese believers throughout the Japanese occupation and then through some of the long Communist era.

Let me continue in the words of Christopher Willis in his book *"I was among the captives"*. "Our landlord had returned home on one of the repatriation ships, and had left the care of his property in my hands. I had quite a few interviews over this. There are three buildings on it. A very old house in rather bad shape, built of brick covered with roughcast. Second, was a bungalow built of steel plates brought out from Scotland; and last our warehouse, or go-down, as we call it in China. It is built of brick. The Japanese sent for me once to know what these buildings were made of. They asked about the old house in which we lived, and about the go-down; and forgot to ask about the middle house, the one made of steel plates. Had they asked about this almost certainly they would have immediately sent and taken all the steel plates of which it was built. Surely this was the Lord's doing; and another of His tender mercies. I might add that our landlord was a dear Christian man, one who commits all his cares to the Lord; and we did rejoice that the Lord honoured his faith."

In Billy Graham's book about Angels, he records a story about this Shanghai book-shop. "A Japanese truck half filled with books and with five marines drove up to their corner shop to seize their stock. The brother looking after the shop was alone. He was very timid and felt it was more than he could endure. The marines jumped down and made for the shop door, but before they could enter, a stranger, a Chinese gentleman, neatly dressed, entered the shop ahead of them. For some unknown reason they seemed unable to follow him, and loitered about, looking in the four large windows, but they did not enter. This was about nine in the morning, and they stayed around until after eleven, but never set foot inside the door. The stranger asked what the men wanted, and the brother explained that they were seizing the stocks from many of the book-shops in the city, and now they had come to seize their stock. They had prayer together, and the stranger comforted and encouraged him, and so the time passed. The brother knew practically all the Chinese customers who used to come to the shop, but this gentleman was a complete stranger. At last the soldiers climbed into the truck and drove away. The stranger also left, without purchasing anything or even making any enquiry as to anything in the shop. When the brother told Mr Willis, he said "Do you believe in angels?" "I do," said Mr Willis. "So do I," said the timid young man.

These stories were a great encouragement to my faith. The Cooks came to Edinburgh because when Mrs Cook read "Daily Light" in her flat in San Francisco, she heard God say to her as he said to Abraham "Get up and go into a country I will tell you about." So she got up, with Celene and van Dyke, and came to Scotland. "I have no more personal possessions that I can pack into a suitcase," she said. "We believe in travelling light." Apart from the land in Shanghai, they owned no other possessions, and always rented accommodation.

Mrs Cook taught me a lovely Chinese chorus which she said her own mother used to sing to her as they travelled on a donkey cart in the Chinese countryside.

"Farther on, yes still farther
Count the mile stones one by one
Jesus will forsake you never
It is better farther on"

Celene joined in the evangelistic activities of our youth fellowship. She was a most spiritual girl and gave me a "Daily Light." "It is the most precious gift I could give you." I learnt from this family to expect to get my instructions for the day from the Bible. I also began to read the Bible through in one year. I found that four chapters a day would cover the whole Bible in twelve months. This has been my practice ever since.

The Cooks returned to USA in 1955. Celene started medical school at Stanford but tragically had a cerebral haemorrhage and died at 9.30 one Sunday morning. In her handbag was a letter from the pastor of the church in New York saying, "We look forward to welcoming you into our fellowship at 9.30am on Sunday morning." There must have been a tremendous welcome in Glory.

22. Learning the china trade
From about ten years of age I had helped my Father every Saturday in Doncaster Market. I would stand inside the market stall, and the other assistants were outside serving customers. I would stand tip toe on a wooden box, so that I could stretch my hand through the display of teapots and cups and saucers, receive the money from the assistants

and return the change. I noted how some customers decided quickly what they wanted to buy, and others took their time about a purchase. I would interject a few comments in the hope of influencing a sale and I gradually learnt the psychology of the retail trade - when to speak and when to be quiet. It was like playing a fish. There was a satisfaction in seeing a customer walk away with a full carrier bag marked "Porter's for Glass and China". I always felt that I learned more practical psychology in the market than in the lectures at Medical school.

When I returned to Doncaster for the holidays I was pleased to help my father again. This was a small way trying to repay him for supporting me at Oundle and in Edinburgh. I would go with him to the potteries on a Wednesday. We would get up early and set off at 6 o'clock to get ahead of the rush hour traffic in Sheffield, and then cross the misty Derbyshire dales, through the stone villages of Longnor and Monyash, and dropped into Stoke when the potteries opened at 9 o'clock.

If we had enough time we would stop on the hill above Monyash and look at the beautiful countryside. We leant once on a dry stone wall and gazed at a dew pond, and my Father who was developing a sermon "I will be like the dew unto Israel," shared his thoughts on the quiet, mysterious and gracious work of God.

As we visited several potteries in the five cities, we would discuss with the potters the wares we needed - a gross of white dinner plates, two gross of Blue Dawn cups and saucers, six dozen basins of five different sizes and some tea pots. We would walk round the factory selecting different items and in the process watch the pots being made. They would go into oval brown clay "saggers" and be carried on top of the men's heads into the brick kilns. Other men would be sealing up the kilns ready for firing. The kilns would soon belch out black smoke to earn these five cities the name "Black Country". More kilns would be broken open to bring out the china ready for the glazing process. Some would be decorated, often with transfers or with delicate hand-painting and then be glazed and re-fired. The packers' room was a hive of busy activity. The air was cloudy with of straw dust as these skilled men and women packed the china safely into tea-chests and baskets.

Doulton was an interesting factory where the rooms were full of women sitting at long tables, hand painting bone china and figures. They would show me the new designs coming onto the market, and my father would buy tea sets and Doulton figures. Shelley and Hammersley were also busy establishments, with a strong Methodist Management, and they producing their own distinctive wares. We would make a tour of six or eight potteries, loading up the van in the process.

We usually headed back home in the early afternoon. My Father was treasurer at Cliff College so we usually made up enough time to stop at Cliff for my father to sign the cheques of the week. I had tremendous admiration and love for my Father and it was nurtured during those journeys to the Potteries. We talked at length about my Father's days as a student at Cliff College, and what God was doing now. Without exception we would stop on the hill just above the College and pray for work of Cliff and the students.

On Thursday I would help unload the van, put some china into the warehouse, some onto the market stall and return some back into the van for me to take to Scunthorpe the next day. On Fridays I would drive the van on the Scunthorpe road singing some Cliff College choruses on the way. At times I would take the elderly Miss Ellis with her large carpet bag full of ironmongery - hammers and screwdrivers, nails and saws, chisels and padlocks. She was a faithful old-fashioned Methodist who made an honest living on the market.

At Scunthorpe I would find Mr Edwards the market manager and wait my turn outside his office until he could allocate me a spare stall for the day. I paid the rent of one pound seventeen shilling and sixpence and then unloaded the van, displaying the china to its best advantage. I put the flat-ware round the outside of the stall - the dinner plates, soups and tea plates - and behind this build up a display of tea pots and basins, tea-sets and figures in order to catch the customer's eye.

There were quiet times in the market with little activity, and times of hectic selling. I would sometimes talk about the china and try to draw a crowd. "We have a special delivery from the potteries this week with a remarkably cheap line in tea sets." I would describe how the china was made, how the burnished gold was applied, discuss quality of the glaze and the durability of the porcelain, and hope for a sale. "Not three pounds for this beautiful tea-set, it's worth all of that. Not even two pounds ten shillings. Here is today's bargain. One pound seventeen shillings for this eighteen piece tea set, and it's only for the first five customers.

I would sometimes have the help of Norman Bromley or Joe Wells and at lunch time we would stand aside from the stall and have a short open-air meeting. The Market superintendent would stand in a corner and listen, and before long he was enquiring about the way of salvation. He asked if he could go with my Father when he was preaching in the Lincolnshire chapels. He had a beautiful baritone voice and he would sing gospel songs before my Father preached.

23. Examinations and outreach

The medical course was beginning to fit together. I enjoyed it all, and especially when I got into the clinical years. It was rewarding to elicit the abnormal clinical signs, and then put them together to make a diagnosis. Mornings were spent on the wards, afternoons at lectures, and evenings occupied by reading the text-books. Steadily I made my way through medical school.

Gus Armstrong was a great supporter. He was twenty years my senior and was a curator at the National Museum for Scotland in Chambers Street. It was only a stone's throw from the Royal Infirmary. I would often find him at coffee-time or in the lunch-break. He would be cleaning the display cabinets of fossil fish, or checking some piece of antiquity. "Richard!" - his shout would echo down the corridors. We would embrace and have a time of prayer together. He took a great interest in my studies and he was a great prayer-warrior. He was interested in all my studies and prayed for everything I did. When I see him in glory, I will give him a big thank-you that I was able to get through the medical course with reasonable ease.

Gus was also the leader of the Open-air meeting on the Mound. He purchased an old Post Office van and decided to use it into a mobile pulpit for open air preaching. I told him that there was something wrong with its registration number of 666. "It's all right brother," he said "It's been converted." He had cut out one side of the van so that it dropped down to make a platform. About twenty of us would crowd together inside this old van for prayer before the meeting - it was a close hot huddle when the east wind blew down Princess Street in January - and then the sides would drop down and we would start the meeting. I was the musician with the accordion, and we had a simple programme - songs, bible reading and testimony, finishing with a word usually from Gus and an appeal for people to give their lives to

Christ. Then we would have one-to-one conversations with any who were prepared to stay.

We had some significant conversations, and we would try to follow these folk over the following weeks, sometimes visiting them in their homes, and encouraging them to get established in church fellowship.

A diverse group of people helped on the Mound - students from the University, girls from the Domestic Science College, nurses, and young people who were working in the city. There was a distinct spin-off for our Methodist Youth Fellowship. At one time we thought that over a hundred people had found personal faith in Christ through the various activities of the youth fellowship. I have kept in touch with some of them over a lifetime.

THE YOUNG DOCTOR

24. Romance

'First I saw her peach complexion, set against golden curls, and next I noticed her legs. Of course, there was more, much more.' I should explain ....

Busy as I was in medicine and in Christian activity, I had no serious girl friend. I once kissed a student nurse in the darkness of the hospital grounds. It seemed a brave thing to do in those days. I went out with a pretty girl from the Domestic Science College for a while, but I knew it was not for real. However, it was during my student years when I was at Cliff College for the Pentecost anniversary, that I first set eyes on Christine - the one who was to become my very best friend - my special love for a lifetime. I was in the College dining-room sitting on a window bench, and the most beautiful girl I have ever seen passed by the window. I discovered her name - Christine Brown. She became part of my prayer life from that moment.

Although I tucked this thought away in my mind, and from thereon I secretly prayed and dared to hope that one day I might be able to marry Christine - if God should allow me that blessing - I was a very slow and dilatory suitor. I think it must have been my nervousness about a relationship with girls, and the hang-ups of having grown up in an all-male school. I continued to enjoy the company of many girls in Edinburgh and Doncaster, but I avoided any special relationship, and I believed that one day, in His time, God would give me the "desire of my heart". It would be some years before that dream was fulfilled and I nearly missed it.

25. A doctor

The undergraduate years passed all too quickly. I took the finals in 1958 - three big examinations in Medicine, Surgery and Obstetrics and Gynaecology. It was such a relief to see the pass board, and enjoy the relief of graduation. On that late June morning we were dressed in our robes and mortar boards, and before graduation we had a service of dedication at Grey Friars Church. The chaplain preached on the Tower of Babel, the foolishness of building a life simply on knowledge and skill, if God is excluded. Then we processed through the cobbled streets to the great McEwan Hall where my Mother and Father, Uncle Clarence and my sister Isabel were waiting to support me. I said the Hippocratic Oath and knew I was receiving a great gift, which I wanted to use to the best of my ability.

I was not ambitious for professional success. Many of my peers had fixed up residencies in the teaching hospitals, but I was content to work in a District General Hospital. It would not provide the prestige or high powered references, but I would get a lot of practical experience. Maybe one day I would work overseas, and hands-on experience would be invaluable. My Mother and Father were also happy to have me in our home town for a while.

My first job was a House Surgeon to Mr David Aitken at Doncaster Royal Infirmary. At 9am on the first day the emergency lights flashed for me to go to casualty. There I found my first two patients. They had been struck by lightning. Medical school had not prepared me for this. One poor guy was dead and the other mildly burnt. I realised that in medicine you have to be ready for anything.

I enjoyed surgery tremendously. I was so impressed with the enthusiasm of my boss, David Aitkin, and I knew I had to become a surgeon. He treated me so well, that I became his personal assistant. In those first six months he taught me to do appendicectomies, bowel resections, cholecystetcomies, excision of ovarian cysts, varicose veins, haemorrhoids and opening skulls to decompress injured brains. I watched a few, and then with supervision I found myself the operating surgeon. I worked for long hours, often covering at the same time for the Casualty Department. The sisters in charge taught me a lot - how to treat eyes and ears, and skin problems. On one occasion I had no sleep at all for 72 hours - but through it all I developed surgical confidence.

For the next six months I was Dr Peter Milligan's House Physician in the same hospital. The wards were full, often with beds in the corridor. It seemed like detective work - matching the history with the abnormal signs, choosing the right investigations, reaching a diagnosis and starting appropriate treatment. And every patient was different. One night a lady was admitted very ill with pneumonia and 36 weeks pregnant. I was hurriedly called from my bed at 2am because this poor lady had died and I had to make an immediate decision about the baby. With the minimum of instruments I did an

68

emergency Caesarian section on the ward, and was at least able to deliver a live baby.

I felt an important part of my job was to talk to the patients about themselves and their families. When appropriate I would also ask if I could pray with them. The ward sisters let me conduct ward services on Sunday evenings. I would have the gramophone, play some favourite hymns and give a short talk about the love of God in Christ, and His care for each of us, and the power of prayer. There were not a few tears.

There were also many heartaches. A little girl with a cerebral tumour was very ill. The Pentecostal pastor had told me he did not know how this newly converted family would cope with her death. My job was to break the sad news to this fearful man and his wife. He immediately dropped to his knees and through his tears he said "The Lord gives, the Lord takes away, blessed be the name of the Lord."

Professor Kennedy, when he gave his psychiatry lectures in Edinburgh, had shown us how to hypnotise patients. He had taught self-hypnosis to our Special Agents during the war so that they could minimise any pain if they were caught and tortured by the Germans. I found it quite fascinating and used to hypnotise selected patients with asthma. I also tried to regain the memory for a man with amnesia, to discover that he was wanted by the police for murder!

26. Christine

Whilst in my residency year in Doncaster, I had the paradox of being very busy and also quite lonely. There were long hours of work, not so much time for prayer and bible study and there were many weekends when I could not get to church.

I began to pray about Christine and was delighted not only to be invited to preach at her church in Darfield, but to find that she had returned home from Charing Cross Hospital to convalesce after an appendicectomy. I was invited to her home for a meal before the service and for the first time we had the chance to meet and talk. I plucked up the courage to ask her to go out with me the following Saturday. I polished my father's van until it sparkled. It needed cleaning because it was normally full of straw and dusty from delivering pots. We went to Clumber Park to watch the cricket match and have tea. We agreed to write to each other, and for some weeks we wrote letters, Christine telling me about the life of a student nurse in

London, and my letters were full I suppose were of hospital life in Doncaster and the hope of seeing each other soon.

Christine invited me to London for a weekend. We went to Westminster Chapel on the Sunday morning to hear Dr Martyn Lloyd Jones, and then had a rather frivolous afternoon by the river. I was foolish enough to write to her and say that I did not think the Lord wanted us to have a serious relationship! How blind can one be! I was too short sighted. I certainly missed an opportunity, because it was some years before we met again. Christine told her father "Richard Porter will never marry. He will become a missionary."

27. Which direction?
At that time I was trying to prepare myself for the possibility of missionary work overseas. It would need a broad experience. So my next six months were spent at the Western Hospital Doncaster doing Obstetrics and Gynaecology. I learnt how to deliver babies, and cope with emergencies. I never remember the time when I was convinced that I should be a missionary, and yet I wanted to be ready if the Lord pushed me in that direction. He never did, and eventually I knew that I should be a surgeon in my home country.

I have an impetuous nature, and I have found guidance difficult. I want to know now, and God's promise is only to give light to our feet, not illuminate the distant path. I took some time to learn that it is better to wait and be prayerful, and God will eventually give a clear sense of peace about the best way ahead. I think peace of mind is God's given method to guide His children.

It seemed to be clear to me that I should prepare to become a surgeon which meant passing the difficult Primary Fellowship examination of the Royal College of Surgeons. How could I get three months paid leave for pure study? It was the beginning of January 1959 and I would be out of a job at the end of the month. Then I read in the British Medical Journal that the Blue Funnel Steam Ship Company wanted a locum Ship's Surgeon from the beginning of February, to go to the Far East on SS Peleus. That was the job for me. I made a hasty journey to Liverpool, had an interview, and was offered the job.

28. Off to the Far East

I was 25 years of age. I bought two sets of officer's uniform - blue for the cold northern climate and whites for the tropics - filled a leather case with essentials and surgical text books, and found my way to the quayside where SS Peleus was berthed on a wet February afternoon. She was a stately merchant ship, proudly displaying her characteristic upright blue funnel. The ship was in fine trim, well painted, with no rust and with her clean flags hanging limply in the foggy drizzle - the Red Ensign at the stern and the Blue Peter aloft to tell all that she was soon to leave the muddy estuary of the Mersey for the clear open sea.

Though totally ignorant about the ways of seafaring men, I climbed the steep gangway and was shown respectfully to my cabin. There was a bunk with high sides to stop me falling out when the ship rolled in high sea, a low couch, a fixed table, sink and toilet. Through the small round port-hole I could see the busy tugs racing up and down the Mersey. The first-mate in the cabin next door introduced himself and the two "sparks" busy with Morse code in the cabin opposite hoped we would have a healthy ship for the next three months. I suspect they had made a quick assessment of this very young rosy-cheeked youth who called himself a doctor, and hoped they would not suffer from any serious illness.

There was a commotion. Someone had arrived in black tails, wearing a shining top-hat. With great deference the officers stood to attention, and I followed suite. It reminded me of the consultant's round in Edinburgh Royal Infirmary. This VIP was one of the Senior Directors from the Alfred Holt Company personally delivering the sailing orders to the Captain. It was part of the company's long tradition. The Captain beckoned me to join the procession round the ship, up and down ladders and companion ways, down into the engine room, across the galley, into the cold freeze, no where escaped this inspection, even my cabin. Everything was apparently in order and we were ready to sail.

The pilot's flag was raised. There were loud blasts on the ship's horn, noises of ropes being stretched round winches, the rattle of the anchor and the clanging of the ship's bells. We were on the move, through the lock gates bound for scores of exotic Oriental places and all the way to Japan.

We pulled out of the dock, moved round into the swiftly flowing river, and headed out into the night, with lights flashing on either side. I knew that it was going to be a great adventure.

There were about 110 souls on board SS Peleus. Maritime law said that if there were more than 99 people afloat it was necessary to carry a ship's surgeon, so that was the rationale for me being aboard. There were about 80 crew and in addition 30 passengers travelling in luxury to distant shores. I hoped they were all in good health and would not need too much of my services. I hoped also for lots of time to read my surgical textbooks.

There were five large round tables in the dining room, and a senior officer sat at the head of each table to be host for six passengers. The captain's table was in the centre, but he was on the bridge that first night. The first mate, the chief engineer, the purser and myself were responsible for the other tables. I found that I had six fascinating passengers to entertain. Colonel and Mrs Gunter starting a world cruise. Miss Peacock, taking a slow boat to Japan where she was joining the British Embassy in Tokyo. Mr and Mrs Jones - just married and on their way to Egypt. And Mr Johnson, whose purpose for sailing remained a mystery.

Conversation flowed easily between this disparate bunch. I knew that they thought I was rather young for the job and must be inexperienced. They thought that the only people who wanted to be a ship's surgeons were alcoholics, men running away from their wives and doctors who had fallen foul of the General Medical Council. They wanted to know where I fitted in. I don't think they were too convinced when I said I was at sea to study for the Primary examination of the FRCS. I suspect they thought that a young doctor who needed to go to sea to study, could not be up to the job in the first place.

29. Life at sea
It was exhilarating to feel a sharp wind on the cheeks and taste the salt in the air as I leaned on the polished rails that first morning, alongside the bridge. The ship was ploughing into a heavy sea and I thought of the opportunities ahead.

- I must provide good medical care for this small community during the next three months, get to know them as friends and, where possible, offer Christ.
- I also had to develop a discipline of reading and learning a lot of Anatomy, Physiology and Biochemistry which was essential to pass the Primary FRCS in Edinburgh in June.
- I was looking forward to seeing the different ways of life of many people along the route – in the Middle East, Ceylon, Malaysia, Philippines, Hong Kong and Japan.
- And I was also open to anything God wanted to say to me about offering for missionary work overseas.

My plan was to read the medical books morning, noon and night, every day that we were at sea. When in port I would stop reading and spend as much time as possible ashore. I had already made contact with missionary organisations who worked in our ports of call. And I would spend time in prayer.

Each morning I had an open-surgery from 9.30 to 10.30 am. After breakfast that first day, I sat in my surgery - a small cabin aft - waiting for customers. There were none. It was obviously a healthy ship's complement. Through the open door I could see the stern of the ship rising and falling as it shouldered the crests of the grey waves and dropped again into the troughs of the Irish Sea. I turned the pages of well-thumbed "Manual for Ship's Surgeons" and learnt about conditions I had hardly considered before - prickly heat, snake bite, venereal disease, malaria, Beriberi and Scurvy. I was ready to deliver babies, but no one was pregnant. I made sure that I was able to cross match blood. There were enough instruments to do an appendicectomy on the Captain's table if my assistant the senior-steward would give the anaesthetic, but he was not very promising. He confessed to fainting at the sight of a needle. We were in for an interesting time.

At 10.30 the First-mate popped his head through the door and advised me to be sharp and ready in my full uniform for the daily ship-inspection. Sure enough, I was expected to follow the Captain and his officers on their daily inspection of the ship. We went from top to bottom, bow to stern, whilst the Captain muttered words of advice. Woe betide any member of the crew who was not at his post. I was expected to give advice about the cleanliness of the galley and the condition of the deep freeze. It was difficult to give an opinion about the hygiene of the dozen Chinese greasers who lived a cloistered life of their own right at the stern of the ship. They were sitting on their haunches eating some exotic smelling delicacy and they stood in deference to the Captain. He ran a tight ship and was obviously a man to be respected. After this inspection at 11am, unless there was an emergency, the day was my own.

It took us a couple of days and nights to round the Scillies, cross the Channel and move into the North Sea. At Rotterdam, I had a day ashore, walking the long cold streets into the city, browsing in the shops and visiting a large Lutheran church. I was thankful to be back aboard out of the biting wind, and having some good hot food. The ship was now low in the water, loaded to capacity with European goods for the Far East. Somewhere in the bowels of this ship was a large piece of textile machinery - a loom - being exported by my uncle Ossian from Barnsley, and bound for Singapore.

30. Outward-bound

I was soon used to the daily rhythm of the ship. Regular meals, interesting conversations with the passengers, making friends with the crew - officers and seamen alike – The ship had its share of hypochondriacs who expected professional advice, and I became proficient in many hitherto unknown minor medical conditions. I also spent long hours in my cabin with the textbooks, as the ship headed steadily south across the Bay of Biscay. Here we encountered a force ten gale, but I never minded a storm. The Captain was a man of experience with the confidence of his officers. This was his penultimate voyage.

He eventually shared with me his own health fears but fortunately he never required my services.

It took us about ten days to cross the Mediterranean. It was getting warmer all the time, and as we arrived at Port Said we changed into "Whites" for the tropics. There was a lot of merchant shipping in the harbour, Arab dhows and boats of many colours. We anchored off shore and soon attracted scores of small vessels with merchants selling leather and brass souvenirs. I was advised to keep my cabin door locked. It took a couple of days to unload the cargo into lighters and take on more. Colonel and Mrs Gunter invited me to join them on a small boat into Port Said. We wandered the streets and Bazaars, took a horse drawn carriage, and drank some thick black coffee under the suspicious eye of a number of Arabs. I remembered the recent Suez Crisis, and the British were not popular.

Colonel Gunter was lost ashore, and he was carried to the ship rather inebriated only when we were ready to sail. Putting this man to bed after every shore visit, was going to be a routine experience.

SS Peleus waited her turn to join the convoy of thirty or so ships sailing south through the Canal. And then we were under way. It required great skill to negotiate this ship down the narrow Canal. All the officers and midshipmen were on the bridge. When I looked out of my open port hole, I could almost touch the little children only a few feet away running along the sandy tow path by the side of the ship.

There was unusual excitement as we waited in Bitter Lake - a passing place for the north bound convoy - and our sister ship SS Pegasus steamed into view. Many of the Liverpool born crew had relatives on this ship of the line, brothers and cousins whom they had not seen for many a year. The decks of both ships were crowded with waving seamen and the ships' horns went mad with excitement.

We continued down the canal. In places there were square shaped dung-coloured houses, some with balconies. At another site where the canal was being widened, there were hundreds of Arabs carrying sand in buckets, reminiscent of Biblical times. Many women wore the Abaya, and frequently men would kneel on their mats and face Mecca. There were camels and villages and the desert stretched into the distance, with the sun setting over a palm fringed oasis.

Next morning there was a brief stop at Port Suez to deposit the pilot and then we were into Gulf of Suez and the burning heat of the Red Sea – the hottest place on earth. We had a good turn of speed and comfortably passed the rest of the convoy. The warm stiff breeze from the Saudi desert was welcome and I was happy to read my books in a sheltered corner of the deck, because the cabin was stifling.

Here my instructions were to issue salt tablets to counteract the effects of dehydration - something I had not learnt at medical school.

We turned round the tip of the Arabian Peninsula into Aden - a landlocked harbour which was once the crater of a volcano. We anchored in a bay surrounded on three sides by high brown hills. This was a bunkering place for international shipping and I had only a few hours ashore. Being quite tall, a European and wearing uniform, I was aware that on this foreign shore I cut a conspicuous figure and I was advised to be careful. We still had a military presence and there was a sense of hostility in the air. I purchased a few duty free goods in the souk and returned to the ship.

31. Illness
The night we left Aden I began to feel ill. I had a fever which increased over the next few days. We were crossings the Indian Ocean and I kept to my cabin. I had a painful throat with pustules developing and decided to put myself on antibiotics. They seemed to have no effect. I looked at my pharynx in the mirror and saw what seemed to be a large abscess - a quinsy. My text books suggested that it should be incised. I dare not do it myself, and my assistant the chief-steward did not have a steady hand.

Back in Doncaster, Jim Smith who was a member of the Hexthorpe Methodist Church, was suddenly propelled out of his bed in the middle of the night. He started to pray for Richard, but he didn't know why. Next morning a Tuesday, he went into the market and found my father. "Luther," he said "I was woken in the night and told to pray for Richard. He is in some sort of trouble, but don't worry, it's going to be all right." When I heard this story on my return, although I could not understand the mystery of illness and prayer, I just thanked God.

By the time we reached Ceylon ten days later I was beginning to eat again and feel more like myself. Off-shore breezes carried the scent of sandalwood and cinnamon out to sea from the palm-fringed beaches and into my cabin, tropical smells from this exotic island. I could see the inviting coast of Ceylon and we were to have three restful days in Colombo.

32. Coincidence
When I was in my final year in Edinburgh I became friendly with a Dr Disanayaka from Ceylon. He was studying for the MRCP examin-

ation, endocrinology being his special topic. He taught me quite a lot about the subject. When I knew we would have a few days in Ceylon I contacted Dr Disanayaka, and he invited me up to his village - Negombo - where he had a small private hospital.

I took the country bus from the busy market place in Colombo. It was crammed full, with people hanging out of windows and sitting on the roof. They treated me kindly and moved up on the back seat to let me sit down. Next to me was a man who wanted to practise his English. He told me that he sold Ivory and he asked if I knew anyone in London who would buy his Ivory. I confessed I did not, but my Auntie Hilda lived in London and knew quite a lot of people. He asked what her name was and then pulled out a letter in his pocket which was addressed to her at 4, Inverness Terrace. We smiled and I told him about the God who plans coincidences.

I found Dr Dysanayaka's hospital in Negombo and was able to greet this friend again. His father had just died and he now had big family responsibilities. We had some delicious food, especially the fresh pineapple. Next day he arranged with a Buddhist friend to take me up to Candy into the cool of the mountains. There seemed to be a gentleness about the Ceylonese life in contrast to the sullenness of the Middle Eastern Arabs. Here were hillsides of tea plantations with the women collecting the leaves, and in the valleys children at play in the river, washing their elephants.

The Buddhist friend was also a respected astrologer. He had been called out in the previous night to give advice to one of the politicians. Apparently no important political decision was made in Ceylon without consulting the stars.

My doctor friend drove me back to the ship, and when he opened the boot of his car, it was packed with about thirty fresh pineapples. One of the stewards helped me put them into the cold store, and I left Ceylon a happy man. But not for long. There was an urgent call to see the Captain. I stood in his cabin feeling like a reprimanded school boy before his headmaster. I could see he was rather angry. "What do you mean by endangering the safety of my ship?" I was at a loss to understand, until he told me that there were strict regulations that no food should be brought on board. If the authorities had known that we were sailing with thirty fresh pineapples in the store, the ship would be impounded for thirty days and the company would lose thousands of pounds. The doctor would not be popular. I watched in disappointment as my pineapples were unceremoniously committed to the sea – all except one which we enjoyed for dinner.

33. Singapore, Philippines and Hong Kong

After a few days I awoke one morning to find the ship docked in a narrow channel in Singapore harbour, where we were to stay for a week. Across the water from our berth was a whole village, with scores of families living in thatched wooden huts built on stilts. Women were washing their clothes and children fishing with lines dangling through the floor-boards. Men were hurrying about carrying heavy burdens and the waterway was alive with boats large and small, fussing about the harbour. Our ship had already started to unload.

I went ashore to visit the China Inland Mission (CIM) language school. Captain Cook had prepared the way for me, and I was expected. I shared meals with the students. These wonderful young missionary recruits had come from all parts of the world, to spend a few months in Singapore, getting acclimatised to the tropics and learning the language of their new sphere of work. A group of them took me into the city, showed me where to eat the best food on the streets, and taught me how to play volleyball. They helped me to buy a new accordion and I fear I used it to bother the ship's complement with hymns for the rest of the voyage. It is not possible to play an accordion quietly.

The next port of call was in the Philippines. We steamed into Manila Bay in the late afternoon, as the setting sun gave the sky the most wonderful colours I have ever seen. I was welcomed in Manila by a faithful CIM missionary who provided me with hospitality for two days. He introduced me to the poor areas of the city, where I met some radiant Christians. Then to the FEBIAS radio station where I heard a Christian broadcast scheduled for mainland China. And to a bookstore where colourful literature was being prepared for distribution. These people were busy about the Lord's work.

The next day I went about fifty miles to the south to a small village on the sea shore. The houses were built on wooden stilts on the sands, sheltering under palm trees. Children played their games on the sands, women were cooking, and the pigs and hens scratched around. I met a fisherman who was a new believer. "When did you become a

Christian," I asked. "As soon as they came and told me," he replied without hesitation.

Back into the China Sea we encountered the biggest storm I have ever seen. Here also I saw my first flying fish, silver creatures, five to six inches long which skim from the crest of one wave to the next like swarms of little silver birds or dragon-flies. There would be several of them on the deck each morning having been blown aboard.

We knew we were approaching the Chinese mainland when we began to pass slow moving Chinese Junks. They were the floating family home of several generations who made a living from the sea. No doubt some were pirates, but we made good speed and soon anchored in the Hong Kong straits half way between Kowloon and Victoria Island. I had instructions from home that this was the place to buy some clothes. A tailor came on board and was delighted to put a tape measure round me and measure me for a suit, a number of white shirts and two pairs of pyjamas. These clothes were in my cabin the following morning.

I was looking forward meeting a special person in Hong Kong. I wanted to meet Miss Willis, the sister of Christopher Willis whom the Communists had recently thrown out of his Bookshop in Shanghai. She sent her representative - Jonathan – to meet me on board. He was a British soldier doing his National Service in Hong Kong. He was working for British Intelligence spending his days and nights on the Peak, eavesdropping on the Mandarin radio from mainland China. This young Christian man believed that he would return one day to be an evangelist in mainland China.

I invited Jonathan aboard and the Captain wanted to meet him. The conversation turned to evangelising the nations, and the Captain expressed strong views that it was unethical to change other people's culture. We tried to explain that the gospel was good news for all and it crossed every culture but he was not impressed.

I was taken ashore on a launch and then through the bewildering alleyways of Kowloon until we reached Miss Willis' Christian Bookshop. It was a combination of a church, a bookshop and also a small industry. In a warehouse at the rear there were about twenty women sitting at tables doing the most beautiful coloured calligraphy. They were Bible texts on gift cards and making calendars which had attracted a world-market. Even in the back streets of Hong Kong I

79

had found a group of dedicated people fulfilling their mission. They were hidden away from publicity but faithful to their calling.

We seemed to be very close to the Chinese mainland as we headed out again into the South China Sea. Behind those mysterious mountains and beyond were one billion people, a third of the world's population, suffering under the cruel dictatorship of Mao. We had heard rumours about the cruelty of the cultural revolution and the absolute atheism that was imposed on this continent. What had happened to the young church founded by Hudson Taylor and the China Inland Mission, the work of David Hill and the Methodist Missionary Society, and the young seeds sown by Gladys Aylward?

I remembered how hundreds like Eric Liddell had given their lives for these people, and latterly missionaries like Mrs Cook and Auntie Hilda had been thrown out of China. Surely there was a still a small Chinese church surviving somewhere beyond those dark hills, but we were in total ignorance, and the door was securely closed.

34. Japan and Malaya

Our ship was scheduled to call at four Japanese ports – Kobe, Yokahama, Shimitzu and Nagoya. I discovered a nation at work, determined to rebuild its war-torn economy. No sooner had we come alongside, than a multitude of dock workers swarmed onto the ship in the early morning to unload our cargo. I had permission to go into these coastal cities. It was fascinating. The small streets were lined with open fronted shops selling clothes, cameras and electronic goods at such low prices. Modest Geisha girls would trot down the streets demurely, balancing precariously on their high heels.

I enjoyed browsing round the bazaars. One day above the chatter of Japanese voices I distinctly heard the sound of George Beverley Shea singing "I'd rather have Jesus than silver of gold, I'd rather be His than have riches untold." I followed the sound of the music filled with curiosity until I came to a small corner shop where a Christian man was selling his wares.

It was here in Japan that I was almost killed. I stood on a railway line to get a cine film of a passing train, unaware that another train was rapidly approaching from the opposite direction. It was coming on the very railway line where I was standing. I kept hearing the horn of a train, but believed it was from the train in front of me which I was filming. I only just moved back a moment before this high speed train flew by. It missed me only by inches. Was it an Angel that nudged me out of the way?

"Angels, where ere we go,
Attend our steps whate'er betide.
With watchful care their charge attend,
And evil turn aside." Charles Wesley

One morning I was sitting in my cabin reading a book when I was called to an accident in the hold. A docker had fallen into the depth of the ship and I thought he had a fractured spine. I administered morphine, and stayed with him until he was firmly immobilised on a stretcher. A little later in the day a delegation of Japanese dockers found me and presented me with a generous gift for what I thought was only my duty.

I caused the Captain a little anxiety one Sunday morning. He had given me permission to go to a Christian service, on condition that I was back at the ship when we were due to sail at noon. I knew that every hour spent in port, cost the company a thousand pounds, so I dutifully left in the middle of the service and strolled onto the dock at about 11am to be on the safe side. I became quite nervous. Everything seemed extraordinarily quiet. The usual noise of the rattling cranes and the lifting gears was quite absent. It was eerie. I hurried round the warehouses to see if the ship had sailed without me, but I knew that the law prevented that. And there was the great hulk of SS Peleus standing silently at the dockside. The whole crew and complement of passengers were looking down at me from the decks, and the captain was pacing the bridge. The loading had been completed earlier than expected and they were now ready to sail. But without the doctor they could not move. I apologised profusely, even though it was not my fault. Anyway, they all knew the doctor had been to church! We cast off, and were bound for home.

We returned again by much the same route, in order to pick up home-bound cargo in Hong Kong and Singapore. Here in Singapore, Jack Riley came bouncing aboard. Jack was in his mid forties, and was the Director of Rehabilitation for Young Offenders in Malaya. He had been a member of Spring Gardens Methodist Church when I was a boy. He had been my Sunday School teacher and was an old family friend. Jack had joined the Probation Service as part of his Christian commitment, and he had taken a Prison Superintendent's post in Kuala Lumpur (KL), quickly rising to be head the whole Probation service in Malaya. He asked the Captain if he could take me up to KL and then I could re-join the ship four days later when she came into Port Swetenham on the west coast of the peninsula. However, it was unlawful for them to sail without their doctor even on a coastal route, so I had to be content with a day's visit to KL, when we moved further up the peninsula.

The west coast of Malaya is a fascinating labyrinth of jungle lined waterways. The roots of mango trees reached down into the dark muddy waters, forming mysterious caverns along the shore line. These were covered with tangles of strong vicious thorned creepers and from the dense undergrowth came eerie cries of birds and predators. A water snake moved across the water. There were flowering trees, and orchids and buzzing insects that came on board as we slowly steamed up a narrow channel to Port Swetenham. This was a one-horse town, with no more than a jetty to unload cargo for Kuala Lumpur. I was given dispensation to go ashore and have eight hours in the city.

I took a taxi and arrived at Jack's house for a spicy meal and loads of fresh orange juice, relaxing on his veranda. He was living in colonial style, with a deferential house boy to do the cooking and wash his white shirts. I always found that conversation with Jack was mind stretching and stimulating. A prison psychiatrist joined us and we talked for hours about the criminal mind, about how much was innate and how much acquired. I almost began to think I would like to be a psychiatrist!

The ship moved across the water for a brief visit to Penang, quite a paradise island for tourists. And then we ploughed our way back across the Indian Ocean, returning through the Canal, and battling with a hurricane force twelve in the Mediterranean, until we were in the Atlantic, travelling northwards for home.

I looked at myself in the cabin mirror and realised I had put on a stone in weight since leaving home. And what had I learnt in those three months? I had seen parts of the world that I never knew existed. I had completed my revision of the Primary FRCS. And I discovered the attraction of the sea. It is a strange paradox that seamen are restless on land, until they return to the sea, but when enjoying the exhilaration of life afloat, they are almost without exception, homesick.

35. Home-coming

It was great to be home, and see my Mother standing on the quayside waiting for the ship to dock. And then to be taken home to Doncaster in the Sunbeam Talbot, with so much to talk about. "You look so well," everyone was saying. "Life at sea has been good for you," and I was sorely tempted to take another trip. I got as far as going to London and I found a shipping office where they had a vacancy on a ship to Burma and to South America, but I knew that another voyage did not make sense.

The immediate priority was to pass the Primary FRCS. I was not wishing to find another medical post immediately, but I had to be sure that I had established my knowledge base and was ready for the coming examination in May 1960.

In May 1960 I presented myself at the College for the examination. Mr Brandt gave me a piercing look as I walked rather fearfully towards him across the examination room, to be surrounded by dissected corpses. He had taught me Anatomy as an undergraduate. "Porter," he said looking at me over his spectacles. "Where have you been in the last few months? I hope you have spent a long time in the dissecting-room whilst you have been preparing for this examination". "No Sir," I confessed, "I have been to sea." So he fired the first question. "Tell me about the surface anatomy of the flexor retinaculum." "Yes sir. It is about the size of a postage stamp," I volunteered and began to draw its position on my hand. He gave a knowing smile, because he used to say to us as students - "The flexor retinaculum is the size of a postage stamp." I was home and dry with Anatomy. When, at the end of the day, the day the College Officer stood at the foot of the stairs and called out my name with twelve other candidates, it was an unbelievable relief to know that I was one of the 15% of candidates who had been able to satisfy the examiners.

I telephoned my Mother and she agreed to join me on a short holiday. She came up to Edinburgh immediately on the overnight train, and at 8.30am we were bound for Glasgow, then boarded the Clyde ferry to East Loch Tarbet. It was a short bus ride to West Loch Tarbet and another boat carried us to the idyllic island of Islay where Captain Cook had been born. It was a most beautiful journey, so quiet with brilliant colours reflecting off the rippling sea. It was a lovely way to celebrate passing the Primary examination.

Returning home I had an important task of finding a new surgical job - this time as a Senior Surgical House Officer. I applied to many hospitals including Edinburgh Royal Infirmary, but was repeatedly turned down. I sensed it was because I had done my House-jobs in a District Hospital rather than in a teaching hospital.

Sometimes my Mother seemed to have a hot-line to heaven and this was one of those occasions. "Wait," she said, "I know you will get a job in Edinburgh." I dutifully waited and before long a letter arrived from the Edinburgh Royal Infirmary. They had received back-word from a candidate for the SHO post on Wards 9 and 10 and they offered me a twelve months appointment to start on August 1st.

36. The Edinburgh Royal Infirmary

I was thrilled to be back in Edinburgh and I gave the job one hundred percent. The "Firm" was made up of two consultants - Bill Adamson and Jim Jeffrey - Ivan Tait the Senior Registrar – myself as SHO, and two Housemen. Between us we looked after about sixty patients on two wards.

The atmosphere on the ward was not pleasant. Bill Adamson the boss, hardly ever spoke to me, although one day he insisted that I alone should accompany him to theatre. He asked everyone to leave the theatre except myself and the theatre sister. Then he demanded a large swab, plunged his arm into the depths of the abdominal cavity and with his enormous hand he pulled something from the peritoneal cavity which he wrapped in the swab. "Incinerator," he shouted. I realised that he had retrieved a pair of forceps which he had left behind from a previous operation. He must have thought that I could hold my counsel. Bill Adamson was a colo-rectal surgeon and I shall always remember the hospital porter rushing down the Royal Infirmary corridor with a glowing red-hot iron held in his extended hand, and hurrying into the theatre, for the surgeon to cauterise the unsuspecting patient's haemorrhoids.

84

Ivan Tait was on our ward doing penance. He had previously been working for Sir John Bruce and had accidently grasped the great man's index finger in a pair of sharp towel forceps. Sir John had cried out in agony and Ivan Tait was demoted at once to Casualty. He was now being rehabilitated on our ward, and he was nursing a grudge against the establishment.

Some of the time I was like a horse champing at the bit, waiting to move ahead and yet being restrained. I spent a lot of time assisting when I could have confidently performed many of the operations myself. And I found that the standard was no higher than in David Aitken's ward in Doncaster. But I had many lessons to learn, and I discovered ample time to read for the final FRCS. In May 1961 I appeared for this examination and I passed. They said that I was the youngest Edinburgh fellow at that time, and the ward kindly celebrated with a party.

I also enjoyed the year because I had time to renew the friendships on the Mound and at Nicholson Square. On my last night in Edinburgh before I moved to a new job in London, we had a prayer meeting in the van on the Mound. My friends gathered round me and began to pray in tongues, that God would anoint me to do great things in London - that He would open the eyes of the blind and release the captives. I recognised the power of the Holy Spirit, and as I went south, I expected to see some spectacular things.

37. Mile End
In 1962 I worked for a year at Mile End Hospital in the East End of London, as Surgical Registrar to Mr Holmes. He was such a kind man, and he soon allowed me to have a free hand to do any operation where I felt I had confidence. I was particularly happy doing gastro-intestinal surgery. My anastomoses were secure, and I thought the patients did remarkably well. There was so much surgery to learn, develop the skill of making diagnoses and learning new operative techniques. Part of the job was at the Hackney Children's hospital where I carried out a number of emergency tracheostomies for children in respiratory distress.

One of the ward sisters was a Christian and we held ward services every Sunday. Quite a few patients became Christian. There was a large Jewish presence in the East End, and one Jewish patient was so excited when she realised that Jesus is the promised Jewish Messiah. She told me that as soon as she had recovered from surgery she was going to Jerusalem to tell everyone that their Messiah had come.

I walked the length of Mile End Road passing the statue of General Booth, and looking at Barnado's Home. In this East London community Hudson Taylor had been prepared for a life in China. My heart was crying out because of the barrenness of the place. Oh that God would come down again with blessing. I had been at Mile End about a month when I invited some friends to come to the East End and help. Joe Wells came from West Wickam, Norman Bromley from Doncaster, Gus Armstrong and another friend Eddie Smith travelled from Scotland and we spent a weekend together in London.

On the Friday night and we had a great time of prayer for revival. I invited some others to join us including the new Methodist minister James Martin, a man who had been an alcoholic in Singapore and now had a wonderful testimony. We spent many hours in prayer on the Saturday. That night we were joined by a number of criminals - a car thief, a drug addict, a couple of alcoholics, and they all found Christ. When my friends left on the Sunday night, there was a nucleus of new believers experiencing God's blessing. Here was the beginning of a work that was going to develop for a many months.

Joe Wells who had become a Christian in Doncaster, and his newly converted brother Tom, agreed to come over the river to the East End every Tuesday and Saturday night. They bought a small van. Joe was an electrician and he rigged up a system to play gramophone records from the back of the van, with a loudspeaker perched on the roof which would carry gospel songs down the streets and alleys of the East End. We discovered a useful corner in Cable Street and for two hours, played gospel music and shared with passers by, the good news of salvation. We would finish up in the West African Rainbow Club, having coffee and talking to homeless men, black activists and prostitutes.

There was a Somali population in Cable Street, and we bought some records of gospel songs in Somali. As they were broadcast into the night, scores of Somali men came out into the street to hear the sound of their native tongue. There was some fruit. Many of these men wanted to learn English. The sister tutor at Mile End Hospital allowed me to use the nurses' classroom on a Monday evening to teach the Somali men English. We had a deal - that I would teach them English if they would let me use John's gospel as a text book.

One Saturday night a young wayward couple, Ernie and Carmel, wandered down Cable Street and stopped by the van. "Can your God do anything for drug addicts?" asked Ernie. I introduced them to Joe. They were challenged by Joe's testimony and we took them to their home. It was no more than a triangular section of the corner of an attic room, partitioned off from some other family by a heavy curtain. It reminded me of Fagin's lodgings in Oliver Twist. We prayed with them and they agreed to come to Cable Street Methodist Church at 11am the following morning where I was to be preaching.

I started the service but was disappointed not to see Ernie and Carmel. Then during the second hymn, they made a noisy entrance. Joe had been waiting for them, standing in the street and praying that they would wake up. They told us that they had been suddenly roused from their bed – almost thrown out of bed - and had come to church without having had any breakfast. After the sermon, Ernie came to the front of the church and put a vial of drugs and a syringe on the communion table. He was giving his addiction over to Christ. We were able to re-house these two and care for them for a while.

As we were closing our open-air meeting one night, I was told about a man sleeping under the railway arches at the Tower Bridge end of the Cable Street. I went down with my car. Everything was pitch black. I called out and someone murmured beneath a bundle of rags. Here was an elderly man, dirty and cold, coughing and flea ridden who needed help. I lifted him up, carried him into the car and drove him to Mile End Casualty Department. A Christian sister was on duty. The nurses bathed him, put him in clean clothes, gave him hot food and admitted him. When I visited him in the ward the next morning he said and he had enjoyed the best night's sleep he had for years. This transformed man was sitting up with bright eyes and pink cheeks reading a bible. He said he had reached chapter 15 of Genesis! I pointed him to the Gospel of John. We started him on Anti-tuberculosis triple therapy but, with no home to go to, we suspected that it would not be long before he was again drinking methylated spirits.

We discovered a lot of homeless men who were trying to rehabilitate themselves. I went with James Martin to the Borough Council and they gave us a derelict terrace house in the Isle of Dogs to use as a half-way house. We recruited a group of enthusiastic nurses and doctors who got busy with soap and water and paint brushes, and before long we had quite a clean presentable property for men who were trying to make a new start. This house offered the men a dry warm room on the cold winter nights, and a place of fellowship and support to those who really wanted to change their lifestyle. There were a few successes and many more failures.

James Martin was a very successful business man in Singapore, somewhere around the late 1950s. He had only one problem which was an alcohol addiction which was ruining his business and his personal and family life. One day, seeking a solution, he attended a Salvation Army meeting in Singapore and the Captain of the meeting was inviting people to 'come out to the drum' which I understand was leaving their seat and walking to the front and committing their lives to Christ. This he did and found release. He told me that one day he had been so drunk he went to sleep in Singapore and woke up in Manila and he was getting quite worried about his condition. However, once he was soundly converted and had committed his life to Christ, he was looking for his mission in life. His mind went to Paul's journey from Jerusalem to Damascus and he felt convinced that he should take the same road, so one day he set off from Jerusalem on foot and walked north through the Damascus gate on the road to Damascus, praying as he walked that God would show him His plan for his future life. When he neared Damascus he had a strong conviction that he should offer for the Methodist ministry but he was now in middle years. He therefore wrote a letter to Dr Sangster asking for advice.

Dr Sangster invited him to London and showed him how he could now become a Methodist minister in middle life and this is exactly what happened to James. We became good friends for a number of years as he ministered in Cable Street in the East End of London and I was a Registrar at Mile End Hospital.

How important to realise that we meet with a God who will reveal himself to those who seek to find him.

38. West London

If I was to progress with a surgical career, there were five difficult years ahead of me. I needed to spend two more years as a registrar in a Teaching Hospital, and then find a three year appointment as Senior Registrar. Every time I had an interview at the London Teaching Hospitals I was told that they thought my Edinburgh FRCS did not compare satisfactorily with the London fellowship. In order to train in the South of England, I therefore needed to pass the London FRCS. The regulations demanded that I spend at least six months in a Casualty post. I dutifully moved from the East End and to work as Registrar at the West Middlesex Hospital. It was a new challenge, because part of the job was orthopaedics, and part plastic surgery where I learnt the importance of handling tissues with care.

During this time I lived with Auntie Hilda in her flat in Ladbrook Grove. I used to drive her back and forth from MIH and learnt so much from her about China and her friends in West Africa. I preached at the final service before the Lycett Mission closed its doors in the East End, and Auntie Hilda insisted on going with me. My text was, "The things that cannot be shaken will remain."

Then I received an SOS from Osmond Mulligan, a desperate cry for someone to go to Nigeria and run a single-handed bush hospital. I knew I was the one who had to go.

39. Nigeria

Osmond Mulligan was a great friend from student days. He was in the year behind me at Medical School. He was a Methodist Ulsterman with a key role in our Youth Fellowship and he had a passion for evangelism. Osmond had married Sylvia and when he qualified, he went to serve the Qua Iboe Church in Nigeria. In 1963 he contracted some tropical disease and was so very ill that he had to return home, leaving an un-staffed Bush hospital.

Before the Qua Iboe Mission accepted me as a locum replacement for Osmond, they wanted to be sure I was "all right". I respected them for this, because I believed that many missionary societies had lowered their standards for the sake of expediency. I took a plane to Belfast and was interviewed by Professor Rogers, the Prof of Surgery at The Royal Victoria Hospital. It is the only time I have been interviewed on a seat in a public park. This godly man took me for a walk, plied me with questions about my surgical experience and my faith, and he was eventually reassured that even if I was not ideal for the job - it was a single handed position and I had no West African experience - I would probably do.

I gave two weeks' notice at the West Middlesex, and soon Auntie Hilda was waving me goodbye as I boarded a BOAC plane to Lagos. We crossed hundreds of miles of arid brown desert and then as night fell the plane came in low over the bush. I saw scores of village fires illuminating the mysterious West African darkness. In Lagos, I stayed with Auntie Hilda's African friends overnight, and the next day I took a very bumpy and scary flight through a tropical thunderstorm, down the coast to Port Harcourt.

Oswald Mitchell a doctor from Etinan Hospital met the plane. He first picked up provisions at the store in Port Harcourt. "We come to town so infrequently," he said, "that we stock up whenever we can". I began to understand what he meant as we travelled north, first on tar roads, and then on rough sandy tracks. We swerved from side to side to miss the major pot-holes and the dense bush encroached on either side.

Women in brightly coloured clothes carried enormous loads on their heads. Some men rode bicycles, others were chopping at the undergrowth with machetes and children romped around on their way from school. As we passed through one village, a goat suddenly darted across the road in front of us. I looked behind. It lay motionless in our tracks. Oswald said, "We must keep going. If we stop we shall be beaten up or worse."

It took several hours weaving in and out of the bush, over rivers and through many villages before we reached Ikot Okoro. This was to be my home for three months until the mission could find a permanent replacement. The guards opened the gates of the hospital compound and we drove through well manicured grounds up to the white single story buildings of the hospital. There was a large water tower in the middle and tall palms around the compound, casting some back shadows here and there, against the brilliant glare of the late afternoon sun. We pulled up outside Osmond's home. Sylvia came to the door, so pleased to see that I had come to relieve her exhausted husband. Osmond could barely stand on his feet. I hardly recognised this young man, thin and gaunt, physically spent – the human cost of

90

sharing the gospel in Africa. I was pleased that Oswald would take Osmond and his little family to the airport the following day. They were in need of rest and probably medical help at home. "Don't worry about the strange diseases you will meet out here," Osmond said. "There will be things you've never dreamed about, but there are plenty of text books, and the nurses will help you." And soon I was alone, with no other doctor for twenty two miles, with no tar roads and no telephone.

40. The bush hospital
The hospital had 110 beds in four simple open-wards. There were many more patients than beds, as extra patients and relatives slept under the beds and on the verandas. There were a lot of sick people about but I was young and undaunted. If I was short on tropical experience I did not lack enthusiasm. I had a head full of basic surgical knowledge, and there were four Irish nurses who seemed to know how to run a bush-hospital.

My first welcome was from the smiling black face of an elderly lady who came to my door with a large oval bowl piled high with oranges. "For the new doctor," she said. This lady was the wife of the local church pastor and was offering the same style of generous hospitality that my mother used to share whenever we had new neighbours at home. Someone else arrived with a bowl of eggs, another with two live cockerels and the pantry was soon full of large yams. I was not going to starve. Local food was cheap, and once a week the sisters would make a major shopping trip to the town of Aba twenty miles to the north. With care I would survive like the other missionaries, on a salary of £23 per month.

Ossie and Raymond were my two house-boys. They assured me that they knew how to wash and iron, and they sported brilliantly starched white shirts to prove it. They would also do my local shopping in the market, cook my food, make my bed, clean the house, boil the water on a wood-burning stove and generally make sure the doctor was comfortable. In fact I had to do no domestic chores - just look after the hospital. These two boys were given a crash course in hygiene, important when dysentery was endemic and everyone was a carrier of worms.

91

Each morning I sat in the out-patients clinic. It was a cool room, off the balcony with open windows. Mr Ekyate was my interpreter. He took the patient's history, and he was delighted if he could make the diagnosis. We would expect 100-200 patients each morning. No one was in a hurry. It was too hot anyway. Provided the patients were seen that day, everyone was happy. In addition to specific medication, each patient went home with a packet of iron tables, vitamins and anti-helminthic drugs for worms.

We admitted about six patients each day, either from the clinic or as emergencies. The most common surgical problem was inguinal hernia. One poor man arrived, pushing a wheel-barrow, and inside the barrow was his large scrotal hernia, almost full of his total abdominal contents. He survived! And almost daily we received exhausted women in obstructed labour. I did routine operating sessions every Tuesday and Friday mornings. I had to give spinal anaesthetic, introducing the needle and procaine in the side room, scrubbing and sometimes adding local anaesthetic. Once we got the system going I could get through six to eight operations on one list. There were various tumours, gall bladders and kidneys to be removed, vesico-rectal fistulas to be repaired - in fact I had to be prepared to do everything, otherwise the patients would have no surgery at all.

The operating theatre had open windows because the heat was stifling. Flying beetles would sometimes sacrifice themselves in the beam of brilliant theatre lights and drop into the wound - probably sterile beetles, because we had a very low infection rate.

The hospital had a maternity village, where women from a distance would stay for the last four weeks of their pregnancy. They received expert midwifery care and shared in bible-study and prayer each morning and evening.

It was not safe to give spinal anaesthetics to women in obstructed labour because of the sudden drop in blood pressure, so I gave a lytic cocktail. I would place the needle in the vein, scrub, prepare the patient and towel-up, and just before I made the incision I would ask the nurse to inject the prepared cocktail of pethidine, phenergan and largactyl. The patient would give a big sigh when the drug reached the brain, and if I was quick I could get the baby out without them feeling any pain. Using this cocktail, I carried out over a hundred

Caesarean sections during my three months at Ikot Okoro and did not lose a baby.

We made a small charge for treatment, but the poor were treated free. I discovered that the standard of care in all the mission hospitals was very high, and patients often travelled many miles to reach us. They knew they were coming to a Christian hospital and they were prepared to hear the gospel. We had four sisters from Northern Ireland, and about forty Nigerian nurses. They were all Christians and these girls with smiling faces conducted morning service in the out-patient hall each day.

I was surprise at the happiness of the people in West Africa. They had so little materially, their life expectancy was short, there was a lot of disease and ignorance, and yet they went about their work cheerfully singing hymns and praising God. By contrast, in Europe with its affluence and security, people walked the streets with miserable faces. I decided that selfish ambition and materialism are the major source of unhappiness.

I preached in the village church every other Sunday through an interpreter and, on Tuesday mornings, I would take a Bible study for the preachers. I would cycle for about five miles into the bush along narrow sandy tracks, until I reached a clearing where there was a small church. There would be about thirty preachers waiting for Bible study. Each week I shared with them the teaching of the early chapters of Genesis. When we reached chapter sixteen I explained that although Abraham took a second wife Hagar, it was not God's best plan. It resulted in broken relationships that lasted for generations. Unbeknown to me, these leaders of the Qua Iboe church had struggled with this very problem for many years - about having more than one wife. They believed in trial marriage, and if their bride failed to produce an offspring, they found another wife. They responded to the scripture in Genesis, and in 1962 presented a motion to the Church Conference agreed, that in future, Qua Iboe Christians should practise only monogamy.

One weekend I travelled to Umahia where I stayed with a gynaecologist. He told me how to do symphysiotomies for obstructed labour, by dividing the ligament at the front of the pelvis, which could sometimes avoid the need for a Caesarean Section. I began to practise this technique, with great effect. After being obstructed for hours, the baby would suddenly pass through the divided pelvis. The mother would waddle temporarily for some weeks, but it was worth it.

Whilst at Umahia, I asked where Don English was staying. I knew Don was working at the Trinity Theological College and wanted to surprise him. I had first heard of Don at Cliff College when a local preacher, "Big Bill Stoddart", told me that he had a young man under his wing, who would be a very great preacher one day. A year or two later I learnt that Don had become the travelling Secretary for the IVF. I wrote to him asking him to speak to our youth Fellowship at Nicholson Square and in a memorable way, he expounded the Bible with a style I had not heard before. And now Don was in the heart of Africa, in Umahia.

I walked up to the front door of his home and it was opened by a worried Bertha. "Come in. Don's very ill in bed." He was, and he looked very poorly indeed with a fever of 102°. My first guess was malaria, and it was right. He was taking an inadequate dose. I changed his tablets. It was routine for me, and thereafter, Don said that the Lord has sent me that day to save his life. For years afterwards, he would repeat the story whenever he saw me in his congregation.

41. The mysterious continent

Africa has been called the Dark Continent. On my first morning at Ikot Okoro I was asked to see a young man who had turned his face to the wall, and he was refusing to eat. He was a pastor's son. They said that ju-ju had been placed on him, that the local witch-doctor had put a spell on him and he would die. I believed none of it and was sure there must be a medical reason for his anorexia. I examined him with a tooth-comb but found nothing amiss. I was so worried that I sent a runner to Etinan to ask Oswald Mitchell to come and give a second opinion. Perhaps this was a tropical disease that I did not understand. Oswald came. "He has ju-ju on him and he will die," he said. I had difficulty accepting his diagnosis and we prayed. His family took him home and the poor boy died. I discovered that I was in the middle of a spiritual battle that I did not understand.

Some weeks later one of our nurses Nwima also had ju-ju placed on her by the witch-doctor. She also refused to eat, and we had to admit her. On the Tuesday evening I was leading the hospital's Christian

Endeavour service. We sang and read the Bible and we heard some powerful living testimonies from the nurses. I felt that this was the time to do something about Nwima.

I remembered a story that my father had told me about his days at Cliff College. In 1928 Samuel Chadwick had called the whole college together to he asked them to pray for Brother Euglow. This ex-student was very ill in Cornwall with a mental condition. Chadwick asked everyone in the college to stay on their knees that night and pray until they were sure that God had healed Brother Euglow. The lights burned at Cliff College long into the night. In the morning, Chadwick announced at breakfast, that he had had a phone call from Cornwall and Brother Euglow was fully restored and in his right mind.

Remembering this story, I made the same request to the hospital staff at Ikot Okoro. We agreed that all of us would pray and not sleep, until we were sure of Nwima's cure. In the morning, this young nurse sat up in the hospital bed, and ate her breakfast. I learnt the truth of the teaching of Jesus, about the man asking for bread at midnight and the unjust judge who responded to the importunate widow's plea.

One of my many tasks was to perform post-mortems for the police. I dreaded looking out of my window and seeing the police making their way to the mortuary. It was a very unpleasant affair. The smell was offensive, even when the windows were wide open and the air sweetened by a perfumed spay, but it brought a little money to the hospital. It was a procedure that had to be carried out as quickly as possible. One day I was asked to go to a distant village where the police were doing an exhumation of the village chief. They suspected foul play. Mr Ekyate suggested he go with me to show me the way. "It could be quite dangerous," he said knowingly. We drove through the bush for a long time eventually arriving at a small clearing where a crowd of villagers had gathered to watch the proceedings. I was told to expect several bodies because the wives of the village chief were often sacrificed when he died, and they were buried with him. There on the hot dry sand was but one shrivelled corpse, six months deceased. They expected me to determine the cause of death.

I gazed at these poor emaciated remains. The man had only one arm. I prodded the other arm and noted that the humerus was broken. "Of course," I said. "I can now sign the death certificate." "Cause of death

- (i) malnutrition (ii) fractured humerus - inability to feed himself." There was no clear evidence of foul play. It seemed to satisfy the authorities and we sped on our way home.

Another time we took the hospital van to a village in the heart of the bush. We were carrying the body of a patient who had unexpectedly died from septicaemia. I didn't want the distraught husband to have to wheel her home on his bicycle, and we offered to help him. As we drove into the deep undergrowth, the path got smaller and ever narrower, and I began to re-consider the wisdom of our decision. We crossed a small river, carefully placing the wheels on two slender planks of wood, and drove on into a jungle village. We were not expected. Rather they were looking forward to the lady arriving home alive and well. As we lifted the coffin out of the back of the van, the villagers who gathered round began a pitiful wailing. The men looked angry and menacing, whilst the husband was holding them back and trying to say something in our defence. The atmosphere was getting tense. We climbed back on board, quickly turned around and sped back towards the river. On the makeshift bridge, one of the planks snapped under the weight of the van, but we were on the right side. No one was following us. We accelerated and were greatly relieved to reach the far bank and be heading home.

The bush can be very frightening. One of our nurses was cycling though the bush and came into a clearing. She was surrounded by a score of Ekpo men adorned in their head-dress of feathers. They were practising witchcraft and ju-ju. She feared for her life, knowing that a girl rarely escapes from their hands. She cried out one simple prayer - "Jesus". And she said that although she was in the middle of this group of men, their eyes were blind to her presence. She dismounted and crept quietly away.

Many villagers did not know about the gospel, even though the Qua Iboe mission had worked along the river for nearly seventy years. One Sunday morning I was woken early by the police. They had brought in the body of a man cut to pieces by a machete. An hour later they brought in another similar corpse. Then they came with a young prisoner who had attempted suicide. His throat was cut from one side of the neck to the other. However, he had missed the large vessels because he must have extended his neck in the process, and he had therefore cut through his wind-pipe. He was almost dead, gasping for breath. This was the alleged murderer. I took him quickly to theatre and made a formal tracheostomy, and tidied up the wound. We nursed him back to health in the isolation hut, which was used for serious infections. He was manacled hand and foot to the bed, and guarded day and night by a policeman. This isolation hut was on the path from the nurses block to the wards, and each day, as the nurses went too and from work, I would see them stop and talk to this frightened man lying on his bed. He had never before heard the gospel. Before long he wanted to receive the forgiveness of God through faith in Jesus. He became a believer. I closed his tracheostomy and off he went to prison. Some weeks later I was a witness at his trial. I knew that whatever his crime, when he stood at a greater judgement seat he would be acquitted.

Africa is also an exciting continent. You never know what to expect next. I was in the clinic one morning when a man arrived with a twenty foot python curled up in a basket. He had caught this creature in his fishing net, and wanted to take it into the village to eat. However the chief would not accept it in the village, until the venom was removed, and the only person to do that properly was the doctor. I promised to help him if he could wait until the end of the clinic.

At lunchtime, we laid the dead python across the operating table. Mr Ekyate assured me the venom would be towards the caudal end of the belly, and he was correct. It was like a small gall bladder. I found and removed the sac and asked about the snakeskin. The fisherman wanted me to have the skin, so I proceeded to remove the beautiful skin, and we were both happy with the bargain. I nailed the skin taut on a long plank of wood and let it dry in the sun for a few days. Then I rolled it up to take home, and it was made up in London into a lovely snake-skin handbag for my mother.

There was a variety of dangerous wild life that kept me literally on my toes. In the middle of the night, I would have to see the emergencies by crossing the hospital compound. I was given a hand torch to scare off any snakes that might be in my path. One morning I was wakened with the cry, "Tiger, tiger." Of course there are no tigers in Nigeria, but they meant that they had seen a leopard spore on the very path which I had used in the darkness only hours before.

We were surrounded by impressive towering red termite hills and from time to time these colonies decided they would move house.

They streamed out in a moving black river of soldier ants. The whole colony would start to march, and millions of them would move purposefully in one rather frightening black mass. There was no other choice than getting out of their way. If they came through your house, they might cover you and eat you alive. I saw a colony move across the compound and towards our children's ward. There was a hasty evacuation of the ward as we let these determined creatures have right of way.

Darkness quickly descended on the compound each night at six o'clock, and the bush became alive with the sound of drums and the noise of millions of insects. Many of these creatures would invade my house and settle on the walls. They were insects of every description. I watched many a praying mantis, and hungry lizards, and was careful to keep an eye out for the dangerous scorpions. I only felt really secure when I was safely tucked inside the mosquito net, and could let the hungry creatures creep and buzz ineffectually outside.

All too soon I was getting ready for home. I received a delegation of Africans begging me to stay with them, but I knew I must be returning home again. Like Osmond, the climate and the pace of life was taking its toll. I could see that I had lost a lot of weight.

SETTLING DOWN

42. A training post in Sheffield

Back from Africa, within a few weeks I was in Sheffield. A strange looking man sat on the other side of the desk frowning at me. I had never seen his like before. Profuse hair was sprouting from his nose and ears, and his dark brow was heavily furrowed, and he had enormous hands. If this was a typical orthopaedic surgeon, was I the person to be joining their ranks?

I was attending an interview for a new two year training Registrar post in the Sheffield Teaching Hospitals. It promised six months training in orthopaedics, six months in paediatrics, six months plastic surgery and six months urology. It was ideal, but the competition was fierce. I had had a lot of practical experience and was qualified with the Edinburgh FRCS. But I had stepped off the career ladder and worked in Africa. Would this count against me?

I need not have been concerned about John Dornan's appearance. He had a kindly voice. "Tell me about your time with Qua Iboe," he said. I waxed eloquently about life in an African mission hospital. I soon began to appreciate that he was an Ulsterman himself. He knew many of the Qua Iboe staff and was in full sympathy with the aims of the mission. I was offered the job, and was expected to begin in Orthopaedics with Mr Dornan in a few weeks' time.

In the very next post, I received what seemed to be a better offer of a general surgical registrar post at the Royal Infirmary of Edinburgh. I thought that the Edinburgh post would have suited me better than the Sheffield job I had accepted, but I was honour bound to go to Sheffield. I had to step out in faith. This was a major cross-road decision, because I think that if I had gone to Edinburgh I would eventually have been a general surgeon rather than have pursued an orthopaedic career.

As I rotated through various appointments, from orthopaedics to urology, then plastics and finally paediatrics, I became increasingly focused on the speciality of orthopaedics. Experience from many previous posts matched the needs of orthopaedic training and this was now became my career path. I also knew that there was likely to be a consultant orthopaedic vacancy in Doncaster about 1970 and I set my sights on that. It would be good to have the opportunity to practise in my home town.

43. Engagement

Whilst in the Sheffield Registrar rotation, I discovered good lodgings with a kind elderly lady - Miss Button - who was a member of Victoria Hall Methodist Church. She welcomed me into her home, and prepared a three course meal for me each evening. She gave me a comfortable room, but I was increasingly empty inside. I worked long hours in the hospital, studied the surgical text books at night, went to Doncaster at the week-ends, but I kept thinking about Christine. Why had I cut short such a promising relationship five years ago? And where was she now?

I heard from Wilfred Brown that his daughter was doing a Health Visitor's course at London University. There had been one or two boy friends and she was quite serious about someone in London. Perhaps I had completely missed my chance?

In January 1964 I went skiing in Austria with a group of Christian medical friends. This was a new and exhilarating experience. I learnt to stay on my feet, and progress beyond the nursery slopes. I wrote to Christine asking if she would go out with me for a meal as I passed through London on my return from Austria, and I was delighted to receive a guarded acceptance. What would she think of the man who had so unkindly broken off a relationship some years before?

We had an Indian curry in Hampstead. I remember following her up the stairs to her first floor flat for coffee and thinking that she had lovely legs! She was so bright and cheerful and her conversation sparkling and full of life. She wanted to know about the time in Mile End and with the Qua Iboe Mission. How could I have been so blind, seven years before? And we kissed. I knew there was mutual affection and I tried to offer an apology for previous years. She was gracious enough to agree to see me in a few weeks time when she was coming to Yorkshire for a holiday.

Christine had a short holiday in Darfield seeing her parents in March 1964. I made sure I had plenty of time off and took her out every evening. On the Saturday we had a day together in Scarborough. It rained all day. Never mind, I had organised lunch at a small guest

100

house where we were the only visitors. The proprietors knew that there was romance in the air and gave us some space. We walked the length of the marine drive and then spent two hours in the cinema watching I know not what. But I do know however that after the cinema, we sat in the car park close together, kissing and cuddling. I said, "Christine, will you marry me?" I asked hesitantly, holding her hand. "I'd like to look after you for ever." She pulled back, looked straight into my eyes and said, "Do you mean it?" "Yes I do. I love you," and to my great surprise and joy she hugged me and accepted my offer. "Yes I will."

I cannot explain the delight and lightness in my spirit as we drove back through the night across the Yorkshire Wolds. I took her to her home in Darfield and returned to Doncaster. Mother and Father were awake, and did not seem at all surprised when I said that I had asked Christine to marry me and she had accepted. As usual my Mother and Father prayed, and I sense Wilfred and Mary were also on their knees in Darfield. We both had parents who had shown us the way of faith and we knew they would endorse our marriage.

When the following day I formally asked Wilfred for his daughter's hand in marriage he said, "Richard, she needs a great deal of love." This I promised to give and the news was out. We planned an early marriage in July.

44. The Brown family
Christine and I have always had complete agreement about spiritual things. We both have a simple trust in Jesus as our Saviour and Friend, and believe the Bible implicitly even when there are parts that are difficult to understand. When Christine was eleven years of age, in an evening service, an old local preacher made an appeal at the close of his sermon, inviting people to come forward and accept Christ. He was not an eloquent preacher but he quoted hymns. Three people responded - an old man in his eighties, a young man Bill Platts, and my dear Christine who was still a girl. She says she has never doubted the Presence of Jesus in her life, since that time. We both understand that others may struggle with doubts, but since those early days both Christine and I have had an assurance that God is in control of everything, and all is well.

Christine had a happy innocent childhood. She was brought up on a diet of chapel, Sunday school and Christian holiday conventions. Her father Wilfred helped to organise the Southport Holiness Convention each July, and each Easter he ran a convention at his own church in Darfield. Visits from the Cliff College trekkers had also stirred her young heart and she used to wonder if God wanted her to be a missionary. In those days there was an unwritten law that first-class Christians became missionaries, second-class went into some full-time work at home, and the rest took secular employment.

At seven years of age Christine contracted acute nephritis and was admitted to the Sheffield Children's hospital. There was much anxiety and she lost a whole year of schooling. It was a great achievement that not only did she catch up academically, but she was eventually accepted for nurse training at Charring Cross Hospital and was finally selected for a Health Visiting course at London University.

Both Christine and I have always felt that our families were rather special. Their interests inter-twined, and before we ever met, both families knew and respected each other. My Uncle Ossian used to preach at Darfield and sometimes he would take Christine and her brother David in his Rolls Royce to the cricket Test Matches.

We were proud that our families had prospered in spite of personal hardship. Wilfred was one of thirteen children and had been brought up in the Depression. Uncle Harry became an evangelist. He played and taught the violin and made much of music in his services. He became known as the fiddling evangelist. He had an effective ministry in Carcroft, a mining village to the north of Doncaster, having open-air meetings in the market square as the pubs emptied on a Saturday night. He also was pastor in Leeds and there he had a renowned healing ministry. When we were married he sent us a post-card covered with texts about the glory of heaven.

Uncle Herbert died in Wilfred's arms having been gassed in the trenches in the first world-war. Uncle Arthur was an Estate Agent, and father of Douglas Brown who later became Vice President of the Methodist Conference. Uncle Fred moved to Doncaster and was a pillar of strength at Priory Place Methodist Church. Emma, Annie and Sarah were spinster sisters who managed a corner-shop in Hexthorpe in Doncaster. They were renowned for a life of prayer. I can still hear Annie singing in a clear voice during the prayer meeting

- "God answers prayer in the morning, God answers prayer at noon. God answers prayer in the evening, so keep your hearts in tune."

This was Christine's family background. Her mother Mary was rather small in stature but she and Wilfred had five children. Gordon was killed in a tank in Italy. Cynthia married Geoffrey who became a Canon in the Church of England and Principal of Whitcliffe College in Oxford. Eunice moved to Mansfield and her brother David settled in Doncaster.

Christine and I knew that there is a sense in which man and wife become one person. "The two become one flesh." We were leaving our father and mother, and yet we were accepting our respective families, and their respective heritage, for which we are continually thankful.

45. Marriage

The sun shone from a cloudless sky on July 16th 1964. Christine at 26 years of age was nervous. I was 29, and full of excitement. I stood at the front of a packed Pitt Street Methodist Church in Barnsley waiting for the chords of the organ to announce her arrival. Here she was, coming slowly up the aisle on her father's arm and followed by her bridesmaids. She was radiant, and she pulled back her lace veil and smiled at me. After the vows I gave her a kiss. Geoffrey preached on Ruth - "Your people shall be my people and your God my God."

The reception was at the Royal Hotel, Barnsley, with 120 guests. We had the sweetest non-alcoholic fruit punch that I ever tasted. There were flowers everywhere and lots of laughter. It seemed a sea of happiness. Many friends wanted to make speeches - some were funny and some serious - and I assured everyone that Christine and I wanted to have an open house where they would always be welcome. We returned to Darfield and were sent on our way by family and a host of friends for a honeymoon in Ireland - without my spectacles! Who wants spectacles on a honeymoon?

We could not have chosen a more delightful place for our honeymoon than the Lake Hotel in Killarney. We were shown to the enormous bridal suite with large floor to ceiling windows overlooking the lake. After the hectic time, leading up to the wedding, we both welcomed the tranquillity and luxury of this beautiful hotel. Words that come to mind are - tenderness - sharing - laughter - oneness. God was good to us.

46. Daniel

We had no sooner settled in our small house in Chorley Road when Christine realised that she was pregnant. We tried to convince the Senior lecturer in Obstetrics that there was a baby on the way but he discounted it. However, Christine was right.

Christine was tremendously hospitable during those months, inviting many friends for meals and running a warm and welcoming home. My mother was relieved that there were no more socks to wash and that someone was cooking for me like she used to. My father invited Wilfred to join him as treasurer at Cliff College and the sun was shining for us both.

Daniel was born on May 7th 1965. It was a difficult obstructive posterior delivery - a high forceps - and we were pleased that Christine had excellent care. 48 hours after Daniel's birth, I was called from theatre because Daniel was fitting. He had a low serum calcium level, and had tetany. The bloods were adjusted. We took him home, and he was put onto a bottle, but Daniel refused to feed. For ten days we watched his weight fall and we were in despair. The professor said that if he did not improve he would have to be admitted. We sat up each night holding a bottle to his lips but in vain. Then Tom Butler arrived. He had a bottle of oil. He prayed for Daniel. He anointed him and we watched. The very next feed Daniel took 12 ounces! He never looked back. We took him to the clinic and the professor asked the nurse to weigh him again. He did not believe the result. But we knew.

47. Early research

I had then started a year's appointment in Orthopaedics at Rivelin Valley Hospital working for Sir Frank Holdsworth and John Sharrard. This leisurely post also gave me time to think about the unexplained areas of surgery, and the need for research. I discovered for the first time that there are more questions in surgery than answers. It led to the publication of four papers during my time in Sheffield.

The first was accepted by the BMJ - "A new test of finger tip sensation". It was uncanny how the idea dropped into my mind. I was driving down to Derby to a meeting of hand-surgeons and I was thinking that there should be a better test of finger-tip sensation than the two-point discrimination test and Moberg's test - good as they were. I simply asked the Lord to show me a better way. I began to think of Braille, how blind people move their fingers over proud marks to identify words. Then I thought of dyes manufactured in Sheffield. They were used to punch letters into metal. It would be possible to ask blindfolded patients to try to identify these embossed letters - letters like A, H, I, M, O, T, U, V, W, X, Y which are identical in reveres - and find the smallest letter they could correctly recognise. We could design a finger-tip sensation test, to be used like an optician testing a patient's sight.

I found a small firm tucked away in the back streets of Sheffield that made these dyes. They were very interested, and they gave me a free sample. I tested them on a series of patients and published a paper. This Sheffield dye-making company went into business selling a box of different sized letters to hand-surgeons for what became a standard clinical test – "The Letter Test."

The second paper in the Journal of Bone and Joint Surgery was a comparison between two different types of finger-tip skin graft. The third described the benefits of a modified bladder operation - the valved Boari flap operation. I had no innovative part but was just responsible for the assessment. The fourth paper however was rather novel. I examined the temperature control of the lower limb in about fifty children with spina-bifida and demonstrated the presence of an undiscovered spinal reflex - an autonomic mechanism to regulate lower limb temperature. Thus began a life time interest in medical research.

48. William
On October 3rd 1966 our second son, William, opened his deep blue eyes to this world. It was an easier labour for Christine than her first. I was in the delivery room and William had the umbilical cord twisted round his neck. There were a few anxious moments, but he finally took a big gasp and went pink. Our cup was full - two healthy little boys in the first two years of marriage - and also a little Lakeland

Terrier called Tessa. The house was scattered with small toys and with much happiness. We joined the Fulwood Methodist Church, led a house-group for weekly Bible study, and we had many young friends in Sheffield. But I had an eye for a new post, and we had to move on.

I had found the English FRCS more taxing than the Edinburgh examination but after several attempts I satisfied the examiners in 1965. My Mother and Father and a very pregnant Christine went with me to the College in Lincoln's Inn Fields and I received the diploma. Sir Frank Holdsworth who was the College President developed a great rapport with my Father and showed him all over the College. Patronage has always been important in British Surgery, and I felt the Sir Frank would support me in a new move. And he did.

In 1966 I applied for a Senior Registrar post at Kings College Hospital London, rotating between Farnborough Hospital and Kings College in Denmark Hill. Remarkably I was short-listed. I sat with seven others in the small waiting room eyeing the competitors. They were all very confident registrars from different London Teaching Hospitals and what chance had I coming from the provinces. I was rather relaxed expecting little from the interview, and was amazed to be called back into the board room and told I was offered the job.

I think two things tipped the balance in my favour. The first was a reference from Sir Frank. The second was the easy rapport I had with Chris Attenborough when I visited Farnborough Hospital, the peripheral part of the rotation. We talked of my friend Kenneth Hulbert - a respected orthopaedic surgeon at Orpington Hospital and son of Rev Charlie Hulbert, who had invited me to accept Christ when I was a boy of eleven years old. Chris Attenborough was the country's leading expert on club feet, and we discussed the way John Sharrard performed his children's foot surgery in Sheffield. Whatever the reason, I was offered the post at Kings, and was expected to start in six weeks' time.

It was going to be a hectic time. My father was recovering from a minor cerebral episode but Wilfred and my Uncle Clarence agreed to have a day with me in London to buy a house. We spent about six hours with an estate agent touring Farnborough and Bromley until we found the ideal spot, a semi detached three bed roomed house – 34 Southcroft Road. I put a down a deposit hoping to take possession within four weeks.

Unfortunately the vendors let us down. They decided to delay their move and I felt I had no choice but to start the job, and live in hospital accommodation, with Christine still in Sheffield. It was not easy for her having to wait with little Daniel and William, until the new house was empty.

49. Family anxieties

I had just started the morning operating list at Farnborough when I was called to the phone. A Christian Registrar at the Sheffield Children's hospital told me that Daniel had been admitted and he was unconscious. He had somehow managed to find a bottle of Largactil tablets whilst Christine was preparing breakfast and had swallowed an undetermined number. He had started to drift into unconsciousness whilst eating his breakfast and Christine hurriedly put him and William into the car and drove madly through the rush-hour traffic to the Children's Hospital. They immediately washed out his stomach and telephoned me in London. I dropped everything and hurried northwards.

I found Daniel sitting up in his little cot bright and chirpy, but Christine was really distressed. I also felt guilty about having left my precious brood for the sake of a career. I should have refused to start the job until the whole family was together.

I remembered how John Wesley was almost lost in the blazing fire at Epworth Rectory - a brand plucked from the burning - and I wondered what would become of our special Daniel. I was soon to ask the same question about William, because he presented us with another serious problem within a few months of reaching London. I was again in theatre at King's College Hospital and was summoned to the phone. William had inhaled a piece of a plastic toy. He was in Farnborough Hospital, wheezing and in respiratory distress. I again sped through the London traffic to find the Thoracic Surgeon about to do a bronchoscopy. He retrieved a small foreign body and to our enormous relief, little William recovered.

When Daniel was born, one of my chiefs said, "Richard, you will never be truly happy again. You will have anxieties for your children as long as you live." I could not accept his philosophy, but these experiences were teaching me there is an element of truth in his statement - that if you really love, you must risk being hurt. And for a

Christian - out of suffering comes hope, and a peace that whatever God permits, it is for the best. We asked ourselves whether these painful trials were a sign of a special work in life waiting for these two boys. I know so.

50. Orthopaedics - learning the trade

Orthopaedics was proving a most satisfying speciality. I spent half the time at King's College Hospital with Hubert Wood, and half the time in the periphery at Farnborough and Bromley with Chris Attenborough. I learnt most from my apprenticeship with him. He was a most innovative surgeon. He was leading the field in his management of club foot, experimenting with a novel design for an artificial knee replacement, and he had a method of spinal fusion to his name. His assistant Dr Drozowski was ex-Polish Air Force, and he was a source of most sensible practical knowledge on the management of fractures. These four years in London were a sound practical foundation for my future orthopaedic career.

We became members of Orpington Methodist Church where I was on the preaching plan, and we appreciated also the fellowship from being on the executive of the World Evangelisation Crusade, but family life prohibited time for open-air preaching.

Christine was a full-time Mum and home-maker, and because of my heavy hospital commitment I was not at home as much as I would have liked to be. One Christmas day I had to leave in the middle of our Christmas dinner because of an emergency and I spent the rest of the day patching up a young man with multiple injuries. Not much fun for a young family. I knew that home-life had a greater priority than work and determined that when I became a consultant, I would so organise my life so that I would spend plenty of quality time with the family.

I had been to Jersey several times with my Mother and Father and I wanted Christine to see this idyllic place. So we spent the whole month of May 1968 in Jersey. She fell in love with it immediately. We rented a flat in St Martin, looked after ourselves and the sun shone every day. I introduced the boys to the country lanes and the sea shore. My Mother joined us for a week, arriving at the Airport wearing an enormous flowered hat, and bearing lots of cakes and pies. It was the beginning of our family love affair with this Channel Island.

51. Florence

One day Hubert Wood the senior surgeon at King's stopped me and asked if I would care to go to Florence for a month to work with Professor Scagliatti. I asked about the family and he agreed that I could take them with me. We contacted the Christian Literature Crusade (CLC) who had a book shop in the city and Miss Henderson insisted that we stay in the flat above the shop. We were grateful for her last minute offer, a welcome place to sleep until we could find something in Florence that we could rent for ourselves. We set off from Orpington in our small Renault car, with two boys in the back and Christine as the navigator. We were loaded with necessities for four weeks, with a calor gas stove, and enough food to feed ourselves on the four day journey.

It was a great adventure, travelling through France, across the Alps and down the Aoster Valley into Italy. The CLC bookshop is in the heart of Florence, in Via Ricassoli, half a block from the Cathedral and baptistery. The traffic was chaotic, and parking a nightmare. We found that Miss Henderson had vacated her first floor room for us, and she was sleeping on a camp bed. And she insisted we stay in her flat for the full time. The international helpers at the shop were living on a pittance and were not really eating very well, so Christine volunteered to be chief cook, making sure that everyone had some nourishing food whilst we were there. Shopping was fun, trying to use a new language and discovering to our surprise that we could be understood!

Close by the bookshop was the monastery where Frere Angelico spent most of his life. It was decorated with his lovely fifteenth century wall paintings, still appearing pristine as though they were painted yesterday in their vivid colours. Michaelangelo's David stood in the gallery opposite us, and all around the city centre was evidence of the Renaissance. We were being educated in a discipline that previously we did not know existed.

Here too I was introduced to the writings of Swiss theologian Francis Schaeffer, who with persuasive logic defended the biblical revelation as the true word of "the God who is there." I was fascinated with his revelations that every discipline from art, literature, music, and theology had been moving on a downward slope from the days of the reformation, and now because society had rejected biblical faith, we were in a culture of despair.

I spent the mornings in the hospital watching Scagliatti. He moved like an actor along a row of nine operating theatres, from one operation to another. One team of surgeons would open up the operation site, and he would dash in and do the essential procedure. He would leave the team to close the wound whilst he moved from room to room down the line. He was a great showman and had some bold and interesting concepts, but I was not too impressed.

The afternoons and evenings were free for taking the family around Florence. Daniel at three years of age was interested in everything. William had a mop of almost white fair hair and the swarthy dark skinned Italians were fascinated by his lovely features.

We were invited by some Miss Henderson's friends, to spend a week with them in Sorrento, south of Naples. I preached at their small Brethren fellowship and we joined them in evangelism on the water front. Here too at the foot of Vesuvius, we were introduced to the treasures of Pompeii.

52. Matthew
In 1968, Christine was pregnant again with Matthew. He was born on a Sunday afternoon on 3rd March 1969. It was her easiest delivery. The midwife thought the labour was not progressing very quickly and gave Christine 100mg Pethidine, but then after only three or four contractions Matthew was delivered, initially a rather sleepy baby from this injection, but he was very healthy. We soon knew he had arrived. The house was getting rather crowded and Matthew was full of life - a most active and energetic little toddler.

Christine had her hands full. It would take her half an hour to get the three boys ready for an afternoon walk, tie the dog to the pram, make sure the Sammy the cat and her four kittens were out of harm's way and then take them all down the hill to the local shops. How she managed to look after the house and cook for me as well, I never knew. We were all waiting for the advertisement in the BMJ about a Consultant post in Doncaster, and it appeared at last.

I was ill at the time, with a painful peptic ulcer, and was most relieved when I was appointed Consultant at Doncaster Royal Infirmary in

January 1970. Life would be less stressful because this was a new appointment and the build up of patients would take time. It suited us well.

53. Return to Doncaster

We had a lovely home at 157 Thorne Road, just opposite the Royal Infirmary. I could walk out of the door and be at work in two minutes. There was a lot of family support from Christine's Mum and Dad who had recently moved from Darfield to Doncaster, and from my Mother and Father and lots of old Doncaster friends.

I taught Christine to drive and bought her a small new green Renault Four car. The first day she passed her test she walked home from town. She had forgotten where she had parked the car and I had to tour the town to find it. She admitted that map-reading was not her strong point.

The boys were forever having minor accidents and some were not so minor. My father suggested that the Council move the pedestrian crossing so that we could make a hurried visit across the road to the casualty department when ever necessary. Matthew managed to drink some turpentine that I had been using for painting and he needed an urgent stomach wash-out and overnight admission. William burnt himself and Matthew almost cut off one of his fingers. Otherwise the family survived early childhood.

We joined Priory Place Methodist Church, and Matthew was baptised there. I preached around the Doncaster Methodist circuit about once every four weeks. With Father and Wilfred we started a branch of the Gideons in Doncaster. I also chaired the committee for town wide evangelism, organising inter-denominational missions and what we believed was culturally relevant outreach.

I also made sure that my first priority was to be at home for three family meals each day, even if I had to return to the hospital again in the evening. Unless I was needed for emergencies, I always stopped work at midday Saturday and did no more medical work until Monday morning. I wanted Christine to know she had a husband and the boys that they had a father. We had decided that our first calling - our major mission in life - was to bring up our little family in the shadow of the Lord. Christine was always there for them, but I knew

111

that if the boys thought they had an absent father, what would they think about their heavenly Father?

54. Orthopaedic consultant

It was a very satisfying experience being a consultant in the town where I was born. I wanted to pay back to this community some of the debt I owed for my happy childhood. Christine also felt she had returned to the community of her birth. We had been pleased to leave the busy Metropolis, and we had no ambitions for a Teaching Hospital position. We felt sure this was the right place to live and practise Orthopaedics.

I aimed for the highest standard of surgical practice. When there was a difficult problem I used to say to myself: "What would Chris Attenbourgh have done here?" I tried to produce a useful research base, identifying a few conditions like club-foot and low back pain where I could keep careful computerised prospective records. And I made sure that I would always have enough time to talk to the anxious patient.

My senior colleagues were Mainland Smith and Archie Sinclair, who could not have been more helpful. We seemed to have an unspoken understanding that we would never criticise each other, even if when occasionally there would be an inevitable area of disagreement. There was a most harmonious working relationship throughout the department. We were blessed with a remarkable team of dedicated nurses, many of whom were Christians.

The work-load steadily increased, until the clinics were overflowing, and my waiting list for surgery was full. I found myself working tremendously hard, but I was young and fit, and I enjoyed the increasing demands of a most satisfying job. First of all Margaret and then Jean were my medical secretaries. Jean became a Godsend - such an invaluable secretary for over thirty years. She was so patient and kind to the anxious patients, efficient and reliable. She made my job so easy.

55. James

Christine was pregnant again and we had a fourth little boy - James – who was born just before midnight on 29th December 1973. He was

112

an emergency Caesarean section, because there was some foetal distress, but he came into the world fit and healthy, although protected in an incubator for a couple of days. We had moved house to 34 Bawtry Road - a house with one third of an acre of grass, which was ideal for kicking a football about and a game of cricket.

James was only about six months old when he had a mysterious infection. He was admitted in a hurry and had a lumbar puncture which, we were relieved to find, excluded meningitis. However, from that time onwards, for about two years, he did not have much of an appetite. He was below the fifth percentile for weight for several years, but eventually he did catch up, to become taller than his three brothers.

All the boys enjoyed, and had an aptitude for, music. They all learnt to play the piano to quite a high standard, and in addition Daniel played the trumpet, William the violin, Matthew the viola and James the cello. We had a lively quartet. I was preaching about once a month, and would take the four boys with me. We tried to be innovative in the services, introducing the congregations to new forms of worship as well as valuing the old. It was well received wherever we went, probably because the boys were in the pulpit with me, leading the singing with their instruments and my accordion. The people used to say "Please come again. We always enjoy your visits because you bring your boys". I always preached for a verdict, pressing home the urgent need to decide for Christ, and my sons realised from an early age that one's parent's faith is no substitute for a personal faith.

Daniel was the first to make a commitment to accept Jesus as his Saviour. Then William was converted under his own preaching! One Sunday afternoon when he was about eight years old he asked if he could conduct a service in our lounge. He gave us each a hymn book. We sang and he then prayed and preached. He went upstairs to his bedroom and then came down again, and said that having preached an evangelist's message, he thought that this was the right time to accept the Lord Jesus Christ as his Saviour. I'd never before heard of anyone being saved through their own preaching!

Matthew was the next to accept Jesus, and then James. I had gone into the post office leaving William and James in the car, and when I got back into the driving seat, William said, "Dad, James has something to tell you." I looked round and James said, "I've accepted Jesus

113

Christ as my own saviour." William at fourteen years of age had been sharing the gospel with his seven-year-old brother, and James had made a clear commitment to give his life to Christ. Christine and I have been thrilled beyond measure that our four sons yielded their lives to Christ at a young age. And having put their hands to the plough, they have not looked back.

56. Mercy mission

We had a tradition at Priory Place Methodist Church, that on the morning of Boxing Day, the men and boys would play football, and then retire to the minister's house for coffee and squash. It was 1980 and the minister was saying that the Methodist Church had issued an emergency appeal for people to take caravans to Italy. The south of Italy had been struck by a severe earthquake. There was a convoy leaving Doncaster in two days time taking caravans beyond Naples. Were there any volunteers?

We discussed this over cold turkey and Christmas pudding at Boxing-day lunch. I had already arranged to have ten days of holiday after Christmas. The boys were not due back at school for ten days. We had never towed a caravan before, but what did the family think? We had a vote and it was a unanimous decision that if we could get ready in time, we would go.

After lunch I made a few phone calls. It was Friday. There was a caravan we could collect the following morning from Sheffield. The convoy was to meet at Dover at 10pm on the evening of Monday 29th and all the necessary export documents could be prepared for us if we were prepared to go. We needed valid passports, a new tow bar fitting on the car and provisions to feed ourselves for several days. There was a flurry of activity that Monday morning, Christine preparing food, bottles of water and warm clothes. The boys helped me to get some maps together, and plan enough in-car activities to keep four boys occupied in cramped conditions during a long journey across Europe. Daniel was nominated to be the navigator.

We knew God had given us a strong nudge to go, and were therefore confident that if we prayed about everything, it would work out brilliantly. It was to be an exercise of faith for all of us, a demonstration of what God will do if we let Him. We learnt lessons that have stayed with us for a lifetime. The first test was getting to

Dover on time. If we missed joining the other caravans at the Channel port on the last ferry of Monday evening, we would probably never catch them up, nor make our destination. We left Doncaster at 3pm, and it was going to be tight.

I drove the hatch-back Renault 30, and had to learn the new skills of towing a caravan. We made a circuit of north east London, crossed the river and headed for Dover. We arrived on the dockside just in time to meet a small party who were trying to decide whether to board the boat, or to wait for our arrival. There was Rev Trevor Noble from Retford and with another man from his church. We were pleased and surprised to see old friend Frank Ashmore - a local preacher in the circuit and his wife Eunice driving a second car. There was also a patient of mine and his wife from Thorne, and also a young married couple from Tickhill. Five caravans were in the convoy. This was to be a group of people we would get to know very well in the next ten days.

We reached Calais by 10pm and drove into a large car park to bed down in our caravans for the night. We had decided that Christine and I, Matthew and James would sleep in the caravan, and we tucked Daniel and William into sleeping bags in the car.

There was a sense of excitement in the air as we surfaced from our slumbers early on that December morning. We ate our bacon and eggs cooked on the calor gas-stove. We agreed that first thing each morning we would share daily devotions together, and Trevor Noble organised this. Then we developed a plan with our co-drivers about how to reach southern Italy without getting lost. We were to lead the way, not going too fast because this was in the days before mobile phones, and if we lost someone there was no way of making contact. Daniel was elected the party's navigator.

We set off for Paris, taking the Arras by-pass and reaching the capital at about 5pm just at the beginning of the rush-hour. We tried to keep the convoy together, not an easy task for five cars and caravans, which had to weave in and out of the congested traffic lanes on the west side of Paris. It was dark and suddenly I had a major electricity failure. The headlights failed. I had to stop on the inside lane. There was emergency prayer, and we discovered that one of our party was a motor mechanic. Much to our relief he quickly identified that it was a simple fuse failure, and we were on our way again.

We headed for Lyon and spent the coldest night I have ever experienced, in a lorry car park at Auxerre, 1500 feet up on the central plateau. We had not appreciated how very cold it was going to be. We all slept in our clothes, hugging pop bottles that Christine had filled with hot water. Daniel and William, who had slept in the car, awoke in the morning to find that their shoe laces had solidly frozen. What were the poor homeless people in Italy suffering without any shelter at all? The newspaper report said, *"A cold blast has gripped Italy from the Alps to Sicily, and caused at least six deaths including an elderly man left homeless by the Italian earthquake. Temperatures dropped as low as minus 28 degrees centigrade in the South Tyrol region".* We were on our way there!

We travelled from Lyon to Avignon and then on the coast road round the Gulf of Genoa. We had been given free passes on the French and Italian motorways, but sorting out the export licences at each of the customs points was sometimes tedious.

It was a little warmer in north Italy where we spent the night on a garage forecourt, and it took us a further day to reach the Methodist offices in Rome. There we were told that we needed to be vigilant. Some of the earlier caravans had been stolen, and in Naples, even a hand resting on an open car window, could be quickly severed from an engagement ring.

We had to make a three hour detour north of Naples when we ran out of currency, but even though we felt vulnerable, we were confident that we were beneath the shelter of God's secure care.

Remarkably our small convoy remained intact all the way down to Naples, then round the bay to Salerno, and onto the narrow roads snaking up into the hilly country towards the epicentre of the earthquake zone. We found that whole villages which had once perched on top of a hill were now a heap of rubble, and their populations were living in tents in the safety of the valley floors. We drove into the camp of one of these populations, from the village of Muro Lucano.

I take up the story as we later recorded it in our church news sheet - the Priory Diary.

"We have been privileged to take one of the Methodist Relief caravans to Italy, travelling with a small convoy from Doncaster. The suffering of these

mountain people left a great impression on us as they struggled to survive one of the worst winters for years. One sixth of Italy is a disaster zone, presenting enormous problems for the authorities. The villages which normally crown the mountain peaks are now largely uninhabitable, with their people living under canvass in the valleys. The elderly huddle round log fires, women pulling shawls around them. Children play in the mud. The priest and social workers busy themselves organising food and sterile water supplies. Into such a camp below the village of Muro Lucano drove five caravans from Doncaster, and life suddenly stopped. There was a stunned silence before they rushed to greet us with hugs and kisses. Coffee and chocolates were pressed upon us, and for an hour we dispersed amongst the crowd. We heard their stories of tragedy, felt their loss and gathered round the village priest who wanted to give a message to the people in Doncaster. He said that Jesus who had no home had joined them at Christmas, and had taught them a greater concern for each other. Eight days after Christmas there still stood in the centre of the camp a Cross and a Christmas tree, which summed up the message of the gospel for us. God's Son not only shared our grief, but carried our sorrows, to bring healing and joy to the nations.

We enjoyed good fellowship travelling 3,700 miles with four other Methodist families, witnessing God's hand in every aspect of the journey. We had less than 24 hours preparation, yet lacked for nothing, (but warmth and sleep says Christine).

We were certainly taught a great deal during the trip to Italy. On the way home we spent a few hours in Rome visiting the Coliseum, and then having what seemed to be a chariot race in three horse drawn carriages charging through the congested streets of Rome. We spent the night north of Bologna, and then the next night at an Alpine Christian retreat centre known to Frank Ashmore. We knocked on their door late at night, and although totally unexpected, these kind ladies welcomed us, and gave us hot food and warm beds for the night. The last night we spent in Arras before taking the ferry home.

Gathering round the stern of the heaving cross channel ferry, I shared with them the words of Captain Cook:

> *"When I behold the shining wake,*
> *Illumined by God's light of love,*
> *In perfect peace I onward go,*
> *Knowing that He Who holds the helm*
> *The course must know"*

117

FLOURISHING

57. Ultrasound measurement of the vertebral canal

Doncaster sits squarely on several prime coal seams, and in the 1970's, the town was at the heart of a thriving South Yorkshire coalfield, an industry employing 150,000 men. About one in nine of my patients were miners and their most common complaint was low back pain. I remember a friend telling me that if you wanted to do useful research, you need either a novel idea or a unique opportunity. We were in the last category. Someone else had said, if you are confronted with a difficult medical problem - like low back pain - you can either run away from it, or face it head on.

With David Ottewell - head of medical physics who later became a parish priest - I started to use ultrasound to look at the size of the vertebral canal. It was on a car journey from Sheffield that David and I discussed ultrasound. It was the time when ultrasound was being used to examine the small foetus in the womb, and I asked David if it would show any echoes from the spine. "Well at least we could look," he said.

We were amazed to recognise echoes from the back and the front of the canal, and could even measure the size of the canal to within a millimetre of accuracy. More significantly, as we built up a database, we noted that people who came to the clinic with back pain had much smaller canals that asymptomatic people, and many of the patients with symptoms from disc protrusion had the smallest canals of all. If our measurements were correct, it looked as though the vertebral canal size was a highly significant factor in back pain. The space available for the nerves within the vertebral canal seemed to determine whether or not some added pathology resulted in back pain. It was revolutionary.

I shared our results with the medical staff at British Coal, requesting a research grant to study low back pain in coal miners. If ultrasound could identify an important risk factor for low back pain, it had potential to help coal-miners to avoid a lot of unnecessary suffering, and also save the coal industry millions of pound a year. The Coal Board responded in 1978 by offering me £10,000 per year, a grant that continued for about ten years, and the National Back Pain Association supplemented this with a further £2500 per year. It allowed me to employ two research assistants.

The Monday afternoon clinic became a dedicated Back Pain Clinic. Every patient had an ultrasound back scan and completed a questionnaire prior to the consultation. About thirty features in the history and examination were recorded prospectively, and after the clinic, the research assistants would add this information to a computerised database. Gradually over the next few years we were able to unravel the importance of the vertebral canal, and the relevance of many clinical features.

In 1979 we received the first Volvo award for Basic Science for a paper - "Backache and the lumbar spinal canal", and this was followed by many publications and invitations to speak and travel all over the world.

I approached the Natural History Museum in London, and asked if I could examine their collection of skeletons from Poundbury in Dorset. Miss Moleson took me down into the bowels of the building, into cellars that has been used as air raid shelters in the war-time. There were rows upon rows of brown cardboard boxes stacked from the floor to the ceiling, containing the several hundred skeletons, beautifully catalogued. I was welcomed by the staff, because these bones were waiting for someone to examine them.

Garry Swann the Hospital Photographer came on board and made a "Photographic Box", so that I could take un-magnified silhouette photographs of the vertebrae and measure the vertebral canal indirectly from the photographs and at leisure. One day every month, I took the train to London, to examine the vertebrae and return home with packets of photographs to be measured. Most of these second century bones were in pristine condition, having been preserved in the chalk of the South Downs. I learnt that this had been a Christian community, because they had been buried east-to-west, without grave trappings and without their boots on. There had been contact with Italy because the bones had a high concentration of lead - believed to have been from drinking Italian wine from lead caskets.

I began to realise that the Roman soldiers in the first two centuries must have been effective witnesses for Christ. As I worked my way through these bones I thought of Paul sent under guard to Rome, *"handed over to a centurion named Julius who belonged to the Imperial*

120

Regiment" (Acts 27, 1). And during the shipwreck, when the soldiers planned to kill the prisoners to prevent them escaping *"the Centurion wanted to spare Paul's life"* (Acts 27, 43). And when imprisoned in Rome for two years Paul had *"a soldier to guard him"* (Acts 28,16). Were these Poundbury bones the remains of the spiritual grandchildren of the Apostle Paul? It seemed to me that it was as much the one-to-one witness of ordinary people - just doing their job for Christ - that won converts, as much as the witness of those great public figures like Augustine, Patrick and Cuthbert.

In 1980 I submitted the spinal research to the University of Edinburgh for the degree of MD. The thesis - "Measurement of the lumbar spinal canal by diagnostic ultrasound" was "highly commended."

After looking at scores of children's spines, I concluded that the size and shape of the spinal canal was determined very early in life and I needed to understand its growth. If environmental factors prove to be important, then growth could be modified, the small canal prevented, and much low back pain could be avoided. I chose as a front-piece of the thesis - *"O LORD, grant me the serenity to accept the things I cannot change; the courage to change the things I can; and the wisdom to know the difference".* This was my mandate for the future.

58. Club feet

I had thought a lot about the problems of club feet whilst working with Chris Attenborough in London. I believed that his method of treatment was superior to any other I had seen. In other centres, children were being treated by forceful manipulation and if this failed, surgery at twelve months of age, which left children with very stiff feet. However, Chris Attenborough was operating on children at a very early age - at only six weeks of age. He would release the soft tissue at the back of the ankle, and when necessary operate on the forefoot at eighteen months.

I was impressed and even dared to think I might improve on his concept. Instead of just cutting the tight tendons, I would formally lengthen the tendons and repair them. In addition, it seemed logical to me to shorten the main tendon on the outer side of the foot because when the foot was corrected, this tendon was always too long. I had been initiated into children's orthopaedics by John Sharrard who had

121

convinced me of the need to rebalance children's feet. Failure to shorten the outer tendon left an imbalanced foot and encouraged a recurrence of the deformity.

From the start of my time in Doncaster I was able to treat all the children in the area who had club feet. There were about eight children born with talipes deformity each year. I would carry out exactly the same procedure on them all, operating at six weeks if the deformity was still present at that time. I kept careful records, always seeing and treating these children myself in a special clinic. I became very fond of these children, spending time with them and their parents, explaining the procedures and watching their progress. I never discharged them, and they returned each year for an assessment.

The club foot work gradually received recognition. In 1984 I was awarded the first Syme Professorship at the Royal College of Surgeons of Edinburgh for work entitled "Surgical treatment of Congenital Talipes Equinovarus". Over the following years, it resulted in about six publications in paediatric journals and in three in the Journal of Bone and Joint Surgery.

In 1988 some of the children wanted to raise some money for club-foot research, so we organised a charity football match with Doncaster Rovers. I was the Doncaster Rovers medical adviser at the time. The children formed two teams, those under and those over ten years of age. These little fellows swarmed all over the pitch and encouraged by the cheers of their parents and friends, they put a few balls into the net past the Rovers goalkeeper.

59. Egypt and ancient history
In 1985 Christine and I went with the Edinburgh College to its first overseas meeting in Egypt. We delayed registering because we were unsure about the wisdom of leaving the four boys for ten days. The decision had to be made on February 2nd, and as we got up that morning we were still uncomfortable and undecided. We sat around the breakfast table and had our family prayers and we then read the daily text on a calendar by the fireplace. It said, *"Do not be afraid to go down to Egypt... I will surely bring you back again"* (Genesis 46 v3&4). We were given Jacob's promise.

In Egypt, we stayed at an old run-down hotel in the back streets of Cairo. It was a hang-over from a previous era. It had a pillared entrance, high ceilings, marble floors, low easy chairs, slowly rotating fans in the ceiling and a background of lush green foliage. Outside our first-floor bedroom sat a robed Arab, who slowly stood to his feet and offered Christine - a dandelion flower! Only dirty brown cold water ran from the bath taps. But we had fun and it was wonderful. Our surgical hosts invited us for a "night in a desert tent", with a scrumptious meal and buxom women performing belly-dancing for entertainment.

I presented our ultrasound work at the scientific meeting, and for the first time saw some Magnetic Resonance Images (MRI) of the brain. I immediately knew that the days of our spinal ultrasound were numbered. Here was a non-invasive technique that would eventually replace all other imaging techniques.

The visit to the Giza plateau and the three pyramids introduced me to a piece of fascinating history I previously knew nothing about – and the mystery of their construction, with the precision of alignment, the narrow passageways into the central chambers, the small ducts pointing to the fixed stars in the sky far beyond. I felt that I could easily change direction and become an Egyptologist.

We were entertained by one of my ex-housemen who had returned to Egypt. He spent a day with us, and took us round the Cairo Museum. He wanted my opinion on a certain mummy. He showed me an x ray of the mummy's chest. "Did this Pharaoh die from drowning?" he asked. Of course it was not possible to answer the question, in the absence of the lungs. "We think this is the Pharaoh that Moses confronted, challenging him to let the Israelites go," he said. I looked at this mummy's face, the hair still on the eyebrows and I wondered. Was it possible I was looking at this very man whose heart was hardened three thousand years ago?

We then moved on to Alexandria for three days, where a piper was waiting for us. He marched in front of the bus, slowly escorting our group of Scottish surgeons into the city. A crowd of curious onlookers lined the streets, wondering who was entering their city.

There was a great storm blowing in from the sea, a north-easter, reminiscent of Paul's eventful journey to Rome. And in Alexandria, we were shown some recently discovered catacombs. Apparently a donkey had been walking across a courtyard. The ground had collapsed and the poor donkey had fallen into a deep cavern, which revealed a labyrinth of caves that had been hidden for two thousand years. We were escorted down into the complex of small chambers, were the ancient dead had been buried, and into an underground sanctuary, where the walls were covered with hundreds of wall carvings and paintings of people with their arms raised into the air. We were told that these were pictures of the early Christians at worship. Perhaps the new way of praise coming to us with the charismatic movement was not so new after all. Paul had said, *"I want men everywhere to lift up holy hands in prayer"* (1 Timothy 2v8). That had been true in second century Alexandria.

60. Jamaica and an example of sacrificial living
Three years later we joined the Royal College again on another overseas visit, this time to Jamaica. Osmond and Sylvia Mulligan came with us. The scientific meeting was in Kingstown. On the first morning, I looked at the list of the surgeons attending, and recognised the name of Daniel Devadah. Was this the same Daniel that I had heard nothing from for thirty years, and was I to have the privilege seeing how he had progressed?

The first morning at breakfast, I stood in the queue next to an Indian. I looked at his neck and there was a transverse tracheostomy scar. "Daniel," I said, reaching out my hand. He was surprised and did not recognise me. "Daniel. Remember Edinburgh 1953. We meet again." It was a great reunion. He explained that he had given half his adult life to surgery in India. This was to be his last surgical meeting and now he was starting on a new venture. In this second half of his life - if he was to be spared – he was going to spend it preaching the gospel. He planned to walk through the villages of India as a travelling preacher. We prayed together, and I have heard nothing from him since.

We then enjoyed a few days relaxing and swimming on the west coast, at Ocho-Rios. I preached at the Methodist Church on the Sunday morning, expecting to find a congregation released in free and joyful worship. Instead we were disappointed to find a rather sombre congregation fixed in a formal Victorian style of worship.

Osmond and I had agreed to visit Albert Guard, who was an ex-Cliff College student and was now stationed as a missionary somewhere in the Blue Mountains. We planned to surprise him with a monetary gift. We hired a car and we found our way up a narrow winding road to the front door of this man's home. What a welcome we received! But Albert's wife was in bed with a bad back, and they had not been able to afford the visit of a doctor. I offered my services. As we left we gave Albert our love-gift. He was quite emotional as he explained that they had no money at all. This was only the beginning of the month, and they would receive no stipend for four weeks. They had given all their money away to the poor families around, who did not have enough to give their children breakfast before going to school.

61. Summer holidays

As the children grew up, we always spent our two-week family holidays at the end of July each year in Jersey. This island attracted us like a magnet. The Biarritz Methodist Hotel was ideal for our family needs with its Christian ethos, and its proximity to the beautiful sandy beach of St Brelade. It was paradise. We met the same families year after year, and watched each other's children growing up from infancy to childhood and into the teenage years. We have returned again and again for the past thirty five years to this sanctuary of St Brelade.

We would gravitate to the beach whenever the sun was shining, which seemed to be most of the time. If we weren't toasting ourselves by the sea wall, we were building sand castles, searching the rock pools, playing rounders with whoever would make up a team, or we were jumping through the waves of the warm sea.

At night we would arrange our own talent concerts or just sit and talk until we almost fell asleep. The young people liked to go for a walk before bed-time. The boys regularly made the girls scream by jumping out from behind the gravestones. An irate Mr Booey - the manager - would wait at the door at 10.30pm each night, key in his hand like an anxious schoolmaster as these guilty young people crept in from the darkness. But they were always forgiven, and somehow in spite of our misdemeanours, we were offered accommodation year after year.

One day James hid with a whistle in the undergrowth, whilst Daniel persuaded the girls that there was a Dartford Warbler in the gorse bushes. "Yes, we hear it," they whispered, only to be teased as the deception was revealed. One of the annual events was to hunt for octopus at Green Island. Each year we would recruit a large search party and would follow the retreating tide, exploring the rock pools, expectantly turning over stones. The fact that we never found an octopus didn't spoil the fun.

On Sundays we would be invited to the morning service at Bethesda Methodist Chapel. The boys would take the service and I would preach. Many a time the church was full with chairs in the aisle. We have gradually become an extended part of this special congregation.

Jersey stole a large part of our hearts, to such a degree that I applied for a Consultant Orthopaedic post at St. Helier in 1987. It looked so attractive. We had many established friends on the island, there was a welcoming evangelical church fellowship, a job tailored to my orthopaedics, and a beautiful climate, were waiting for us. Our parents and sons were supportive, but I had increasing unease. On the Friday afternoon three days before the interview, I was so restless I had to withdraw my application and I had immediate peace. I came to the conclusion that God had something else for us, however attractive as the post may have seemed.

62. Education
In the 1970's we were faced with a decision about where to find the best education for the boys. My time at Oundle had been a distinctly unhappy experience, and we had difficulty trying to compare the benefits of State and Private education.

In favour of a public school education
- it produces independence and resilience
- it gives a wider education than is available at home
- personal faith can become experiential
- benefit from the challenge of high flying peers
- learn the cut and thrust of debate

Benefits of State education
- Parents share in their son's adolescent years
- Boys benefit growing up alongside less fortunate children
- Less stressful time for many children
- Parents able to give day to day counsel

The balance seemed to tip in favour of the private sector and we therefore sent all four boys to Oundle. We tried to minimise the trauma of leaving home by buying a derelict cottage at Glapthorne,

126

three miles from Oundle, and we tried to go down every alternate weekend. However, we always wondered if sending the boys to Oundle was one of the big mistakes of our life. They learnt resilience and their faith was challenged and refined, but we lost out on sharing the intimacy of those growing years.

Daniel assured us that he was happy at Oundle, but in retrospect I think he was rather lonely like his Dad. Daniel has a very strong character, and he is uncomplaining, uncompromising and unassuming. He will persevere irrespective of the pain. He was in the School's cross-country eight and was prepared to push himself through the pain barrier to win the races. He joined a school party to Papua New Guinea and trekked for eight days across the inhospitable Kokuda Trail.

When Daniel was in the lower sixth studying Ancient History, I arranged for him to go with Christine on a Swan Hellenic cruise round the Aegean. They had a great time exploring the archaeological sites of Ancient Greece. When they arrived in Athens Christine had a headache. "I'll stay in my cabin this afternoon," she said. "You go with the tour to the museum, Daniel." She was no sooner lying on her bunk than a message came over the tannoy. "If anyone would like to go into the city for a shopping tour, the bus is about the leave now." She was up in an instant and was soon on her way into Athens. They were in a traffic jam and looking out of the bus window Christine was surprised to see an equally amazed Daniel looking at her from a bus that had drawn up alongside.

Daniel developed a love for Ancient History and following that trip he wrote an excellent paper on "The origin and value of currency."

Daniel helped to form the Christian Union at Oundle which met at School House on Friday evenings, and wrote of his excitement as one after another, many of his peers became Christians. He had wanted to be a doctor from his earliest years and came away from school with straight A's. He had no difficulty getting a place at Edinburgh Medical School. We attended his last Speech Day at Oundle and heard the Headmaster say they had created a special prize for an exceptional boy - "For the boy who has done most for the school whilst seeking the least publicity."

When William was six years of age, the music teacher came to see us one evening. "You have an exceptional child," he said. "He has

127

perfect pitch. I have never known this before in a boy so young." He wanted us to send William to a choir school, but we declined and instead we offered to encourage him to learn two instruments. I would waken William at 6.30am so that he could practise the violin for an hour each morning. It took him three years to realise that this discipline was not expected of every child! He had grade eight in no time and became leader of the Doncaster Youth Orchestra.

William is exceptionally bright, with a most retentive memory. When only ten years old and asked to read the lesson at church he surprised us that rather than reading it, he recited the whole passage from memory. He went to Oundle a year early. When it was obvious however that he was not settling we transferred him to Wakefield Grammar School - much more to his liking. He continued his music in Doncaster spending many evenings playing duets with Mr Bear, Director of Music. He pursued a music/classical career, and eventually secured a place at the Royal College of Music in London, before hearing God's call to become an evangelist at Cliff College.

Matthew was always a lively little boy, an extrovert and so sensible and reliable. When he was six years of age we were on holiday in south-west Scotland staying on the top floor of a five story mansion. Matthew locked himself in the toilet and try as hard as he could, he was unable to turn the old key to open the door. He was rather distressed, and I was talking to him through the keyhole. I knew that we could not get him out through the window so we paused for a moment. "Matthew, let's pray about it." So through the door we prayed that God would give him strength to open the door. We both prayed and then he tried again. The lock turned immediately, and Matthew never forgot this remarkable answer to prayer.

Matthew took to Oundle like a duck to water. He was a fast runner, and his 200 metre record held for 20 years. He ran for the County, and was a useful rugby player. He became fully involved in the school Christian Union, when scores of boys turned to Christ. He, like Daniel before him made a strong and difficult stand at school, against drinking alcohol. I think they were respected for this when it was thought "macho" for the boys to drink beer on Saturday nights. Matthew was unsure of the direction of his future career but moved to Nottingham University to read history.

James began at Oundle as Matthew left. He picked up the activities of the Christian Union from Matthew, like a runner exchanging the baton in a relay race, and the momentum was maintained. However, James still ploughed his own furrow, enjoying rugby and rowing. He took good care of himself in the Glapthorne Cottage at the weekends. He excelled in the sciences and it seemed natural that he chose to study medicine at St Bartholomew's Hospital in London.

So many people have said to Christine and me, that we must be proud of our sons. We can only reply "No, we are just thankful." We think of John's words *"to all who received him, he gave the right to become children of God - children born not of natural decent, nor of human decision or a husband's will, but born of God."* And again. *"You have not chosen Me, but I have chosen you."* We have seen God at work in the lives of our sons as they have grown into manhood, and we can only be humbly thankful.

63. Reflection: Obed-Edom

Obed-Edom was a most fortunate man in the bible. One day to his great surprise he saw a procession passing the front door of his house. King David was passing that way. There were people dancing and priests blowing trumpets and everyone was having a good time. David was bringing the ark of the covenant back to Jerusalem. It had accompanied the Israelites though the desert, it had been taken into battle as they conquered the Promised Land. Even when it was captured by the Philistines it caused them so many plagues they agreed it should be returned to the Israelites. And now it was being taken to its rightful place in Jerusalem. It was on an ox cart being carried with great ceremony and celebration to the city of David.

Suddenly the procession came to a halt, and the dancing and the trumpets stopped. The oxen had stumbled on the rough road, and the sacred ark was in danger of falling onto the ground. A man rushed forward and tried to support the ark, and everyone gasped in disbelief, because no one was permitted to put a hand on the sacred ark. It was only moved by the priests if two long poles were first inserted through the golden rings on its sides, so then even these priests could maintain a respectful distance. This man had dared to touch it! They looked at him dumbfounded, and watched in fear as he fell down by the side of the road. He was dead!

Here was a dilemma. What were King David and the priests to do? They obviously needed time to think about it. They looked at the house of Obed-Edom where the oxen had come to an undignified halt.

"Obed-Edom. We want you to look after the ark for us, until we decide what to do." This man took it in his stride. Maybe God was in this. He cleared his best room of its furniture and they took the ark into Obed-Edom's house. It stayed there for quite a long time and God blessed Obed-Edom and all his family, and his many sons.

Since 1970 Christine and I have been reading the Bible through once every year. Every day we read one chapter from the New Testament and three chapters of the Old Testament. It is a quick journey through the whole of the scriptures getting a bird's eye view of the redemption story and of God's dealing with the children of men. We dip into other parts in more detail at different times, but this broad sweep of scripture is a distinct blessing to us.

I can't explain why, but every time I get to the story of Obed-Edom I find myself identifying with him. He is mentioned several times. He becomes a gatekeeper in Jerusalem - a porter - and his sons also have other sons. It says in 1 Chronicles 26 that his son Semimah had four sons and they looked after the East gate - the golden gate - the gate where the Messiah would one day enter in glory. This family were gate-keepers for the city of Zion, *"for God had blessed Obed-Edom."*

God has blessed our little family first with the sacred altar in the home, and he has given us the responsibility of being gate keepers until the Lord returns. One day he will come through the gate. Psalm 24 says, *"Lift up your heads O ye gates, and the King of Glory will come in."*

64. Israel

Daniel lived at the Edinburgh Medical Missionary Society (EMMS) Hostel in 1982 during his first year in Edinburgh. I greatly respected this organisation when I was a student thirty years earlier, and knew many of their past students like Dr Meleca who helped me get into Edinburgh Medical School in 1952 and Osmond Mulligan whom I replaced in West Africa in 1962. The EMMS have a hospital in Nazareth that has been staffed by Edinburgh graduates for about a hundred years. It has a great reputation for excellence.

Daniel asked us if we would like to go to Israel as a family, joining a party from the EMMS. We had always planned to make a family visit to the Holy Land when the time was right, and this seemed to be the moment. We agreed and joined a rather select group of about 50 pilgrims - led by Dr Tester who had previously been a Medical Director at the EMMS Hospital, Richard Bewes - Rector of All Souls and his wife, and Rev Gordon and Mrs Bridges, who became Principal of Oakhill Theological College and was later a member of the church in Cromer where James is to be Curate.

We started in Jerusalem. The first impressions of Jerusalem are always momentous. This is the city of our God. When we walked towards the city from the YMCA where we were staying, we came over a small incline and there before us was the west wall of Jerusalem. I stopped in amazement. I had the distinct feeling that I was coming home. We walked lazily and reverently through the David's Gate with large blocks of stone that must have been quarried two thousand years ago. Into the labyrinth of narrow streets and alleyways, mingling with tourists and merchants, Jews and Arabs, Coptics and Armenians, and to The Pool of Bethesda with its five porches. We could sense the crush of the crowd where Jesus met and healed the invalid man of thirty eight years.

This was the ground made holy by my Saviour, who called the lost and healed many, and yet was rejected and suffered. We visited the house of Caiaphas and saw the courtyard where Jesus probably looked at Peter, and Peter wept. Below was a prison where Jesus may have been lowered and retained for a few hours before he was taken to Herod. The pavement where He may have been scourged was chipped with Roman gambling marks. And these were similar streets where He would have been led out to Golgotha.

Beyond the city, is the Mount of Olives where we sat in the shade of the olive trees, and across the valley we could three gates on the east wall. "Obed-Edom's family were responsible for one of those gates."
"What's that one in the middle Dad?"
"It's the Golden Gate - sealed for now - but it will be opened one day for our returning Lord."

The Sunday service at the Garden Tomb made the site feel so authentic. It was peaceful and cool in the early morning, with the white rock looking like a skull peering across to the city walls. Was this the very place where He rose in power? We sang of His victory. And somewhere in this city was the place where the Holy Spirit was poured out on the disciples; where He had filled a people with fire, who had then gone to the ends of the earth.

We looked back to the very foundations of Old Testament times, and saw the newly excavated part of Nehemiah's 30 feet wide wall which the great choirs had circumvented, singing their praise to God.

Before leaving the city we walked through Hezekiah's tunnel for half a mile under the city from the Kidron Valley, until it surfaced at the Pool of Siloam. We were knee deep in water, and bending low because it was only 5 foot high. With the torch I could see the chipping marks on the tunnel's wall, made hastily by men who in 701 BC were about to be besieged by Sennacherib's army. The excavation was as fresh as if the rock were cut yesterday. The water supply held out and God miraculously delivered them - *"That night the angel of the Lord went out and put to death a hundred and eighty five thousand men in the Assyrian camp and Sennacherib returned to Ninevah"* (2 Kings 19 35). I had been told in medical school that this was a classical example of the plague that could sometimes decimate besieging armies.

Dr Tester took us to Mount Carmel where we stood like Elijah looking out to the great sea for a cloud as big as a man's hand. Then down into the Meggido Valley where Elijah ran from Ahab. This was the same valley where Deborah led Israel against Sisera; and where Ezekiel pictured the dry bones coming to life. Nazareth sits on the hillside top the north of the valley not far from the Sea of Galilee, and we spent one night at the EMMS Hospital.

I lectured to the staff on "back pain" and we settled down for the night in a couple of rooms overlooking the valley. A great thunderstorm was building up to the south, and we could see a darkness sweeping towards us with flashes of lightning, tremendous roars of thunder and the torrential rain. We gathered as a family and sat in awe looking out of the window at this tremendous storm and we read together from Revelation 16 from verse 16 *"They gathered together to the place called Armageddon"* - we were at the very place - *"Then there came flashes of lightning, rumblings, peals of thunder and a severe earthquake. From the sky huge hailstones of about a hundred pounds fell"*. The day was coming when it was going to be just like this.

I don't know how Dr Tester managed to pack so much into two weeks in Israel. We were on a whistle stop tour - Capernaum's synagogue and recently excavated fishing boat - and a sail across the calm Sea of Galilee on a beautiful sunlit day. Our Orthodox guide spoke of the storms that can suddenly descend on the lake. He thought the storm that all but swamped Jesus was demonic and that we still have to contend with devils. To Qumran where the shepherd boy discovered the Dead Sea Scrolls, and an earlier shepherd - David - had hidden from Saul. A swim in the Dead Sea. And a walk around the ruins of Jericho - where were those collapsed walls? And a cable car to the top of Masada. To Caesarea Philipi where Peter confessed his faith in Christ. And Caesarea on the coast where Paul was imprisoned for two years. In spite of this hectic schedule Dr Tester always found enough time for us to stop and think and pray. I don't know why he was not so keen on letting us stop for the toilet!

I think there are three groups of people who visit Israel. The unbeliever sees nothing but stones. The liberal theologian thinks there is a little truth but it is a bit of a tourist bonanza. And the Bible-believing Christian who sees God's hand in this place – which is still the apple of His eye.

65. Osteoporosis
In the 1980's there was an interest in osteoporosis. This physiological age-related reduction in the density of bone is responsible for quite a large proportion of the orthopaedic workload - fractures of the hips, wrist and spine. It occurred to me that we should be able to use ultrasound to measure the density of bone, and hopefully start preventative treatment for those at greatest risk.

Chris Langton was a young physics student who was looking for a job. I suggested that we try to find a research grant for him to study the use of ultrasound in osteoporosis. We visited Stuart Palmer, a Reader at Hull University, who was an expert of the industrial use of ultrasound and we developed a proposal to build a machine that would send broadband ultrasound across the heel bone. It meant building a water bath, resting the heel very carefully in a defined position, and picking up the transmitted sound on the opposite side of the heel. We believed that the amount of sound that was attenuated during transit, would be related to the density of the heel bone.

There were several uncertainties. (1) Would the sound go round the heel and not through the bone? (2) Could the heel be positioned so that the sound always crossed the bone at the same site? (3) Was the heel bone representative of other bony sites, like the hip and wrist and spine? (4) Was the density of the bone related in any way to the risk of fracture? We applied to the Medical Research Council with high hopes and with these uncertainties, and received a very positive response and a generous three year grant for Chris to build and test a machine.

These were exciting times. We looked at several hundred heel bones from the Natural history museum and identified the best place to use for transmitting the sound. The machine was built. We found a 2.5 MHz transducer was best. The sound was attenuated. The level of repeatability was useful and it did relate to the density of the bone. The next big question was "Is it clinically relevant to the risk of fracture of the hip or wrist?"

Even when we were still uncertain about the clinical relevance of the ultrasound measurements, an American Company heard about us and wanted to buy our patent. The three of us had put several thousand pounds of our own money into the project and although I wanted to keep the patent and hope for a useful return one day, my two colleagues wanted to sell. We lost control and there are now several hundred machines in use across the world.

I obtained funding for a prospective study of 2000 elderly women in Doncaster, and employed a young Christian researcher - Tony Miller - to take the ultrasound machine into the old people's homes, measure the heel bone density, and then watch these old ladies over a two year period to see which ladies fractured the hip. We found that there was a subgroup where 10% fractured the hip in the two-year period, and low ultrasound of the heel was an essential predictor. We were the first to publish in the BMJ that ultrasound was a simple, cheap non-invasive test that would give a strong prediction of risk of hip fracture.

66 Spinal surgery

About half of my orthopaedic workload was in spine surgery and I was especially interested in spinal stenosis. In the 1950's Verbiest had described a condition which he called "Neurogenic claudication" where patients had pain when they were walking because of a small spinal canal - spinal stenosis. This was not easily detected by x-rays because of the many overlapping shadows but we could identify the stenosis easily by ultrasound. Patients began to come to Doncaster from all over the country, referred by other consultants, and sometimes from abroad.

If one could be confident of the diagnosis, we found that the results of surgical decompression for stenotic patients were very good. Patients tend to recover quickly. A peer of the realm telephoned from Westminster. He was having difficulty walking across the floor of the upper house and had heard about our work for patients with spinal stenosis. I operated on this octogenerian, and within a few days he was walking long distances again and encouraging friends with similar problems to come to Doncaster.

Mrs Carson from USA heard of our work and came across from California for spinal surgery. She responded well to a spinal decompression and could walk again without pain. Some months later she was standing next to a nun at a bus stop in Exeter and they began a conversation. Sister Adeline realised that she was suffering from the identical symptoms that had troubled this lady from USA and they discussed whether the same operation would help her. Sister Adeline knew a man who had moved into her village from Doncaster. Perhaps he would know something about this young orthopaedic surgeon. "Know him!" said Jack Riley. "I used to teach him in Sunday School."

Sister Adeline came to Doncaster, and she also had successful spine surgery. Thus began a great friendship until this dear lady died fifteen years later. She prayed for me and our family three times every day when she went into the convent chapel - I shall only know the debt I owe to her, in eternity.

We had a winter holiday in Sidmouth - Christine and the four boys, my Mother and Father and Wilfred. Christine's Mum had died the previous year. We were invited to tea at Sister Adeline's Convent at Ottery St Mary. It was a tremendous spread of cakes and pastries, enough to rival any Methodist Chapel tea. Rome and Epworth had finally embraced each other.

I was frequently being approached by the television companies. I would travel to Leeds after a heavy operating list and take part in the evening chat show. I suppose I was initially flattered, but it did not take me long to understood that their motives were different to mine.

I was trying to complete a clinic and at the same time help a TV company prepare for a short interview. I was unaware that I was still wearing a mobile microphone and muttered to my registrar "Finish your job first. You will learn that the media is interested only in ratings and not in education." The presenter came through and adjusted my mike. "I'm afraid you are right," she said "but this is our job."

The BBC invited me to do a half hour programme in the series "Your life in their hands." They wanted to film a man with disc protrusion, before, during and after surgery. It was risky for me, because although most patients recovered quickly not every operation goes well. About ten percent of patients will continue with some leg pain, and about 2% will be significantly worse. It is never possible to eliminate surgical risk. I prayed about it and reached the decision that I could try to do this programme and bear a witness for God.

We identified a miner with disc symptoms, and filmed him in his home where he was confined to bed. We showed him having an ultasound scan. His vertebral canal was small. The myeolgram showed a large disc and the day came to film the operation. I stopped before making the first incision and said to my assistant, "Let's pause to remember that he's in better hands than our hands," and then we operated. I was so thankful that we quickly found a large disc and were able to remove it without complications. Our prayer was answered, and this man did well. The programme was shown across the English speaking world, and I had many letters from people thanking me for my small witness which the BBC did not edit out.

67 Author
About this time I thought patients were in need of some simple written advice and I wrote a patient handbook about back pain, which Churchill Livingstone published it for me in a simple question and answer format. It sold very well.

Mike Alcock made the book available on the internet with the following testimony. *"I suffered for ten years from severe low back pain and sciatica - some days I could hardly walk. I was told I would have to live with it! In 1985, whilst working as a Medical Representative for a major British pharmaceutical company, a meeting with the author of the book led him to perform a discectomy on my spine a few days later. After two weeks in hospital and a month taking it easy I thought I had been reborn. I'm in my later forties now (2001). I scuba-dive, play squash twice a week and never get sciatic pain any more! I get the odd painful episode when I do something stupid (like dig the garden) but having followed the advice in "Understanding Back Pain" thankfully they are rare. I will always be grateful for the surgical skill of Richard Porter and his team."* Thanks like that make a big difference to a surgeon.

68. Motivation

During these years I struggled with motivation. My life was surrendered to Jesus Christ. I had promised to give one hundred percent for Him. I was trying to witness in my work and I was preaching in Methodist churches once every three or four weeks but I was no longer preaching in the open-air. Sometimes I was too busy to attend the branch Gideon meetings and too busy to present Bibles in the schools. Was I getting off track?

I felt that I had a four fold mission - family, evangelistic witness, high surgical standards and research. I knew that my family was my number one mission field and this was going to be a long haul - a life time process. I tried to give priority time to Christine and the boys, to listen to them and be there when they wanted me.

Day after day I was meeting anxious patients and their relatives, and I was trying to provide them with a first class orthopaedic service for them. We were blessed with a team of committed people, my efficient secretary Jean Reynolds, who was a wonderful communicator and a Christian, and quality nurses and ancillary staff. I also committed every operation to God in prayer before we started. I would just pause for a moment with a bowed head before I made the first incision. I was sometimes asked, "Why do you pray before you operate?" and I would reply "Only surgeons know the answer to that question."

I had the opportunity to pray with many patients at the bedside before they went to theatre. I would sit by the bedside with the curtains drawn around the bed, as we would talk about the procedure. If it seemed appropriate I would ask if we might have a short prayer together. On only one occasion over a period of 30 years was this offer refused - by a patient I respected who was a closed brethren and who treasured the closeness of his own fellowship. There was no doubt that a doctor is in a privileged position, being there when so many patients need spiritual help.

I was also responsible for training many young doctors. In this apprenticeship I hoped they were learning the principles and practice of good surgery. Were they also learning good attitudes?

I also wanted to my research to count and show that Jesus is Lord. I prayed that I would be asking the right questions and be able to design research to provide the right answers - answers that would relieve someone's suffering. The research was proving to be productive. But there was a certain amount of publicity that came with it and this could be dangerous. Was it possible that I could lose my focus and seek glory for Richard Porter? How could I sort out the real motivation in such a complex situation?

Here was little me getting something of a reputation, when my Master had made Himself of no reputation. Patients and staff were offering me a degree of respect, and even the dog. There was a danger that I could become a little king in a small domain, puffed up and full of empty air. The main influences that I hope kept me on the right place were my time of daily devotions, Christian fellowship, and especially Christine's common sense and spiritual wisdom. How important to have a sensible wife!

In spite of this I never resolved to my satisfaction the question of motivation. I knew the priorities that were expected of me as a follower of Jesus Christ. Seek first the kingdom of God, and all other things will be added. I just had to be obedient day by day, but I never sat comfortably with success. I was conscious of its dangers and had to leave it with the Lord.

GOD OPPORTUNITIES

69. Angels

Christine had a hysterectomy a few years after James' birth, and during the first post-operative night she had an experience of the intimate Presence of the Lord. She said that she was so sure that He was with her in the room that she could have put out her hand and touched Him. This experience carried her through to a remarkably rapid recovery.

I thought she deserved some convalescence and so I arranged for her and my Mother to go on a Mediterranean cruise. I took ten days holiday to look after the boys and with my Father's help we managed very well. It was also a time when Mother and Christine became great friends. One evening a gentleman asked Christine if she would join him in the bar for a drink. She said she would be delighted to have a soft drink and she would also like to bring her mother-in-law along. My Mother's comment was "He was a very nice man." They locked their cabin door at night. "You can never be sure in these ships you know," said my Mother. We were pleased to see them home. One poor lady jumped overboard on that trip, but Angels watched over my loved ones.

I had given a lady from Tickhill a hip replacement who occupied the same room in the Nursing Home where Christine had been, following the hysterectomy. This lady surprised me when I visited her on the morning after the operation. "There has been someone with me in this room all night," she said. "It is a lady dressed in white." The nurses wore blue uniforms and there was no one on the staff in white. This lady was a faithful member of the Tickhill Methodist church and I could say to her "I think you may have seen an angel. *"Are they (angels) not all ministering spirits, sent forth to minister for them who shall be heirs of salvation?"* - Hebrews 1v14.

It was only a few weeks later that I listened to another patient telling me about an angel. I had carried out a meniscectomy for him and had sent him home with instructions about exercises. When he returned to have the sutures removed at ten days he said, "Do you believe in angels Mr Porter?" I replied that I had never seen an angel but the Bible clearly stated that there are thousands of angels that watch over us and minister to us and I did believe in angels. He then said, "There has been a young man with me day after day helping me to do my exercises, and I think it is an angel." He did not confess to being a Christian but he had reason to believe in angels.

A lifetime of surgery has convinced me that medicine is not only dealing with the physical ailments but it is practised close to the spiritual realm. On one occasion I was examining a lady with neck pain. I explained to her that she had some degenerative changes in the cervical spine and that these were responsible for pain and stiffness. We discussed how the symptoms should settle down with appropriate treatment and sensible care. The consultation had finished and I had an uncanny urge to talk to her about the occult. I risked an unpleasant response, but I gently enquired if she had had any contact with the occult. She opened her handbag and showed me a lucky charm and how she had dabbled in black magic. After some discussion she gave me the charm and I gave her a New Testament.

Just as I believe in angels, I know there are demons, but I have always avoided getting too close to the occult. As a medical student I was driving from Sheffield to Doncaster with two Christian friends. For some reason we pulled up at a transport cafe in Conisborough for a cup of tea. I was ordering the refreshments when the lady behind the counter asked me what I did for a living. I explained that I a medical student. She said, "Do you know Stanley?" My immediate response was that I did not know anyone called Stanley. She said, "He knows you and he is helping you a great deal in your studies." I realised that she was a spiritual medium as we drank our tea. The house we were living in at 21 Town Moor Avenue was called Stanley House. The previous owners had called it after their son who had been a medical student at the Middlesex Hospital in London, and he had died as a young man from tuberculosis. I decided that my single room at the front of the house had probably been Stanley's room, but I did not share this piece of information with this lady medium.

70. The miracle of the moment
A young man was about to leave the clinic. His femoral fracture had healed and I was discharging him. He then turned round and sat down again. "I want to tell you what happened to me," he said. "I was flying through the air at 60 miles an hour. I had left my motor bike seat and was about to hit the tarmac. In that split second, I thought I

140

was going to die and I accepted Christ. I had been told about the gospel but had rejected it. God has given me my life back and I have now started to live for Him."

I recollected John Wesley's words "Twixt the saddle and the ground, redemption sought and mercy found." As hundreds responded to Wesley's preaching and were immediately changed, he knew that it was possible to be saved even in the brief second it takes to fall from a horse.

God can change a life in a moment of time. I had witnessed to this from my teens. But we were attending a large Methodist church where evangelicals were in a minority. Sunday by Sunday we listened to sermons about how to overcome doubts, how to come to terms with a Bible that was at odds with science, how to be good citizens, and how good works are the evidence of faith. We believed that God had put us there to be a witness, but we saw little fruit and it was hard going. Few of our church members really believed in the New Birth. For many of our friends at church, Christianity was about living a good life and trying to do your best.

One of my patients - Ada Mann - became a pillar of strength in our church. When I first met her she was lying down on her living room floor with severe back pain. I was a new consultant and I knew she needed a spinal fusion, an operation I understood but had not previously carried out alone. She was a woman of great faith and she agreed to be my first patient. Coming out of the operating theatre she opened her eyes, grasped my hand and said "Thank you." She turned out to be a miracle cure. She had many years with total relief of back pain. She joined our church, helped in the evangelistic work across the town and eventually travelled the country with the evangelist Don Double, sharing in his nation wide campaigns. Ada worked tirelessly for the Lord. She was a radiant witness, wonderfully baptised in the Holy Spirit, and encouraged many people to speak in tongues.

We organised a church prayer meeting with about eight people attending each week. We encouraged our friends at church to share in the town-wide evangelistic efforts, but we had little response. We persevered. I chaired the Doncaster United Christian Fellowship which organised a large evangelistic event each year. One year we sent an invitation to every home in town inviting people to join a correspondence course on "Becoming a Christian." A few people came to faith. Another year when David Watson had caught the media's eye with his popular meetings in York Minster, we invited him to speak at Doncaster Race Course. Another year we sponsored Dick Saunders who brought his 1000-seater tent to the town and in those ten days, several hundred came to Christ.

Billy Graham came to the UK again and had a most effective mission in Sheffield in 1985. We filled buses to go to the stadium each night. Christine sang in the 1000 voice choir. The best of all, for me, was James responding to the appeal on the final night. He wanted to make a public confession of what God had started in his life when he was a small boy.

There was a gradual improvement in the temperature of our church and the leaders took the unprecedented step of inviting an evangelical minister. Unfortunately the medicine was too strong! Half the congregation signed a petition to remove him because he was upsetting too many people! We sensed that our days were numbered in this particular church.

I wrote a book for Methodists calling for a change. Methodism was a declining denomination, and in my view it would continue to decline because it did not have a relevant message for the new generation. The wind of the Spirit was beginning to blow across some of the British Churches. Renewal was in the air, with new songs, new styles of worship and new expressions of faith, but it was hardly touching Methodism. I sent my literary effort to a variety of Methodist publishers with no response. The Epworth Press was advised by one reviewer - "Whatever you do, don't publish this book." It still lies in a cupboard and will never see the light of day.

My Father said "Life is like the weather - sunshine and showers." There was some encouragement but many times of disappointment especially in our church. But we were never despondent because we are only called to be faithful. We may never see much success. The detail may look confusing but God sees the big picture. Christine and I could rejoice in what God was doing with our family. And I was aware that God was at work in my job.

71. Secretaries and daughters in law
In my professional life I have been surrounded by a bevy of most helpful and able women, from ward sisters, wonderful secretarial help

and research assistants. I could have done nothing really if I had not been surrounded by so many helpful women over the years. Some of them, especially my research assistants, must have felt that my expectation of them was too great, but they always rose to the occasion and produced the results (over 220 publications in peer review journals over the years). Thanks to the hard work and loyal support of these people.

In family life Christine's role has always been paramount and I have always valued her sensitive suggestions, many of which would elude me many times. We have both tried to show the boys that their masculinity is something to be proud of as they wait for their Eve to be their God given beautiful help mate and share their adventure of life, being prepared to take risks to win the battle. I was never very good at that as a boy but I have learnt its importance for boys growing into men.

Christine started to pray for the future wives of our boys when they were still quite small. Her prayers have been marvellously answered. All our boys flew the nest at an early age and they have lovely partners. Daniel married Barbara when he was twenty four. They met as students at the EMMS hostel in Edinburgh. She was one of four sisters, and the daughter of a general surgeon. She has been a tremendous spiritual support for Daniel in his busy life as an orthopaedic trainee first in Scotland, then in Oxford and now back to Edinburgh where Daniel is Senior Lecturer in Orthopaedics.

William was twenty five when he married Karen. She had been a student at Cliff College and then a lay worker in a London Church. They both have a passionate heart for revival.

William served on the evangelistic staff at Cliff College for five years and then became an evangelist at Hexthorpe Methodist Church, Doncaster before starting training for the Methodist Ministry in Durham. He did his MA degree from Manchester and his first ministry was at Holmfirth Methodist Church, whilst still leading country wide conferences on "Approaching Revival".

Matthew and Sam met in a House Church when they were students in Nottingham and were married when Matthew was twenty two years old. He worked as a legal assistant wondering about a career in law before offering for the Anglican ministry and training in Oxford. He is now vicar at Woodseats in Sheffield.

And James was twenty four when he married Katie, a fellow medical student from Barts. After doing his residential year James offered for the Anglican ministry and did his theological training at Oakhill in London.

One of life's great joys is to sit around the old dining room table sharing a meal with children and grandchildren. Ada Mann had been given a prophetic vision that one day we would be sitting round our dining room table with lots of grandchildren, and it has happened. We are blessed with six grandsons - Ben, Joel, Luke, Isaac, David Luther and Joshua – and five granddaughters – Sarah, Bethany, Rachel, Jemima and Rosanna Abigail.

72. A Chinese connection

During Daniel's final year as medical student in Edinburgh, he had to spend eight weeks in an overseas country. He asked if I had any contacts in China. I was giving a lecture in New York and was introduced to a Chinese doctor. I asked if he could arrange for Daniel to spend eight weeks in his home hospital and before long I received a letter from the Principal of the First Teaching Hospital in Beijing. They would be delighted to look after Daniel for eight weeks if I would take one of their doctors for a year in Doncaster. In due course I arranged for Dr Teng (name altered for safety) to do a year's research in Doncaster, and Daniel went to China in 1987.

Mao's Long March in 1934-36 had gained political power through the barrel of a gun, and thought reform replaced grace. A host of missionaries with my Auntie Hilda were pushed out of China, in the 1940s. There was to be no religion. In 1956 the Hundred Flower Movement introduced criticism. In 1958 the Great Leap Forward destroyed China's agriculture and 30 million died. In 1960 I had looked at the forbidding Chinese mainland from the deck of SS Peleus. We knew that in 1966 to 1976 the Cultural Revolution closed every church and fear gripped one fifth of the world's population.

When Daniel went to China in 1987, it was two years before Tiananmen Square. The door was just beginning to open again, but I knew foreigners would be treated with suspicion. Daniel was naturally a little anxious.

"I go as a delegate;
God's work ahead.
A heart of fear yearns
Peace instead

How can I cope with it?
Everything new.
My means to do well
Are so few.

Yet the Lord wants to be
My only power.
I'll delegate back
every hour.

My Father will show
All His care
With my unequal burden
His share.   DEP 27.07.87

Daniel was welcomed, and he made a good impression in the orthopaedic department of the First Teaching Hospital. He lived with the students and competed in the University games, coming second in the 2000 metres. He thinks he would have won if they had given him the right sized shoes, but he knew it would not have been acceptable for a foreigner to win the race, with Chinese loss of face.

Daniel was befriended by a final year student Dr Nie, and was taken to his home in Shanxi province for the two weeks annual holiday. He says, *"Before I set out to Shanxi I prayed that the journey might be a blessing"*. He was treated as a special guest, and given roast dog at the family banquet. On the Saturday they asked where Daniel would like to go the following day. He said he would like to attend church. There was a church in a nearby town and they agreed to borrow a vehicle and drive across the mountains.

He wrote home on 19th August 1987:
"We left Yong Quan setting off early through the mist of a mountain down to Taiyuan, capital of Shanxi province, 100km to the west. With siren wailing, we passed slow trucks with ease, and as we climbed, a beautiful day

145

blossomed. We descended to a great river plain, and Taiyuan, a city of a million people. Our quest - to find a church for worship".

"At 9.30 within the narrow streets of the ancient walled city, a public notice reading 'Taiyuan Christian Association' led us into a small courtyard and hall, gradually filling with three hundred people... more would sit outside".

"For half an hour, we practised two hymns in Chinese... one of them read 'Jesus is my everything'. My companions sang heartily. Soon an elderly pastor and his wife aged 80 and 82 prayed and led us in song. Some young girls at the front played the old piano and sang beautifully. My eyes blurred as I recalled their rich Christian heritage ...., Shanxi, model province of China, evangelised by the CIM and David Hill of the Methodist Missionary Society. Here pastor Hsi converted Confucian scholars, and set up opium refuges for addicts. Here demons were cast out. In Shanxi the Boxers killed thousands of believers, and put missionary's heads on piles next to their children's. In Shanxi, ravaged by wave after wave of Japanese assaults in 1935-45, Gladys Aylward led her band of children to the Yellow River and beyond. And then the door closed to the outside world. But now, in an official church, a large band of believers maintain that witness".

"The pastor's wife preached on Luke Chapter two 'Behold we bring good news to all mankind'. After the service, a little knot of radiant raced people engaged my companions in conversation - with one purpose in mind - and the results are great!"

"After the service I played some tunes from their hymn book including 'The day Thou gavest Lord is ended'. I thought of people in Britain, in Doncaster, Priory folk, going to bed maybe not thinking that in the heart of China, a band of similar believers would be gathering to maintain that unsleeping witness of the church that rests not day or night".

Daniel later told me that Dr Nie had become a believer that day as they sat by the side of a mountain spring which *"made the whole area an oasis and I told the story of the Living Water that wells-up unto eternal life".*

73. Doors open

I created a research post for Dr Teng in Doncaster. He was an experienced general surgeon but his training was not recognised by the GMC and was therefore not able to do any clinical work. He meticulously examined a group of my patients with neurogenic claudication and wrote a useful paper on the "Walking and cycling test, in patients with spinal stenosis."

During the Cultural Revolution, Dr Teng had been sent to the country to reform. As an intellectual he had to stand day after day with bowed head, be slapped about the face and humiliated until he could recite the words of Chairman Mao. He became a reformed character and was reinstated in the First Teaching Hospital as a trainee surgeon. The Party agreed to let him spend a year in UK because he was now reformed and was considered to be of low risk.

We welcomed him into our home on Sundays. He would go with us to church, have lunch with us and we would take him for a walk in the afternoon. He was quiet, observant and full of fun. On November the fifth he amazed our boys by holding the lighted rockets in his hand and only letting them go up into the sky at the last minute. He kept feeling our boxer dog's leg and we were convinced he was estimating the amount of meat on the bone.

He had rather an unusual view of history. As we were travelling in the car one day he said, "What you need in England is a revolution." I asked him why, and he said, "It's the French. You have to get rid of the French." He explained that we had been conquered by the Normans in 1066 and the French had ruled our upper classes ever since.

As I put him on his plane at Heathrow on his return to China he was rather tearful. "I have to give you this," he said. It was the Bible I had given him some months earlier. "I can't take this home." I assured him that irrespective of the oppressive system, one can always have a free mind.

In 1989, six months after Dr Teng returned to China, student unrest began in Beijing. Dr Teng went to Tiananmen Square to see for himself. There were thousands of students camped in the Square, waving banners and calling for reform. The population was sympathetic and the city was in ferment. Even the soldiers were smiling and accepting garlands of flowers from the students.

There was tension in the air but Dr Teng thought that this was the moment to be counted. For thirty years he had dared voice no opinion about anything. He had learnt that it pays to keep quiet and get on with your job. But now he returned from the Square and went round the hospital saying "The students are right. The government is corrupt. We need a new freedom. Support the students."

Then the Party cracked down on the insurgents. They showed a frowning face and sent tanks to surround the Square. Having lost their patience, the leaders ordered the soldiers to fire on the students and clear the Square. There was panic as young people ran everywhere. Many injured and dead were carried on makeshift stretchers to the First Teaching Hospital where Dr Teng and his colleagues worked through the night in terrible conditions.

A few days later when order was restored, every member of the hospital staff was placed in an examination room. They were ordered to write down what they had done, what they had said and what other people had said to them during the time of unrest. It became apparent that Dr Teng had advised rebellion. He was brought before a committee, and would have been sent to prison had not his chief, Prof Ling, put in a good word for him. His privileges were removed. The computer he bought in UK was confiscated. He had been in line for a professorship but he was now demoted to the ranks of junior doctor.

I met Dr Teng a year later. He had bowed shoulders and was a disillusioned man. I assured him "You will never regret doing what is right. In the short term it may be painful, but in the end it will work out for the best." I am pleased that those words were fulfilled. As the years have brought prosperity to China, with some new masters, Dr Teng has been reinstated and he is now Professor of Vascular Surgery.

74. Romania

The head of Romania's Secret Police was travelling in a fast car with Madam Ceausescu in 1986 when the car turned over. It was a serious road accident reported in the world press, and this man fractured his hip. The primary surgery was not successful and this man was transferred to the Fiosor Hospital in Bucharest for hip replacement surgery.

Philip Trailescu was the Resident doctor on the joint replacement ward. He was naturally apprehensive because a few years earlier, Philip's father had been murdered by the Secret Police. Philip was called to the bedside of this big man. "Is the professor the best surgeon to carry out my operation?" he asked Philip. "The professor is excellent," replied Philip honestly, and then looking over his shoulder, "but Dinu Antonescu is also a very good surgeon". The head of Secret Police understood the coded message, and he asked

Dinu to do the hip replacement. Philip assisted. It was a great success.

When this man was about to be discharged from the hospital, he asked Philip what gift he would like. "I don't want any gift" said Philip. "Come, come," said the great man, "Every doctor likes a gift." It was the practice of the Romanian government to pay the doctors a very small wage, which everyone knew was supplemented with gifts and bribes. Some doctors would not treat a patient until a gift had been given. Others were prepared to accept a gift when the patient was discharged. It was exceptional for a doctor to refuse a gift.

Philip took a deep breath. He knew he was taking a big risk, "There is only one gift I would like," he said Philip. "I would like to leave Romania." "I can't arrange that for you" he replied. Then he paused, and lowering his voice, "I can tell you who to contact, when to apply and what bribe to give." Philip made his application at the right place and time, and he could hardly believe his eyes when he received a permit to go to Germany. It also allowed him to take his wife and child and mother with him.

In 1987 there was a shortage of Senior House Officers in the UK. No one replied to our advertisements. I therefore had advertised in the German press for a trainee. One young man applied - Dr Philip Trilescu - and I made arrangements to interview him in Munich where I had been invited to give a lecture. Philip convinced me that he would make a good surgeon, even if his English was not brilliant, and I offered him the job.

Philip worked very hard and he was willing to learn. He did an excellent piece of research for me showing for the first time that the Straight Leg Raising test - a clinical test routinely carried out for patients with disc disease - has a diurnal variation throughout the day. Philip had a room in the Doncaster Residency which was next door to Dr Teng. Philip, who was not without resources, paid Dr Teng to do his laundry and cook Chinese food for him. It was a happy working arrangement, and a strange meeting of political extremes, European Fascism and the Communist philosophy of Mao. They became the best of friends.

Philip was not only a good colleague but he also became part of our family. We travelled to Scotland to watch the Rugby International and he was mystified to hear the Scots booing Daniel and a few

English supporters as we stood to upright and at attention, to sing God save the Queen. We also took Philip to Oundle to meet James, and he decided that when his son was old enough he would send him to England for his education. He has been blessed with a boy with an IQ of 150 who is now at a private school in Scotland. Philip now practises orthopaedics in Hamburg and most importantly, Philip has gradually opened his heart to the Lord Jesus. He also introduced Christine and me to the fascinating country of Romania.

75. Surprising spiritual encounter

In about 1989 my son Matthew encouraged Christine and myself to attend a worship conference in Brighton, being run by American healing evangelist John Wimber. I have never attended a meeting like it before, nor since. It was a large conference hall full of about 6,000 people and we attended every day for worship and ministry. One afternoon John Wimber stood on the platform with his Bible held high in his right hand and was about to preach, but said nothing for about 5 minutes. The hall was silent and I watched in amazement. I was very embarrassed to find a man in the gallery to my right beginning to laugh. I thought 'you rude man. Here is John Wimber waiting to preach and he cannot quite get started, and you are laughing', and then a ripple of laughter broke around the meeting and spread like a wave. I suddenly found myself laughing uncontrollably and weeping. Christine leaned across to me and said 'pull yourself together Richard, you are making an exhibition of yourself' but I could not stop laughing. John Wimber said, 'You are experiencing something most unusual, that you may never encounter again'. It was clearly a movement of the Holy Spirit releasing tension and certainly doing something in me. I have been thankful for that unusual experience ever since.

76. Further visits to China

I made four or five visits to China in the 1990's, and have had wonderful relationships with many of their doctors (names below changed for safety).

When Philip Nie became a believer, Daniel encouraged him to read the Scriptures every night. He shared a room with two young orthopaedic trainees and he promised to teach them English if they

150

would listen to him read the Bible. Dr Wang Hai Zhou was one of these young men. When Jonathan Redden and I were in Shang Hai lecturing at a conference, a young man came to me at the end of the lecture asking if he could talk to me. I invited him to our room that evening. He came to the 32nd floor, and told me that he wanted to become a believer, that Philip had been reading the Scriptures to him, and he wanted to know how he could become a Christian. We knelt on the floor together, and this young man accepted Christ at that moment. He was eventually promoted to an important hospital in central China, and his hospital President invited us to spend a week lecturing there.

We took in a team of surgeons. Patients came from 100 miles around to see the Western doctors. It was a long time since any Western surgeon had visited the hospital. I gave them a New Testament and a tie. We thought we were going to get into trouble afterwards but he was undoubtedly very pleased to see us all and sent us home bearing many gifts. Dr Wang Hai Zhou is now not only head of the department, but head of the hospital, and is providing a great spinal service to the Province.

On the Sunday we were there, the communist leaders said we could go to church, but we must not talk to anybody, we must not give them anything. We were led into a large church full of worshipping people and understood that they had 4 services every Sunday. Here was evidence of the strong new Church in China, clearly in parts an underground Church, but moving in the spirit of God. We now know that many of the Chinese Christians are getting prepared for a march to Jerusalem, to travel through Muslim lands with the Gospel. They believe they have been prepared by persecution. What a privilege to have had a very small part in encouraging these young believers.

I recollect being in Aberdeen and reading my Spine Journal with an article by Professor Bian from Urumqi about spinal stenosis. I wrote to him explaining this was one of my personal interests and received an immediate invitation to travel to Urumqi. I took Jonathan Redden, fellow orthopaedic surgeon from Doncaster. When Jonathan and I would go to China on a medical trip, we would claim a little Christian song for our own and sing the words as we walked along the dusty lanes of China. One of these was the song 'Here I am, wholly available, as for me I will serve the Lord.' Another was 'Thank you, O my Father, for giving us your Son, and leaving the Holy Spirit until the work on earth is done'. These little theme songs burnt into our hearts as we carried pockets full of bibles and waited for opportunities to develop.

When we conducted the week's seminar of teaching, after each lecture we would invite people to come forward and receive the New Testament if they wished, and the front two or three rows would be full of Army men, having appreciated there would be a danger, but they would rush out to claim the New Testaments each time. Professor Bian asked where his New Testament was. We said they had all gone, but we found him one in our bedroom.

We went up to Urumqi again whilst we were visiting him and I met his daughter Yin. She was having a cup of tea with the Principal of the University and the hospital President. I was given a boldness to tell them about Christ and Yin became a radiant Christian, being baptised and marrying a Christian man. There was a premium on baptisms in Urumqi at the time, with only a limited number being allowed to become Christians in any one year.

I invited Professor Bian to Doncaster and he spent a few days with us. One Saturday evening the telephone rang, would I go to the hospital and meet him and tell him how to become a Christian. He told me he had slept with his New Testament under his pillow ever since our visit and his daughter Yin said he must not return to China without becoming a believer, and he returned full of faith. We maintained a happy friendship ever since.

I remember a special moment we shared together a few years later. Professor Bian, his daughter Xia, David Knight, Richard Aspden and I had been to the hospital in Hainan and spent 2 days lecturing and looking at a few patients. They then wanted us to have a small holiday on the island of Hainan, a most beautiful rocky outcrop, on the most southerly part of China, surrounded by beautiful golden sands.

One morning before breakfast we were all sat on the sand having a light snack. The sun was beginning to rise about Korea on the eastern horizon, scattering the mist of the early morning. The sea was calm, lapping the shore. We were about the same number as the disciples who sat on the sands with Jesus, recorded in John Chapter 21, 'Jesus had lit the fire and prepared some fish'. We sat together eating a similar meal, talking about the transforming power of Jesus to change

152

the ordinary into the extraordinary. The failure of a night's fishing into a bountiful catch. His presence seemed so real to us as we sang a song and shared a prayer.

Professor Bian eventually started a hospital in Hainan with a Christian ethos, run by Christian medics and staff, providing free care for the poor and quality care for the population.

On subsequent visits to China, another friend Professor Ling made sure that the wheels of our journey were well oiled. He would meet us at the airport with an entourage, expressing great welcome, and would make sure that we had a comfortable hotel the first night. He provided a translator in Zhou Fang and Fang was always by our side to ensure that we had no problems, which could easily occur whenever passing across one border to another, from Province to Province. I think he knew that we had scriptures, and needed to be cautious. Our bags were also full of medical books and instruments to share with medical people along the way. Whenever we went from one place to another there seemed to be some doctors about hosting us.

Beijing University honoured Jonathan and myself with an honorary professorship. We were invited to receive this award. The University lecture auditorium was packed. I was able to say that in the UK we believed in holistic medicine. We treat the whole patient, not just the disease, and by the bedside in every hospital there is usually a New Testament because we believe the words of Jesus speak to the whole person, not merely for time, but for eternity. I had about six UK academics who were travelling with us. Their eyes were wide and their mouths open, wondering what kind of response my remarks might produce, but Fang Zhou interpreted faithfully and we were very well received with these University leaders, also requesting New Testaments and being very open about the Christian faith. One man secretly told me that he was attending Church now in Beijing each Sunday. I would encourage Christian travellers in China and in similar countries to be bold and expect God to have gone before them, to claim the way. That has been our experience and tremendously rewarding.

I remember going to Shanghai when the Chinese Orthopaedic Association had a large meeting. The orthopaedic hierarchy were on the platform and it was a big day. They were going to choose their new President for 3 years. There was great excitement when Professor

Ling was selected and this in fact occurred on a second occasion and I understand this was quite unique for someone to be appointed for a 6 year term.

Professor Ling became the most influential orthopaedic surgeon in China and was highly respected by surgeons of all disciplines. This meant that whatever he requested seemed to happen. When we travelled by train we were given first class seats. When we attended a restaurant someone tasted the food first for us and made sure that we had beautiful fresh food. I recollect we once went into a restaurant and were offered turtle. It was chopped up into small squares and I thought it tasted beautiful until it was quickly whisked away from us and another one brought, because someone thought it might be substandard. They had great fun feeding us with all sorts of delicacies that might offend the Western palate but this never happened.

Everyone was so generous and kind and this made our stay so easy every time we went to China, so that we could concentrate on trying to help them medically and sharing the things that count most in our lives. Again and again we kept hearing the message, 'please tell us how we should live'. We endeavoured to answer that question in conversation and particularly by example. We were aware that we were examples of fairly affluent society visiting a very poor country at the time. Our emphasis was always on priority in medical care and the essential requirement of a privileged young doctor in China is to help the poor and disadvantaged who surrounded them in their clinics and busy hospitals. Clinical excellence is fine, but even more important is clinical attitude and the love that must be expressed, shown to us in the life of Jesus.

I remember giving a lecture on that subject in Shanghai to about 3000 medical students and young doctors and a Professor came to me afterwards and said he thought that was a model lecture he was going to translate and send across China.

From that conference in Shanghai a lady came to see me as I was about to board the plane in Beijing back to UK. She had travelled several thousand miles to talk to me before I boarded the plane and she had one question: 'why are you doctors so kind?'. I said to her I did not know that we were particularly kind, but if we were, we were kind because God is kind to us. She said 'what is that religion, I have never heard of it?' I told her about Jesus. She begged me to give her

154

entrance to the UK for some training.   She was a hospital administrator. I promised to do my best.

Six months later she was in Aberdeen on a 6 month placement in hospital management which was followed by a further 6 months in Sheffield.   As soon as she arrived in the UK she wanted to find a Chinese church which she did without too much difficulty.   She joined the Chinese church in Sheffield and became a believer.

Not only did we go as a team of doctors into China but the hospitality was reciprocal.   Visiting us thereafter several times were high delegations of mayors, university principals and hospital leaders.   I would try to place these delegations around the country as they travelled, visiting the colleges, GMC, etc. and they would stay with Christian doctors who would offer them hospitality in their homes. Invariably they would ask at the end of their stay whether they could have a Bible to take home.

Then there was Dr Yung, whom I got to know on one of our trips. One night we chatted long into the evening and he asked me about my approach to death.   I tried to explain that I had no fear of death for God so loved the world that He gave his one and only Son that whosoever believes in Him should not perish but have everlasting life. We stood on the pavement and with a hand torch we looked at these verses.   I asked him to put his name into the verse, 'For God so loved Dr Yung that He gave his one and only Son, and if Dr Yung believed, Dr Yung would not perish but Dr Yung would have everlasting life, if he believed'.   I then said 'Do you believe, Dr Yung?' He looked at me with a gleam in his eye, 'I do believe' he said.

Dr Yung and I have kept up a lovely friendship since that time and we brought him to the UK for some haematology training.   He started a transplant unit in Shi-he-zi which is now quite a prestigious unit in China.

Whilst in Beijing we were walking around the Summer Palace and I had a young man on my right hand, Dr Ku, whose uncles had been believers in the cultural revolution and had suffered greatly.   I think one had been executed.   We discussed some of the truths of the Gospel.   Professor Bian recognised that Dr Ku had great academic potential and wanted to come to the UK for training.   I was able to bring him over to Doncaster and Aberdeen and whilst in Doncaster he came to our church at Hexthorpe.   One day he asked me if he could be baptised. We arranged for a pool because Methodists have frequently not baptised by total immersion, but we arranged for him to be baptised at Hexthorpe. His wife, Bai San, said she would also like to be baptised, but she was very afraid because of the fear of persecution in China for her on return, and for her family back home. She said she had a terrible dream one night. Everything was black and she thought she was going to die, and she saw Jesus who welcomed her and said it was alright, and yes, she would be baptised. When the morning came she was rather frightened because she is terrified of water and cannot swim, but she was very courageous and was baptised one glorious Sunday morning. Now Dr Ku is a surgeon in Canada. He is an elder of a thriving Chinese church and a preacher of the gospel.

Dr Lee Son Heii was senior lecturer in orthopaedics at the University of Singapore. I met him at a conference in Liverpool and we talked about osteoporosis. I found that he was a Christian believer and he invited me to Singapore. We encouraged him to join our China team of academics and went into China with him several times. It was helpful because he was able to speak Cantonese. Dr David Knight, orthopaedic surgeon in Aberdeen, also became a member of a team. He was my Senior Registrar when I went to Aberdeen and needed a placement in a third world country for orthopaedic training, to fulfil his UK accreditation. He already had a heart for mission and readily accepted the invitation to go to Beijing for 3 months. He also has become a great ambassador for the Gospel in China and returns 2 or 3 times a year with a team of colleagues to lecture, operate and share the good news.

Dr Richard Aspden, now Professor Aspden, also became a member of the team, joining us to talk about Bio Engineering, and he frequently returns, maintaining these friendships. There must now be 8 or 10 Senior Academics in Chinese orthopaedics who have had training in the UK, Aberdeen/Doncaster/Nottingham/Royal National Ortho-paedic Hospital.

Mike Edgar, who is an international scoliosis surgeon, also joined us from the Royal National Orthopaedic Hospital and he also frequently returns to China and has been a great help, as has Professor Sean Hughes from Imperial College. I regard these people as my great friends and have valued their support.

It has been a privilege to return to China on many occasions, loaded with Bibles and supported by the prayers of our local Church. Every time we were walking in the experience of miracles.

77. A professorial chair

Christine was reading the Daily Telegraph in 1989, and saw an advertisement for a new Professor of Orthopaedics in Aberdeen. I enquired about this position and learnt that the Special Advisory Committee had visited Aberdeen and was not satisfied with their orthopaedic training. They said that unless the University introduced a chair of Orthopaedics to bring the training up to standard, they would withdraw recognition. Here were ten orthopaedic surgeons doing excellent clinical work, but the training was not acceptable. The University agreed to create a chair with good financial back up for research facilities, and they hoped to attract a good candidate.

I had reached the stage in my career where there was an opportunity to put my research into a higher gear. There were questions I was asking that could not be answered from my limited research base in Doncaster - particularly questions about spinal stenosis, club feet and osteoporosis. I also had something to offer in the training of surgeons that could be expanded in a teaching hospital environment. In addition I would also appreciate the opportunity to say something on the international orthopaedics scene.

Aberdeen seemed a good opportunity, but I knew that most surgical chairs were filled by people who had travelled on a different road. Most had climbed the academic ladder – from lecturer to senior lecturer in an academic unit, and then to professor. What chance had I coming from a District General Hospital? However, after talking if through with the family, and after a lot of prayer, I applied.

I went up to Aberdeen on the train and read in my Bible "*I am not sending you to a people of strange tongue, whose language is difficult to understand*". God was giving me a nudge, and I appreciated His sense of humour. Even other Scots have difficulty understanding an Aberdonian! I was offered the job. I hesitated for a few days to be sure, discussed it again at home, received a couple of phone calls saying they needed me in Aberdeen, and that was hard to refuse. I started on May 1st 1990.

78. The old folk

Mother and Father, and Wilfred were getting older and we could not expect them to move from Doncaster, so we decided to keep our home in Doncaster, and also have a pad in Aberdeen. We bought a small one-bedroom cottage, close to the university in Old Aberdeen and planned that Christine and I would spend the week together in Aberdeen and we would return to Doncaster at weekends. James was still at Oundle and it was important that we visit him on alternate weekends. We make our plans, and God overturns them.

It was not long before Wilfred was ill and needed a lot of home care. So Christine needed to spend more time in Doncaster and less in Scotland. Wilfred began to fail physically and spent the last months in bed, but he maintained his mental faculties, reading a library book each week. He was a spiritual giant, cheerful and faithful to the end. I was there when William prayed by his grandfather's bedside and then I saw Wilfred gently drift peacefully into his final sleep.

Mother became ill in 1992. She had an abdominal swelling that proved to be a cancer of the pancreas. My heart ached as I watched her get weaker and I told her that she set us such an example of faithfulness and trust. God clearly told me he would take her home "on the 29th". I thought He meant the 29th July. I had returned to Doncaster in mid-June and decided I would not return to Aberdeen until she had gone home, and within a few days she died on - 29th June. We had a lovely service in the home and I read Proverbs 31 (10-31). *"A wife of noble character who can find? Her husband lacks nothing of value. She brings him good all the days of her life. She selects wool. She works with eager hands. She opens her arms to the poor. She makes linen garments. She speaks wisdom. She watches over the affairs of her household. Her children rise up to call her blessed. Many women do noble things but you surpass them all. A woman who fears the Lord is to be praised. Give her the rewards she has earned".* There were tears of sorrow and tears of joy that my wonderful loving Mother was now in the arms of Jesus. The night before she died I had knelt by her bedside and she put her hand on my head saying, "Lord, bless my dear Richard".

We then cared for my Father every weekend, bringing him to our home for meals and taking him out in the car on Saturdays. In order that he could stay in his own home we had arranged for two different ladies to sleep in his house at night and there was a rota of friends who called in during the day. He was rarely left alone. He was very patient in his infirmity - wheelchair bound for the last five years because of peroneal muscular atrophy. He said that my Mother had gone to glory ahead of him in order to help prepare a place for him.

When I went off to Scotland each Sunday afternoon, my Father and I would pray together. He prayed as easily as he talked, and in those days, he generally finished with the words:

"and if our fellowship below in Jesus be so sweet
what heights of rapture shall we know
when round His throne we meet"

Then as I walked down the path to the gate, I would see him sitting in the bay window in his wheelchair waving to me with his hand in the air signifying the victory of Jesus.

In June 1993 I was in the Edinburgh Royal Infirmary examining final year medical students. I was conducting the clinical part of their final examination, when I was called to the phone. Isabel said that my father had died peacefully in his sleep that night. Heaven was ready for him at last. I left the Infirmary, and travelled to Doncaster that day to try and help sort out the necessary arrangements.

MATURING MINISTRY

79. Aberdeen

For five years I lived the life of a nomad, travelling to Aberdeen on Sunday afternoons and returning to Doncaster on Fridays. Christine joined me about one week in four, and we would then travel together by car - a lovely six hour journey over the Cheviots and the Lammermuir hills, by-passing Edinburgh, round the Tay estuary, and then up the Grampian coast to the granite city. We used to take Rosie our Boxer dog who lay on the back seat of the car. She instinctively knew when we were turning the last corner into Old Aberdeen. She would then sit bolt upright on the back seat and begin to pant in excitement. She loved Aberdeen, and the beach walks where she would romp with Christine and dig enormous holes in the sand. In an evening we explored the Dee valley and found our way into the hills up the winding Don. I tried a little estuary fishing and usually brought home a couple of fish for supper.

If Christine was not with me I travelled by train. I would find a corner seat and work steadily for the whole six hour journey. It was a valuable time when I could plan research, write papers, organise training, read PhD theses. The train journey was particularly useful because I was uninterrupted.

If I was alone in Aberdeen, I worked for long hours. I was in the university from seven in the morning to nine at night. Christine and I would talk on the telephone at 9am and again at 6pm each day, but I greatly missed her cheerful company.

My first job was to reorganise orthopaedic training. I had the consultants on my side. They were delighted when the SAC re-visited Aberdeen and not only gave us full marks, but they held Aberdeen up, as a model training programme for the rest of the UK to emulate. This paved the way for a happy honeymoon with my colleagues for about six months.

The four fold responsibility of a clinical professorial unit is to teach, conduct research, do clinical work and make a national contribution. It is important for a Prof to try to keep these four in balance. I soon noticed that my professorial colleagues tended to major in only one or two of these areas and they neglected others. Some did no research at all, and then the University was critical because they did not bring in academic credits. Some failed in their teaching responsibilities and were criticised by the undergraduates and the Dean. Others could not keep up with their clinical responsibilities and their colleagues grumbled about an unfair distribution of the department's clinical workload. The fourth responsibility - having a contribution to the discipline's professional bodies and the Royal College - was expected by one's peers nationally. I thought I had been sent to Aberdeen to try to make a contribution in all these four areas, but it proved to be very demanding and costly.

There was a cost to Christine - she coped remarkably well and helped me through innumerable difficulties. There was a cost to the old folk - they were supportive but wisely told me not to live this kind of lifestyle for too long.

We needed a lot of spiritual support and prayer backing from Doncaster. We did not receive this at Priory Place Methodist Church, we so we moved our membership to Hexthorpe Methodist Church. Priory had been pluralistic, but Hexthorpe was firmly evangelical. We explained we were in an unusual situation, in a sense we were missionaries to academic orthopaedics. We shared our vision with the church at Hexthorpe, and we were promised much prayer. One weekend in six I was on call for emergencies in Aberdeen, and we found an excellent Presbyterian church. Willy Still's church at Gilcomston, on Union Street, was just what we needed. This saintly old man in his eighties, preached his way through the whole Bible each decade. His exposition was riveting, both for older folk like us and for scores of young students who sat with pen and note book recording his every word. His prayers took us to the throne of God and made us weep. On a Wednesday evening I would attend his Bible Study and it was as bread to a hungry man. I bought tapes of the sermons we missed, and played them on the long car journeys travelling north and south. This foundation made it possible to work in Aberdeen for five years and fulfil what I think and hope was God's calling.

80. Grandchildren
The prophetic word given to Ada Mann was wonderfully fulfilled. We frequently often sit round the dining room table and enjoy a meal with our eleven little children, our children's children. We were given

several promises. I was given a promise before Benjamin was conceived, that my Father would be with Jesus before Matthew's first child was weaned. And so it happened.

Sam gave birth to Benjamin at the Royal Infirmary in 1992 when **Matthew** was working as a legal executive at Nabarro Nathanson's in Doncaster. Joel followed when they were in theological training at Wycliffe Hall in Oxford and Luke arrived during their curacy at Dore in Sheffield. They were all baptised by full immersion. Isaac - laughter – was born in March 2002, and David Luther came tumbling along to join his brothers in May 2005.

William and Karen waited some time for God's promise to be fulfilled, and when Joshua was born in 1999 they composed a hymn and sang it at his dedication.

> *The focus of so much hope and love,*
> *A baby to call our own,*
> *A birth that came through tears and joy*
> *And promises faith had sown*
>
> *So we pray with thankful hearts*
> *chorus... May Your blessing rest on all his ways;*
> *Give him the grace to follow You.*
> *May he live his life with courage and strength,*
> *Share in the length and breadth and height*
> *Of Your love for all the world.*
>
> *The future lies open, road unknown,*
> *His passions and skills to find,*
> *May we mirror the life of Christ to him,*
> *Help him grow in heart and mind.*
>
> *So we pray with hopeful hearts*
> *Chorus.....*

William and Karen were blessed with a beautiful second baby, Sarah, born in March 2002.

James and Katie conceived Bethany miraculously (whilst Katie was on the pill) in Nazareth in 1997. James was working in the Mission Hospital for the elective part of his medical course. There were enthusiastic celebrations for the birth of the first girl in the Porter family! For about twelve months in 1999, Christine and I travelled to

London on Sunday nights or early on Monday mornings, and we cared for Bethany for a couple of days until Tuesday evening, whilst James was doing the Cornhill theological course, and Katie was completing her medical training at Barts. This was a precious time for Christine and me as we got to know Bethany and her delightful ways. And Rachel added to the family when she joined her sister in 1999, with Jemimah in 2003 and Rosana Abigal in 2004.

So what a quiver full of blessings for Granny and Grandpa. The legacy we would like to leave them is a prayer that they may each have a personal relationship with Jesus Christ - that they will bow at the cross and know His salvation - that they will grow like flowers facing the sunshine into beautiful lives for God - and fulfil every purpose He has for their lives. We can already see the grace of God in their little lives as they sing and pray and are generous in sharing their love.

81. Clinical work

I like to think I was a good surgeon. At least this is what my patients used to tell me, but then they would, wouldn't they! I enjoyed being in the operating room. I operated quickly and cleanly and treated the tissues carefully. I seemed to have few complications. I had introduced hip and knee replacement and spinal surgery to Doncaster, and I felt what clinical skills I had were needed there in the 70's, 80's and 90's.

In Aberdeen it was different. My ten orthopaedic colleagues in Aberdeen had clinical skills that covered the whole range of orthopaedics. If I had any special expertise it was in low back problems and in the management of club feet. Douglas Wardlaw already provided an excellent service in spine surgery and in this area we were able to complement each other. I held one specialist back pain clinic each week seeing patients especially with spinal stenosis. Tom Scotland wanted to retain the management of club feet so I did not stake a claim. I was prepared to accept the whole spectrum of orthopaedic referrals in order to be able to teach the medical students and junior trainees, and also hope to retain my skills and be able to think about new techniques.

The pressure on my time increased and on-call commitments were difficult when I was travelling back and forth to England most weekends. I needed to relinquish some of the clinical workload, especially the trauma commitment, and this caused a little resentment amongst some of my colleagues. I was assured by my fellow professors that none of them had an easy ride, and I should expect the same. However, it was a little disconcerting having come from a harmonious unit in Doncaster then to find a degree of unpleasantness in Aberdeen. However I knew I could not excel in everything. I could not please everyone and I was led by my conscience.

I was constantly thinking about new procedures - new ways of dealing with old problems - and I developed a number of new operations. One never knew if they would work but, provided the ethical committee thought the benefits were likely to be greater than their risks, they were approved.

The first was a spinal ligament that could replace spinal fusion in selected patients. Whilst in Doncaster I had used stainless steel springs to treat instability back pain when some of the spinal segments might be moving erratically. The springs were fixed to the laminae and spinous processes and two or three patients having this procedure eased their back pain. I recruited the help of John Shepperd, an orthopaedic innovator in Hastings and an engineer and we refined the system using hooks and bollards with crimped looped cord. It looked promising. They were manufactured by an Orthopaedic company and we called the system "Orion" - didn't Job say, *"Who can loose the cords of Orion"?*. The first twenty patients compared favourably with similar patients who had a spinal fusion - 60-70% success rate. The procedure was fairly simple and patients were only in hospital overnight. The operation, similar to a system that was developed in France, gained favour.

A second new operation was a magnetic toe joint. I had been playing with the idea of putting magnets on the opposite sides of arthritic joints - magnets that opposed each other. The distraction should abolish joint friction and hopefully reduce the pain and disability of arthritis. I discovered a remarkable man, John Bevan, who worked in his garden shed in Wales. He helped me to design and produce these magnetic joints, and with ethical committee approval, I inserted a number of these in people with arthritic big toes. If it worked in the big toe, I hoped it could be developed for larger joints. I think the patients were pleased with the results, but I left Aberdeen before it was published and as far as I know no one else has taken this concept any further.

A third new operation was intended to lengthen the life of hip replacements. Currently the average life of a total hip replacement is fifteen years, because they tend to loosen in the bone and need revision. I was impressed with the two stage procedures for dental implants, first inserting a foundation in the jaw, and at a later stage when this was secure implanting the tooth. I therefore designed a two stage hip replacement. The first stage involved inserting a metal plate with an angled cylinder projecting into the femoral neck. Over the next six months this would become surrounded by strong new bone and it would become very secure. Altering the blood supply of the bone should also relieve some pain much as does an osteotomy. The second stage involved removing the femoral head and inserting a mushroomed shaped prosthesis into the cylinder. In theory the femoral component should never work loose. I had two of these devices manufactured, but I moved on from Aberdeen before I could test them and they are probably gathering dust in a theatre cupboard.

A fourth procedure involved inserting ceramic material into osteoporotic hips to prevent them fracturing, but more of that later.

82. Teaching
When I arrived in Aberdeen, the teaching of orthopaedics to medical students was not very good. That was the view of the students and of the SAC committee. I decided it was because the organisation was poor and the consultants were short of time. I greatly enjoyed teaching and set about redesigning the programme, getting more teaching time for orthopaedics (we eventually had more time for orthopaedic teaching than in any other medical school in the UK). I also needed more help and the Dean was tremendously supportive. The university provided me with a lecturer and two senior lecturers.

We put together a programme to teach students in small groups. I worked on the principle that people learn best when they are interested. The policy was to vary the style of teaching as much as possible. We presented about ten large lectures each year for 200 students, but I preferred to work with small groups. Sometimes we would have formal tutorials, and teaching about clinical assessments - how to elicit abnormal physical signs. We would get students to give short talks to their peers, and invite others to produce a small exhibition on a special topic. We would take them on a ward round, let them sit in clinics one-to-one, and give them a short period in the operating theatre.

I would advise the students not to believe everything they were told, and to question the textbooks. They were now adults and not school children. I reminded them that many of the great medical discoveries had been made by students and they should constantly be thinking of questions and how to solve them. I think a sign that we succeeded was that for the first time students wanted to do an intercalated degree in orthopaedics - we managed to look after about four each year.

The teaching of the trainees was also changed. I insisted that our trainee surgeons should be released from clinical responsibilities every Wednesday afternoon and we designed a programme of teaching that covered the whole subject in three years. I invited about ten guest speakers each year from across the UK and I think Aberdeen started to lose its parochial flavour.

I think the success of the Higher Surgical Orthopaedic Training programme could be measured by the high numbers of applicants we had for the training posts. The message that was buzzing round the UK that Aberdeen was the place to train, and the fact that the National Manpower Committee increased our training numbers from four in 1990 to ten in 1995.

The opportunity to help train a score of young British orthopaedic surgeons in Aberdeen was a privilege, trying to show them that following Christ is the best way.

83. A research base

An early priority for me, in Aberdeen, was to build a secure research base. Before going north, I prayed about recruiting someone to organise an orthopaedic basic science laboratory and my thoughts turned to Richard Aspden who was a lecturer in Manchester. Richard and I were both members of the International Society for the Study of the Lumbar Spine. We both thought about problems in the same way, probably because Richard was an evangelical Christian. I offered him a year's salary from money I had saved in Doncaster and we had faith that we could get him a permanent grant thereafter. He agreed to

167

bring his family up to Grampian and they bought an old cottage fifteen miles to the north in Pitmedon.

Once Richard was in post, we applied for soft money to recruit assistants. Richard's own basic science research was on articular cartilage, and we added to that with projects on osteorosis, bone healing and lumbar spine problems. We submitted lots of research proposals and before long we had a laboratory employing half a dozen people that was humming with activity. We had six or eight research workers at any one time - basic research assistants, BSc students, and a couple of PhD's in addition to medical students doing intercalated degrees.

After two or three years the university told me that we were bringing in more money to the university than any other clinical department - approaching £1.5 million by 1995. I was not concerned about the money, but grateful that it did reflect the measure of research activity we were doing and the number of young people being trained. I was able to get Richard Aspden promoted to Reader in 1995 and he was given a well-deserved professorship in 1998.

Research has many facets and I was often asked to lecture on the subject of "research". I believe the first step is to ask an important question. An unprofitable way to do research is to purchase a new piece of equipment and then ask what you can do with it. Much better to ask a big question - formulate a hypothesis - and then think of a way of refuting it.

Our team talked together at coffee breaks and at lunchtime. We mulled over problems, and there was a great expectancy in the department that we were moving forward the frontier of science in our small area.

84. Spinal research

I encouraged our team to discuss ideas with people in other disciplines, and this resulted in innumerable projects we shared with other departments. One was with the Department of Physiology; I discussed the problems of neurogenic claudication with Professor Kidd and we visited Gothenburg together, bringing back to Aberdeen an animal model to look at the blood flow of the nerves of the spine. Andrew Baker, one of our trainees took a year out to do the experiments and for the second time, we won the prestigious Volvo Award for Basic Science in 1994.

I had recognised, in Doncaster, that patients with neurogenic claudication tend to have two levels of spinal stenosis. We didn't know why. This new animal research in Aberdeen showed that two levels of stenosis impair the venous blood flow much more than a single level. We also had evidence that with this venous engorgement, when the nerves need to respond to the challenge of walking, the arteries which normally dilate are unable to do so. This seemed to mirror the clinical situation, and we argued that patients with two levels of spinal stenosis probably have difficulty walking because of this impaired arterial flow. It had surgical implications, because a single level of decompression should and does relieve the symptoms.

From time to time young doctors from overseas wanted to come to Aberdeen and train in our department. They would spend a year in doing research and during that period apply for registration with the GMC. In this way I helped Tibor Papp from Hungary and Trian Ursu from Romania. We attracted grants to support Tibor - to look at the Spittalfield collection of children's archaeological spines in the Natural History Museum, and Trian - to examine the foetal spines in the Anatomy Department of Cambridge University. As we had recorded how the vertebral canal grows from intra-uterine life to adulthood we discovered that the canal is mature in early infancy, and it was obvious that any environmental factors causing spinal stenosis would have to be at work in-utero.

One of the advantage of being in Aberdeen was that little is ever thrown away. Even the obstetric records of the 40's were available to study and we obtained more funding to compare the adult canal size measured by MRI with the foetal records. Tibor discovered that small premature babies, small placentas, mother of low social class and first born babies were independent factors responsible for small vertebral canals in adult life. I employed Jan Jeffreys to look further at a cohort of 200 ten year old children and Tibor's results were not only confirmed, but other factors like maternal smoking had an effect on the canal's growth. Thus we were able to show how adult spinal stenosis - itself a risk factor for low back symptoms - is largely determined by environmental factors in pregnancy. It means that the enormous problem of low back pain could be diminished if we had the will to do something about maternal care.

169

85. Osteoporosis research

I was fortunate that the Rheumatologist - David Reid - was in Aberdeen with an interest in osteoporosis. I received a big grant from the Scottish Office and, with David's support, we purchased two ultrasound machines to measure osteoporosis and compare them with other assessment methods. We established an Osteoporosis Unit and employed a research assistant for five years carrying out many different projects. We established that our ultrasound machine had distinct advantages over the more expensive DXA equipment in predicting women at risk of fracture.

Raj Murali was a young Indian doctor who had just passed his FRCS. I was impressed with this young Hindu who had tremendous energy and a new research idea popped into his mind every day. I employed him first as a research assistant and then as lecturer. I helped him with a number of projects on the spine and on bone metabolism. One day he told me, "Prof you have saved me ten thousand pounds". I looked puzzled until he said, "When I came to Aberdeen I wanted to buy a Jaguar car. Then when I saw that the Prof had a ten-year old Volvo 340, I began to realise that materialism, appearances and worldy values do not matter. So yesterday I bought a cheap second hand car." He was learning fast!

On another occasion Raj told me that at last he had begun to understand what I was doing in Aberdeen. He said he realised that I had a secret agenda. He had married a Christian wife and his heart was slowly turning to Jesus.

Raj came to see me one day asking what we could do about preventing old ladies fracturing the opposite hip when they had already fractured one side. Whilst we were treating the fracture, could we insert a metal pin to strengthen the unfractured side? We thought about the problem and I suggested that we might think about injecting a ceramic material to strengthen the unfractured hip. It might provide immediate strength and if it was osteoinductive - stimulating new bone - and osteoconductive - providing a scaffold for new bone, it might be very effective.

We received funding to test the idea. Raj spent a year in the laboratory experimenting with different components to make an injectable paste. We designed instruments to inject the paste and finally received ethical approval to inject Calcium Phosphate and

170

growth hormone into osteoporotic, unfractured hips when old ladies were having the first fractured hip fixed with metalwork.

We also employed a lady to administer the study, and to discuss the risks and anticipated benefits of the procedure with the patients and relatives, and we thought we had a good watertight study to test a novel method of preventing hip fracture.

86. Full stop

When Raj injected the hips whilst the fractured hip was being treated, it added too much extra time to the procedure. The study was then modified to offer the injection as an 'out-patients' to ladies who had had one fracture. Raj did about ten of these under local anaesthetic and asked me if he could give an injectable sedative to reduce any discomfort. It seemed a humane thing to do. Sedation was a simple and safe procedure being carried out in thousands of people every week for unpleasant procedures like gastroscopies, and it was to be carried out under the supervision of an anaesthetist.

One day I shall never forget was when I went into the operating theatre to begin my Thursday afternoon operating list, expecting Raj to have finished his procedure on one volunteer lady. Raj came hurrying out into the corridor saying that the lady had arrested. I helped him and the anaesthetist for about an hour but it was not possible to resuscitate this lady with cardiac arrest. The anaesthetist who had given the injection was shocked. It had never happened to her before. She said that when she offered the lady the injection the patient had said "Yes please- lots of it".

We were a sad dejected bunch of doctors sitting in the surgeon's room. I broke the distressing news to the lady's daughter and we sat together again going over the disaster. Could the injection possibly had found its way into the blood stream and caused a cardiac arrest? Could the material have been toxic in any way? Was it an unforeseen heart attack? The post mortem would tell. Over the weekend I thought again and again about this tragic event. Were we in any way to blame? Could it have been foreseen?

I could not eradicate from my mind the conversation I was having a few moments before I had gone to theatre to see how Raj was progressing. Richard Aspden and I had been discussing an interesting project with the Senior Lecturer in Obstetrics. This man wanted us to

171

test the idea that divided traumatised spinal cords could be made to regenerate using stem cells. It had tremendous potential to help paraplegics who had severed their spinal cord during spinal injury, and we were enthusiastic. We had the laboratory facilities and it seemed to be a promising study. I asked him how he obtained the stem cells. Were they from the umbilical cord or from pregnancies that had miscarried? "Neither" he said "They will be from aborted foetuses". Richard and I looked sadly at each other and quietly said that we could not be part of a study using aborted foetuses. However worthy the results may be, we could not condone the means of obtaining the stem cells, and we could not take part.

This man was so angry, "I know you people," he said, "You are so sanctimonious but you are the first to come to me for an abortion when your daughters get pregnant". I looked into his eyes and they flashed with a fiery red colour. He stormed out of the room leaving Richard and myself rather breath-taken. We've done the right thing, I said to Richard, and I went off to theatre.

Why did I connect this incident with the unexpected death of the old lady having the injection? Was God saying something? Was He unhappy with our research, and saying to me that our work was not quite ethical? Were we on an ego trip putting vulnerable people at unjustified risk? Or did I see the Devil in those red eyes and I was deep into the arena of spiritual warfare?

Whatever the reasons for this lady's death, this particular research of trying to strengthen bone by injection of a ceramic paste had to come to a stop, until we had some answers.

87. The Procurator Fiscal

In Scotland, the coroner is called the Procurator Fiscal. This lady's death was to be investigated in his court. I was greatly relieved when the pathologist came to see me on the Monday morning to say that the cause of death was a heart attack. There were marked atheromatous changes in the coronary arteries. She had had a previous heart attack, and it seemed a straight forward cause of death. The injected material was in the right place and there was no evidence that it had migrated. The relatives requested a second independent post-mortem. I thought that was rather uncanny but it confirmed the same results.

However Raj came to see me the same morning and explained that, although we had ethical permission for the original procedure, and we had returned to the ethical committee for permission to give the injections under local anaesthetic as an out-patient, we had not requested ethical approval for giving intravenous sedation. I said that we had been remiss, and I applied at once retrospectively, for this permission. I was assured by the chairman of the committee that if we had applied, permission would have been given and I hoped that would have been the end of the matter.

It took many months for the case to come before the Procurator Fiscal. The Medical Defence Union suggested that Raj and I had legal representation. I arrived in Aberdeen rather breathless late on the Sunday night to find a solicitor and impatient barrister waiting to offer me advice. The barrister suggested his presence in the court might give the wrong impression, that I had done something wrong and that I needed some high powered serious defence. He advised me to rely on the solicitor alone. I accepted that advice little realising that I was employing a man who turned out to be a chronic alcoholic and this was to be his last case.

It began to look a little more serious than I first thought, when I found that my lady research assistant whom we had employed for over a year, to recruit the patients and tell them about risks and benefits, was going to be called by the deceased's solicitor. I found her in court for the opposition. Furthermore they had also called one of my orthopaedic colleagues - Tom Scotland - who at the start of the project had expressed some reservations about the safety of the procedure. I was going to need all my wits about me.

The case dragged on for five days. They were not consecutive days but were spread intermittently across several months. When I was in the witness box I was asked why we had suggested on the patient consent form that there was a one in ten chance of a second hip fracture within two years. I explained that our figures in Doncaster had suggested that degree of risk, but my lady research assistant went into the box and said my estimate was inaccurate! She said that we had been misleading the volunteers exaggerating the true risk of a second fracture. She also said the information sheet was inaccurate when the patients were told it was a painless procedure. Even with local anaesthetic some patients were having pain, and for that reason we

173

added the option of sedation. It took about a year for the Procurator Fiscal to reach a decision. It was scathing, blaming me for reckless research, which was of unproven value, and an information sheet which was grossly inaccurate. I had not listened to the warnings of my colleagues, and I was partly responsible for this lady's death. The Scottish national press made a lot of it. And I was deeply embarrassed. I believed I had not been given a fair hearing, but there was no opportunity to reply. I had to take it on the chin.

Worse was to follow. The decision of the Procurator Fiscal was sent to the General Medical Council for them to consider whether Raj and I were guilty of professional misconduct. What a burden to be carrying at the end of my professional career! We waited for months, and then I received a phone call, that the GMC had considered the evidence, and there was no case for me to answer. The file was closed, but it left me with some very painful memories. At a time like this, you learn who your friends are.

I concluded that we had made one mistake by not obtaining ethical approval for every step in the procedure, particularly the addition of sedation, however humane it was. I could not believe we had done anything else wrong ... and from one mistake, mountains can rise and threaten to engulf us. We are not ignorant that there is an enemy of souls who is not slow to magnify one mistake and then try to create disaster. There needs to be a lot of prayer. And we have to accept that we are not exempt from attack. We have to be prepared for our reputations to be martyred, but it hurts.

88. Korea

I was surprised to receive an invitation in 1995 from Professor Kim in Soeul, South Korea. He had been elected President of the South Korean Orthopaedic Association and had the freedom to invite an overseas guest to give a lecture when he was installed President. Very generously he invited me and asked me to bring Christine.

Professor Kim is a strong Methodist, and on the occasion of his inauguration as President, it was also the celebration of the beginning of an important chapter of Christianity in Korea.

In 1895 some American Methodists had visited Korea and implanted the first seeds of the Gospel. The church rapidly grew and over a

174

hundred years, 40 per cent of the population of South Korea had become believers.

It was a very great privilege to witness what God is doing in the land. For instance, when travelling by train we would look out over the housetops in an evening and see hundreds of neon crosses rising high above the skyline of the towns. During the day-time, looking on the flat roof tops we would often see groups of Korean Christians meeting together around an open Bible to sing and pray together.

We attended Xhou's church on the Sunday. There were about 10 sequential services. The one we visited was packed with 10,000 people singing and praising God, often all praying together on their prayer mountain. It mattered nothing that we did not understand Korean, because the language of worship is universal.

After the preaching, when Xhou invited people to come and accept Jesus, there must have been several hundreds standing on their feet from the front of the auditorium. Young women ran down into the congregation with arms outstretched and ran back to the platform with the new enquirers. It was so fresh, alive and vibrant, and amazing to think all this had happened in the last hundred years – surely an answer to Wesley's prayer 'give me the praying love that longs to build thy house again'.

89. The Royal College of Surgeons of Edinburgh

I have always had the warmest regard for the Edinburgh College. I was an examiner in Anatomy for many years and then in examiner in General Surgery and finally in the Orthopaedic Intercollegiate examination FRCS (Orth). I was elected a member of the College Council from 1991. It was a tremendous privilege to be invited by the College to travel and examine overseas, and to inspect training schemes for the College in countries like Syria, Saudi Arabia (four times), Oman (four times), Kuwait, Singapore, (three times) Hong Kong (four times), India, Nepal and Libya . Usually I would be able to take Christine with me, so we are able to share a host of memories.

In 1995 I was encouraged by several of the College executive to apply for the newly formed position of Director of Education and Training. It seemed a good time for me to move on from Aberdeen, and I was fast becoming interested in medical education. I was a member of the Council of the British Orthopaedic Association, (BOA) and was the

Chairman of the BOA Education Committee trying to introduce innovative orthopaedic education programmes across the UK. I also enjoyed being a member of the Specialist Advisory Committee (SAC) that visited and accredited orthopaedic training programmes throughout the UK. So began many lasting friendships with colleagues around the country.

In addition, if I was offered the post in Edinburgh, I could expect life to be easier in Edinburgh than in Aberdeen. We already had a flat in Edinburgh. I negotiated with the President and the interviewing panel, to accept a half salary and work for two and a half days a week in Edinburgh, and I promised to try to establish a new high quality department of Education, that would serve the College well into the new millennium. I stepped into this new post in August 1995.

Life at the College between 1995 and 1997 was great fun. I created two departments – Education and Training – and had the help of a wonderful staff. We proposed some novel ideas, which I was able to implement. I was able to start a Surgical Skills Course, and a Course in Critical Care. I was responsible for a series of College lectures. I wrote a book of "Multiple choice questions and answers" to help candidates prepare for the FRCS College examination. And I also wrote a book for the College on "Choosing a career". We made plans to inspect all the overseas hospitals and those home hospitals that wished to have College recognition for training. It was proving to be a full time job. I worked far more than my promised "half time" but I enjoyed it.

One sad feature of life at the College was that I had a personality clash with one of the senior College Officers, and he made life very difficult for me. I never understood why and how this happened, because never before in my career have I had a problem with professional relationships. I think it must have been because for many years, if I had a new idea that I thought was good, I would try to develop it, sometimes without reference to other people. This was no problem in Doncaster and in Aberdeen where I enjoyed great independence, but the College likes to have every idea passed and agreed by committee. That's not how I work best. So I resigned from the College in August 1997 and was so pleased to be able to retire at 62 years of age. And live full time in Doncaster with Christine.

90. Overseas doctors

I brought about eight Chinese doctors over to UK and five have returned to their own country. All but one came to faith in Christ. I was also able to help a number of Muslim doctors get UK training, and establish real friendships with them all. Sabubah came from Kuwait and said, "There is no Muslim doctor who would have helped me like you have done". Kuffash, from Saudi, said that no one had helped him get established in UK until he met me. Saied from Egypt said that because I as a Christian had been willing to employ him - a Muslim - in Aberdeen, he appointed a Christian doctor in his Cairo hospital contrary to the usual protocol, because he remembered how I helped him. None of these Arabs have openly expressed faith in Christ, but I hope they have thought about the real Jesus.

I was examining for the College in the final FRCS exam in Kuwait at the time of the end of the war with Saddam Hussain, and was faced with a candidate called Dr Sabuba. He performed very well in the examination and I was able to give him a pass. He then asked, now that he had his Fellowship, whether or not he could come to the UK for training.

Dr Sabuba had been trapped in Kuwait when Sadam Hussain invaded from Iraq and he was the only doctor working in the hospital in Kuwait, with bullets flying around through the windows in the operating theatre. He rescued his family and placed them in the hospital for protection for several weeks. This brave man came to Aberdeen and he was in need of a training number. I recollect asking if he believed in prayer. He was a strong Muslim and we prayed together in the surgeons room. I asked if it were possible for God to find him a UK training number so that he could stay in the UK for orthopaedic training. I shouted through to my secretary in the next room, could she get me a telephone line to the College Education Department, who held the numbers. I intended her to get through to the Edinburgh College. She said the College were on the line but I later discovered it was the English College. I asked if they had a spare training number. They said one had been returned that day and I could use it for Dr Sabuba.

Dr Sabuba had his training in Aberdeen, Doncaster, Nottingham and London, and is now a Senior Staff Grade doctor in one of our Midland orthopaedic hospitals. We often talk about that experience, trying to obtain his training number, and the wonderful answer to prayer.

Sometimes I knew of Christian overseas doctors, whom I wanted to help gain valuable experience in the UK. I was always most careful not to abuse a professional privilege I had at the College and through the British Orthopaedic Association, and seek placement for people who were academically unsuitable for this high quality training. It would have been an offence to me and an abuse of my privilege. Fortunately we had been able to set up checks and balances through various committees to make sure that assessments were fair and accurate and everyone was operating on a level playing field. I think the results and current positions of these men today justify the decisions made about them in their earlier training, and that we were confident of operating on a level playing field.

One example is Ben, the husband of Lucy, our Chinese translator from Xin Dow who often helped us on our trips to China, is now working in the most prestigious endoscopic surgery unit in Europe. Professor Cuschieri, who was a member of Council at the Royal College of Surgeons of Edinburgh, was most interested to hear about Ben. He was interviewed and then offered a research placement at Ninewells Hospital, Dundee, to conduct research and help develop the endoscopic unit. Ben settled well in Dundee and particularly in one of the evangelical churches. He returned to Doncaster to be baptised before settling in Dundee. Christine and I have considered him as one of our best friends.

Shunan Zhou was a young Chinese surgeon who had arrived in the UK from Urumchi. He entered my office one day asking if I could help him get established in a UK training post. I listened to his story with amazement. He told me that when he was a student in Xian, he met a patient who had invited him to his home to study an old book. He explained that this was God's book and that if he wished to visit his home once a week with one or two of his friends, this Chinese gentleman would explain the stories of Jesus. So Shunan Zhou took a few students and then the numbers increased to about 20. When the authorities of the University heard of this illegal meeting in Xian, they said they could still continue to meet but as a result they would face very serious consequences as students. The numbers reduced to about 6 and Shunan remained faithful. When the students were allocated their hospitals after their final exams, Shunan was sent to the far north west to Urumuchi where there were few prospects of promotion. However, by some means I never understood, Shunan managed to come to the UK and find himself in my office asking if I could help him have training in the UK.

I invited him home to Doncaster where Christine looked after him for the weekend. He attended church and we had lovely fellowship together. Eventually he was able to obtain a training number and was finally placed in Liverpool Royal Infirmary where he still continues to do excellent research in the field of vascular surgery. He has met a lovely Christian girl and they are now married and working happily together in Liverpool. I am always pleased to receive a Father's Day Card from him and last year a block of Toblerone Chocolate which said 'to my Dad'.

91. Recent research

Back in 1995 I started to think about scoliosis. My best ideas seem to come whilst lying back in a hot bath. After all the work we had done on the spinal canal, it was obvious that the spinal cord is a most powerful force determining the shape of the surrounding bone. The bony canal matches the size of the spinal cord. It's counter intuitive, because you tend to think that the soft spinal cord will be moulded by the hard bone, but it's the opposite way round.

I started to think laterally about scoliosis. What if the spinal cord was moulding the vertebrae into a twisted shape? How could that happen? It came in a flash. If for some reason the spinal cord was to be short and did not grow as fast as the length of the bony spine, first the curved kyphosis would straighten out, then the spine would bend over laterally, and finally it would twist and buckle. As I thought about it, and read as much as I could find, that's exactly what happens.

I measured about 20 scoliosis spines in the Edinburgh and London College museums and found that the length of the spinal canal was always shorter than the length of the bony scoliotic spine, in proportion to the degree of scoliosis. I then read everything I could find on scoliosis, and wrote a paper for JBJS. They turned it down, but eventually I got three papers published in Spine and European Spine. The generous conclusion of the experts is that nothing in the hypothesis is denied by all the current research.

Professor Burwell found that someone had thought of this in the 1960's but it was not considered seriously. So maybe this time it will be accepted as a good working hypothesis, and who knows, one day a spinal cord growth factor may be given to prevent scoliosis.

In 2001 I was awarded the DSc by Edinburgh University for the work recorded in 50 or so papers on spinal stenosis and disorders of the lumbar spine. The scoliosis papers came too late to be included. Unfortunately I was too ill to travel to Edinburgh for the degree ceremony. It would have been nice, because it was the only DSc given at the summer graduation. Anyway the family were not over enthusiastic about these ceremonies.

92. Creation

In the 1980's I began to think about the meaning of "time". It started as I thought about the amazing way athletes kept breaking the track records. I remember being a student in Edinburgh in 1954 and reading about Roger Bannister running a mile in less than four minutes. That record seemed to be the peak of achievement. But then people seemed to be running faster and faster every year. Was it really that people were running faster, or was there another explanation? Could it be that time was getting slower, and with more than four minutes in which to run the mile, it was possible to find hundreds of people to run like Roger Bannister? It seemed a crazy idea, but outlandish ideas are worth thinking about.

The only way I could explain time getting slower was if the Earth was revolving more slowly. And it would do that if the Earth was getting bigger. That would mean a lower gravity on the surface of a larger Earth and it would explain how athletes could jump higher and throw further.

When I was at the Natural History Museum, Miss Molam said, "We've got an odd chap down the corridor, Dr Owen. He thinks the Earth is getting bigger." I made an excuse to meet him, and requested some of his reprints about an expanding Earth. We talked for a while surrounded by fossils in his little office. I asked him why he believed in an expanding Earth.
"Europe and America give a much better jig saw fit if you reduce them in size by one third. You could explain that, if 100 million years ago,

180

when Pangaea split apart, the Earth was one third smaller than it is today."

"Have you any other evidence to support the idea?" I asked.

And he explained that he had done work on fossil fish that he thought had come from two separate lakes before the continent split up. They could only have been separate populations if the Earth was smaller in the past. I didn't say I had similar thoughts about an enlarging Earth.

I remembered the patriarchs in the Bible who lived to such great ages, and how they only had their children when they were quite old, and that too seemed to fit with shorter years in antiquity. I let the concept simmer on the back boiler. My secretary opened a file in 1988 called "Mr Porter's theory of an expanding Earth!" and between orthopaedic research, I kept adding to the file.

In the 1990's I began to buy every book I could find on "time". I started to read about cosmology, astrophysics, geology, and evolution. Until then I had accepted that evolution was probably the best explanation about how God had made living things. Genesis days were really epochs as he created the species slowly over millions of centuries. It was not a matter of chance, but by intelligent design. I thought God had done it that way, and when the first human evolved - Adam - he was infused with a soul and was finally made in the image of God. It meant stretching Genesis to accommodate evolution, but then it was written for a non-scientific people, and that was okay. I fudged the issue of the origin of evil and thought God could have anticipated the fall of man once he had received free will. It was a bit messy theologically, but it seemed the best fit between the Bible and science.

When I started to think about "time" I realised that if I was right, and time was slowing down, there probably wasn't enough time for evolution.

One of my best academic friends was Vernon Wright, Professor of Rheumatology in Leeds. He was a passionate creationist and travelled anywhere to share the gospel and his belief in a literal Genesis. This man was the most prolific researcher I knew, and he believed in a six day creation. I asked him to come to Doncaster and share in a debate on Evolution vs Creation. He said he would come if it was a one sided presentation. He would present the evidence for special creation, Nigel Cameron, a theologian from Edinburgh would talk about the

181

theological reasons for accepting the literal truth of Genesis, and I would chair the meeting.

We had 200 people at Priory. I started by saying this is an area where Christians disagree. "Christians are at an advantage. They can take either side, and have the freedom to be open minded. On the other hand the atheistic evolutionist has no choice."

In my journey over the following decade, I began to think that evolution was too unreliable a theory - a set of assumptions that have been accepted by an indoctrinated population. I came to think that we were doing an injustice to the Bible to accept it.

As I thought and read more about the subject of "time" I also came to think that the cosmos may be very young, in fact as young as the book of Genesis claims - perhaps only a few thousand years old.

I remember one week receiving my copy of Creation Magazine reporting a three page interview I did with one of their editors. "Standing upright for creation". I used to be an evolutionist, but have steadily changed. It was strange though, how uncomfortable I felt wearing an academic hat and saying evolution is probably wrong. So powerful is the media pressure.

James encouraged me to put some of these ideas on to paper, and when I retired from the College in 1997 I began to write. In the next few years I read and wrote, and modified the ideas. I thought I would never have the concept of a slowing down of time accepted by a scientific journal, but I could write a novel incorporating the ideas and see if a publisher would take it. It took two years to write.

The first submission of the novel was to the Creation society in 2002. After 6 months I got a blunt reply that they didn't want to publish it. They thought the science was flawed, and the example of my heroine Sophie, taking a lead role in the conversion of Jon her fiancé was not scriptural! At least I got some useful advice about improvement and was able to revise the book further.

Next time I sent out eighteen letters to different publishers. Christine and I were having lunch and I was saying that I'd had a phone call from a publisher in Belfast a week before showing interest and offering to look at the book, but there had been no further contact. Christine suggested I phone Leo at McCall Barbour's in Edinburgh.

He was a friend from student days and an owner of a Christian bookshop.

"Leo, how are things? I've been writing a book on creation and haven't got a publisher. Any ideas?"

He thought for a while and said, "I have a friend in Belfast - Sam Lowry. I'll give him a ring." I am humbly amazed that God works in such wonderful ways.

"Leo. That's the very man who phoned me a week ago."

Theo was back on the phone in ten minutes, "I've spoken to Sam and he's interested in your book. I told him we were good friends and that you were theologically sound!"

Things began to move. I called it 'Journey to Eden'. Sam was sent a revised copy and we waited for his response.

I enjoyed writing this book. The story developed in a remarkable way, almost writing itself. As it proceeded, my own ideas changed. I realised that time is only a measure of motion - the rotation of the Earth, the swing of the pendulum, the circuit of the Earth round the sun, the motion of electrons and the decay of atoms. We measure one motion and relate it to the motion of something else. If all the rates of motion are keeping pace with each other, we say that time is uniform. If one gets out of step, like a slowing down of the rotation of the Earth, we have to add a millisecond to the day from time to time.

It became obvious that if all motion was slowing down together, we would not know about it. Time might be slowing down, but unless there was an outside clock such as a previous clock years ago, or a parallel clock beating at a different rhythm we would remain in ignorance.

There could be two clocks to help us. The quality of light from nearby stars may be different to the light from far away stars which left in a previous era when time was faster - and the red shift gives just that hint of a different beat of a previous clock. And secondly, a parallel clock could be biorhythm. What if the biological clock was stable and uncoupled from a physical clock that was slowing down? So there was the hypothesis. Uncoupled physical and biological time.

In addition to athletes apparently running faster and men seeming to live longer in antiquity, there were two more clues that biological time may be out of sequence. The circadian cycle is just a bit more than 24 hours, and could have been programmed at an earlier time when 24 hours has now changed to 25 hours. Perhaps the clock in the DNA is constantly being reprogrammed with each generation.

There was another interesting observation, that young DNA is found in old rocks. DNA is said to last no longer than 50,000 years even in ideal conditions and yet remnants are found in rock of millions of years old. That's also compatible with two uncoupled clocks.

I don't know if it's right, but there's a hypothesis to test. It's a novel idea that could harmonise scientific observations with a literal reading of Genesis. But that's not why I now believe in a six day creation. I believe it because God was there at Creation, and for too long science has been over-confident in claiming the high ground.

'Journey to Eden' came off the press in October 2003. We did a launch in Jersey at Ottakers, who said it was one of the best they'd had. Jersey radio did an interview that was repeated six times during the day. I hoped that there would be a good readership and people would begin to think about time and a young universe.

93. Health problems
In 2000 Christine was diagnosed as having carcinoma of the breast, intraductal, and she had a left mastectomy in November. Professor Eremin (who had been Prof in Aberdeen) moved to Lincoln, and he looked after Christine so well. We were so thankful for a good prognosis, and helpful positive follow up appointments.

Over the years I had a few scares with my health. Prostatitis in about 1982 when I was very ill with urinary infection for three months or more. Prostatic hypertrophy in 1997 which began with infection and then a TUR in about Feb 1998. I was ill for a whole year. The histology was clear.

The disadvantage of being a medic is that every symptom is examined and the enemy puts the worst possible scenario in front of me. Especially in the night hours. Why should that be? Was I more frail than most men?

I was diagnosed as having caricinoma of the prostate in February 2001, had a painful biopsy and then radiotherapy for five week in September/October 2001. So, at the close of 2001 we were left wondering about the days ahead, and praying for grace to be a witness in the days.

James and Katie were with us in Doncaster for a few days over Christmas 2001, and it was a delight to have them. Little Bethany - so beautiful - is a lovely girl and to have her in the home is a delight. Rachel has quickly followed in her sister's footsteps, with a personality of her own. Christine and I were always so pleased to have our sons and their wives and families with us, even for a short time. William and Karen came over for Christmas day, and Joshua was showing us what a bright boy he is going to be. Matthew and Sam invited us to spend Boxing Day with them. Christine and I went over after lunch, because we both had problems in the night. Christine kept getting paroxysmal tachycardias, with her pulse racing at 130 per minute, and they went on for a couple of hours. It was quite distressing.

I had also had a paroxysm of fast atrial fibrillation in October 2001 and it corrected in a couple of hours but I was admitted overnight. No infarct, but I was put on Beta blockers. It slowed my pulse and I thought all was well, until Christmas 2001 when I started with paroxismal tachycardias and the occasional extra systole. In the night it would start with a tachycaridia again and I would get up to work on the computer for a couple of hours until it righted again. These things reminded us of our mortality, as if we didn't need to know. Christine and I both looked forward to going to glory, but the passage makes one a little apprehensive.

Billy Bray put it beautifully. *"We're sons of the King. He's given us white clothes that will never wear out, the promise of a crown and he's told us we shall be with him for ever and ever."*

94. Family gatherings

A year went by! Christine had three monthly check ups at Lincoln and all was well. I had the PSA test in May and could hardly believe it was 0.2 - well below the upper normal limit of 0.8. The uncomfortable pains I had been having in the groin and perineum have slowly gone away. The old heart would still go "bumpity bump" for several days on end, and then correct itself. We're still here and tremendously thankful. I started on double strength beta blockers for hypertension, which helped the heart, but made me very tired.

One of our greatest joys has been gathering together our lovely family of four sons, daughters-in-law and eleven lovely grandchildren at our home. When Christine had her 65th birthday celebration here, everyone came (except our dear Barbara who couldn't make it) and we have a lovely photograph to remind us what a happy day it was.

2002 was a very productive year for grandchildren. There was the birth of Isaac in February, for Matthew and Sam, Sarah in March for William and Karen, and Jemima in August for James and Katie. We prayed much for these little ones that they would all come to faith in the Lord Jesus early in life, and live for His glory alone. We pray also for their future partners in marriage, that God will guide them all through the generations.

95. Samaritan

In the 21st century, doctors and health care workers are naturally a little reluctant to stop at road accidents because of the failure of insurance companies to cover the doctor making a clinical mistake. The increase in litigation has not been helpful to our western society.

In January 2004 Matthew and I were driving along the Baslow Road into Sheffield when we discovered that a motor cyclist was trapped under a heavy goods vehicle. We pulled to a halt and I got out and knelt by the side of this motor cyclist who was partly crushed and trapped under the wheels of the lorry. Amazingly, the first passers-by who stopped were me and an accident and emergency doctor. We held his hand, examined for vital signs and made sure of Airway, Breathing, Circulation. His neck was secure and we kept him warm. Eventually the helicopter arrived and we left him in capable hands.

Months later I received a little letter:
'I am Andy, the one involved in the motor cycle accident in January last year when you stopped and helped.

"Matthew, we met after my discharge from hospital. Richard, I never had the privilege of meeting you whilst I was conscious. I just want to say 'God bless you'. Thank you from my heart. Stay strong. I know that you two touched my life and made it better. Thank you, Thank you."

Andy is now much better and is sure that God saved him for a purpose. I really do not think the health care worker who is a follower of Jesus has any alternative in spite of the unpleasantness of our current litigation minded society (Luke ch10v17).

REVIVAL TESTIMONY

"Here I am wholly available
As for me I will serve the Lord"

96. Small beginnings

In the autumn of 2001, two young Iranian people came to our church at Hexthorpe. They had arrived in Doncaster that week, and had heard the gospel for the first time as they passed through London. They could speak no English, but said to the settlement lady in Doncaster "Christos". The translator realised they were asking if there was a church in Doncaster, and she telephoned a friend of hers - Joan Reasbeck - who agreed to collect them on Sunday and bring them to church. They sat in front of us. I saw them reading the Bible in Farsi and we looked at a few verses together. They came every week and their English improved. By Easter 2002 they wanted to be baptised and I hired a birthing pool so that Gorgin and Rashin could be baptised by full immersion.

Gorgin asked me if it would be all right if he brought some Iranian friends to church. "How many I asked?" "Don't know but there are several hundred in Doncaster." So began Gorgin's zealous recruitment of Iranians to come to church. Gorgin worked night and day making Pizzas, and he bought a small car to collect Iranians and bring them to church. Bahman was the first one he found. Bahman was a large surly man who eventually confided in me one day when we had invited him for Sunday lunch. "Richard, do you know anyone in MI5?" I paused, it's not every day you're asked that question. "Why?" I enquired. He told me his story. He had worked in the Iranian Nuclear Power Industry, a sensitive job, and had been asked to travel to Russian for contracts. He had knowledge of the plans and purposes of the Nuclear programme in Iran, but had been trusted to visit Russia. There he met a Christian lady and they corresponded by email. It was intercepted, and he found he was now a security risk. He fled the country with nothing except documents to prove his case. He wanted to see MI5, not to divulge total secrets, but to share something and obtain assurance from them that his asylum case was true. I did, in fact, know someone who worked for British Intelligence and told him I knew ****** and would contact him by phone.

I spoke that evening with ******** and he in turn spoke to another branch who said they would visit Bahman in Doncaster. I kept all Bahman's documents here at Bawtry Road for security, because he was terrified that some secret agent from Iran might be on his trail.

The day came when I had to appear in court on his behalf. John Wiltshire was also there to testify that Bahman was now a true believer and had been baptised, and was now our translator at church. John was amazed to find the court was sitting in camera, and the story unfolded like a James Bond drama. Bahman obtained asylum.

Other Iranians also came to church, and I suggested to John that it would be helpful if they moved into the church lounge half way through the service for their own meeting in Farsi. It was agreed, and I was given responsibility to preach each Sunday, with Bahman translating. We would start with welcome and notices - including one about the Monday afternoon Bible study at Gorgin's house - and then Gorgin would play his guitar and we'd sing a Farsi gospel song. We would read the Scriptures - a verse from everyone, and then I'd preach. We'd finish standing up in a circle and holding hands, and different people praying.

So began an amazing work; unbelievable really, that Christine and I were able to share in what became a mini revival. Christine has such a sensitivity and compassion that makes her able to get alongside people in need, and it has been so apparent to the Iranians.

Amin joined us, a keen ambitious young man who wanted to be as English as possible. He was soon convinced of the truths of the gospel. He shared with Christine and me over a meal, that he had been sure the Koran was wrong when it said you can beat your wife. He came to Doncaster, went to the library and borrowed a Bible to see what the Bible said. Then as he walked the streets, he saw a church with as notice about Sunday service at 10.30am. He arrived at that church and asked the man at the door if it was all right for a Muslim to come in. He was welcomed and started to attend for a few weeks. Then he met Gorgin in Doncaster and came to Hexthorpe where he now had a few Iranian friends. He was baptised. Drying himself afterwards he was so excited. "Richard, it was wonderful. Can we do it again?" Amin became our reserve interpreter. John and I spoke for him at his asylum hearing. We had to convince the court that he was first an open believer, and second that he was an evangelical believer.

It was not difficult, and they granted him asylum in the court which is quite unusual.

Reza and Zari also came to church in 2002, with their three children Amir, Elham and Mohammed. Reza was a tall strong man from the Iranian army. Christine and I took them in the car to Epworth and we had a great time looking at the church and sharing the story of John Wesley. Zari told us she had become a believer in Iran whilst Reza was in prison. He returned home to find he had a new wife. When he came to UK he looked for a church, and found one with about six old people sitting in solemn silence. Then he discovered Hexthorpe with our lively singing, clapping, laughter and lots of love, and they were firm members thereafter. We organised a free taxi to bring them 12 miles to church and Christine and I paid for Amir and Elham to spend a week at the Easter People Christian Conference 2003, and they were baptised with great rejoicing.

This was the first little nucleus and they all started to have a concern for their Iranian people in Doncaster. A small family of Sohila and her two girls Marian and Mehrnoosh came for a while. We shared food in each other's homes together, but then the pull of Islam drew them away. A young 15 year old also called Amir, joined us for a while and seemed to be making good progress, but when he went to school his Muslim teacher said, "What religion are you? No you can't be a Christian. You're a Muslim and always will be," so he stopped coming to church.

Immanuel was a triumph. This young man came to faith in Jesus but he had problems with his sexual orientation. I went to hospital with him and after extensive tests it was found that he was in fact a true male although he felt he was female. We talked this through at length and he was finally baptised with much happiness. He then went to the Elam Bible College in London for full time training.

Ali started to come to church in 2002 and has been a regular attender, but never quite made a strong stand for Christ until the summer of 2003. Some come to believe quickly and others are slow movers. But the end is the same. Alfred now is getting ready for baptism. John and I went to court in Birmingham for him (three times with the adjournments) and took Colin Reasbeck (a retired minister in our church) and he got a positive.

189

John Wiltshire our minister with four churches to supervise quickly developed a heart for the work. Colin also, rather reluctantly at first, started to listen to the Iranian's problems, and became fully involved and deeply moved to help all he could.

97. One by one

In 2002 we had a few problems. Bahman was troubled that three men were coming to church to make fun of the others. There would be small asides that I did not understand, but it was ridicule directed towards some of the believers. Bahman was also unsure whether there was a plant in the meeting, sending information back to Iran, and as a result their families might suffer. Bahman asked me to speak to those concerned and tell them not to come to church, otherwise some of our new believers might well leave and form their own church. I explained that the church was open for all to come, but we would keep the Monday Bible Study for believers only (like the early Methodist class meeting). I promised to speak to Arta (not real name) whom he said was the main culprit.

Arta is a man that Christine and I have come to love and covet for the Kingdom. He became a half believer if that is possible, and eventually went to Bristol to study law. He is a big man and has a smiling face - some of the time - and on other occasions looks very sad. His name means "hope" and he says that he has no hope. I have visited him in his immaculate bed-sit on many occasions, and I had to visit and share with him my concern. "Arta, you are saying things that are bad, that hurt other people, and it must stop." He denied it with tears in his eyes. However, I said that he must identify the person he had hurt and ask forgiveness. "How can I when I don't know who it is?" he asked. I said he should think about it and he should not come to church for three weeks. Then he would be welcome again and we would all make a new start. "Can't I come to church?" he asked. "You're always welcome Arta, but give it a break for three weeks." I thought I'd lost this man who was still claiming to be Muslim but was somehow drawn to Jesus.

Arta returned to church after three weeks and then most Sundays. After a while it was once or twice a week to our home as well, to be an interpreter for first one and then another. Some weeks later he said "Richard, I'm a Muslim, but how is it that when ever you speak of

190

Jesus, the hairs on my arm stand on end?" "That's the Holy Spirit touching you, Arta." He returned again with Ibrahim, who wanted to tell me that he had become a believer in Jesus. He had first come to church at the invitation of Ali and he had found for himself to wonder and beauty of Jesus. He had been challenged by the singing and the joy of Christian worship and by the love shown by all the believers. He listened intently to the preaching, took notes and then went home to read his Bible about the subject. He came with Arta to ask questions. (1) What was this passage in Matthew about the wide and the narrow way? We looked together at the passage and how you can so easily miss the small gate. Not many people find it. That gate is Jesus who said, "I am the gate for the sheep". Then (2) he asked about the meaning of the salt and the light. I said that when we know Jesus, we get a little bit of salt and small amount of light and we will see what a difference it makes to everyone around us. Let the light shine. "Arta has some light," I said. "Me?" he replied in unbelief. "Sure Arta, you're looking towards Jesus and His light is beginning to shine in your heart". (3) We also looked at the promise about asking and seeking and knocking and (4) about playing the flute and no one dancing and singing a dirge and no one crying. However God's word comes to us we have a choice.

The three of us got on our knees and bowed with our heads to the floor and held hands and prayed. We asked for faith and for the Lord to hear our feeble knocking and then Arta declared, "I have faith". He hesitated. "I think I might have faith". I've learnt that I must never push these men. Let the gentle work of the Spirit flow into their lives and watch in wonder as the Lord shows His face.

Two of Arta's friends who had been causing some disturbance were Ali and Reza. More about these two wonderful men later. They have both come to know the reality of Jesus Christ and have both been baptised. That's a tribute to Arta.

I represented Arta in his asylum claim purely on medical grounds. There were medical reasons to believe his story is true. He claims to have been in the Iranian Navy and he got lost in a small boat at sea. The USA Carrier told the Iranian Navy that he was adrift, and he was picked up by the Iranians, imprisoned, and tortured with his arm being broken. He was to be arrested again and he fled the country. I went to court and he got a positive.

Ali, who introduced Ibrahim to Christ and many more, was so excited when he came to church for the first time. He said, I thought someone important must be coming because everyone is happy and singing. He was right. He got a negative at court in 2002/3 but kept coming to church each week and to the many Bible studies. Now he goes into town witnessing to Christ in the open air. He asked the mayor's permission and was told there was no problem. You cannot keep this man quiet! He is sold out to Jesus. He says that it does not matter if he is sent back to Iran, he will just keep on telling people about Christ, and trust Him.

Reza has been able to show Haseen the way. Haseen came to me after church as we were drinking tea and said he had seen such happiness in Reza that he wanted to know why. "I'm no longer a Muslim. I'm a Christian" said Reza smiling from ear to ear. "I want to know that too" said Haseen and Reza introduced him to Jesus. "Are you reading the Bible?" I asked. "I have no Bible". So I found a New Testament and he started to read. He visited us at home full of the thrill and the first love of new found faith and we prayed together.

Reza's father in Iran is a Mullah. Reza's job was to climb the minarette and call the village to prayer. He clearly has an influential family, and they have constantly requested that he converts back to Islam. When he told his father he had been baptised, his father said that he now has no son, and would not talk to Reza. It caused Reza great distress. We prayed long with him for his father. Then in the middle of the night his father phoned. "It's all right son. Keep going". Then he said, "What do they think about me?" "They love you dad." "They do?" "Yes they are praying for you." "Tell Richard that if he keeps praying for me, I will pray for him." And we do keep praying for this dear old man.

Reza did not wish to involve the church in supporting his asylum claim. And he got a negative, when we would clearly have represented him and I guess he would have been given leave to stay. He wrote to Tony Blair and offered to serve in the Iraq invasions, but got no reply. He wrote to the Iranian PM and said he would convert to Christ.

Mehdi started a web site for the congregation. Reza put his testimony on the web site and received a lot of life-threatening replies from security men on the chat page. He just continues with a deep passion for Jesus and for evangelism.

Many of our people have been threatened. Mehdi and his wife became very vivacious believers. They were brought to church by Benny and Zorah. Zorah brought them to me. "Pray for them Richard. They are Muslims, but I know they are going to come to Christ." And very quickly they did. Then some weeks later when collecting her little children from school, some Muslims surrounded her. "You are a bad woman. You have converted to Christianity. You were baptised last week. We are going to kill you and your children. Wherever you go in the world we will find you and kill your family."

She came weeping to me, saying that she knew Jesus would protect her, but still she could not sleep at night. Of course we prayed, and God gave her peace. She continues with the same fire in her heart and brings many others to church.

Back to Reza. For months he would not go into the black economy and NASS removed his accommodation. Homeless and without finance, he survived for months living by faith. Eventually we put him as a guest in one of the ex-offender church houses in Bentley Avenue. He found a small job, and came up smiling from ear to ear. He has about twelve letters supporting his asylum claim and we found a solicitor to take his case on (after failing with our MP).

We have found that some solicitors are in the asylum support business because of their Christian faith, or simply because of their humanitarian concerns. One adjudicator said to John and me at the end of the case, "Keep up the good work!"

One adjudicator who gave Ali Corda a positive on the day said, "I'm not a Christian, but I can recognise true faith when I see it." There is no doubt that our presence in court is a witness to many people that the church cares.

Reza asked if we could pray for a lady called Shahfa who is a Moslem living in London who has not walked for 20 years because of MS and her legs are very swollen. "She's a Muslim you know!" "Certainly" I said, "Jesus told us to preach the gospel and heal the sick. He'd help us. We'll all pray next Sunday." The room was full on Sunday, and I asked Reza to tell them all about Shahfa. Then we all prayed, several in Farsi. Next evening I received a phone call from Shahfa in London, thanking us for praying for her, and she said that for the first time in many weeks she had woken up on Monday without any pain.

98. The Afghanistan movement

Two Afghanis came to church, because they can speak a little Farsi. Mohktar smiled showing all his white teeth and hits his chest saying "Jesus, Jesus". His friend Kabir is about 5 foot tall and he has a rosy smiling face too. He first heard of Jesus at Hexthorpe and was amazed at the happiness of the people. He started to read the Bible and try to follow Jesus, but received a lot of abuse from his Muslim flatmates. "You are doing a very bad thing changing your religion," they said. Kabir worked long hours in a shop. He had his asylum claim turned down and he was living in the black economy, getting a small wage and sleeping on the shop floor. "I decided to ask God for a sign," he said. "If Jesus is the way, give me a dream about him tonight. If Mohammed is the way, may I dream about him. If there is no God, may I have no dream at all." And he went to sleep on the floor.

In the night he had a most wonderful dream of Jesus. "He stood there, so tall and brilliant," he said. I went to my Muslim friends in the morning and said, "I'm a Christian." He said that they have stopped talking to him, but he knows the friendship of Jesus and he is not alone. He says that his asylum claim was 50% lie and he wants to tell the courts now that he is a believer and under new orders. He has had another similar dream about Jesus and radiates the joy of the Lord.

Syroos is another man who is full of happiness. Syroos came to church and I told him he was very special in God's eyes. We looked at Isaiah 44:28, 'Cyrus, he is my shepherd' and 45:1 'Cyrus whose right hand I take hold of'. He accepted a Farsi Bible that Sunday and started to read it at 3pm. He kept reading and reading, captivated by the message. At 3am he was still reading and had had nothing to eat or drink and no cigarette. That week he was working on the factory production line putting some small components together. "I was suddenly so overcome with the glory of Jesus," he said, "I had to stop and worship Him". The whole production line came to a halt and the boss wanted to know what had happened to Syroos.

Syroos says that baptism is a family affair. Whenever an Iranian is baptised in UK the family will often know back home. Some of them will want to know what has happened, and will want to start reading the Bible for themselves. After Syroos' baptism he said that his eldest son in Iran had said he wanted to be John Wesley to Iran - telling people everywhere about Jesus.

One Sunday Syroos came to Christine as we were having a cup of tea after the service. "Christine, will you pray for Nilu, my wife? She has been waiting for a visa to come to UK, but the British Embassy in Tehran has been closed for six months." They prayed at 12.30pm. Then at 3pm the phone rang. It was Syroos saying that Nilu had been asked by the Embassy to go there next day. She received her visa and quickly came to UK to join Syroos. Two weeks later we heard that her father had died in Iran. We prayed together and arranged a memorial service at church. She then told this story – that her mother said that her father had been praying in the Name of Jesus, ever since Nilu left Iran. Nilu became a strong, beautiful believer. She was baptised with great celebration.

Syroos grew tremendously in his faith. He believes God wants him to return to Iran one day and preach the gospel.

99. The work grows

Soon we had three preachers in training – ("on note" as we say in Methodism). Syroos, Gorgin and Ali Corda all began to preach. I let them take the Bible studies twice each. It is a slow process growing leaders, but they progressed very well. There were petty jealousies, some justified, others frivolous. I kept calming the waters.

After three years I was able to identify eight "leaders". I found that the Iranian culture makes them ask *me* to identify leaders. If they elect them, there will be trouble. So after much prayer I asked; Syroos (drama), Ali Corda (music), Ali Boda (Security), Reza (Prayer), Sima (Women and prayer), Ahmad (IT) and Amin (Admin) and then Gorgin (Social sec) to make a leadership team. Straightaway it worked well. They met in our home, talked a long time in Farsi and then told me what they have been talking about.

It was rather awesome to find myself a "father figure" to so many of these brothers and sisters in Christ. They looked to me for advice and accepted it. What a responsibility, and what a dangerous place to be in. Dangerous because without humility there will be no progress. Dangerous, because we know there is an enemy. Ali Corda said that his family know a security man in Iran who has told them they know all about the work in Doncaster, and Richard Porter will be eliminated! We know that there is also a spiritual enemy who is clever, but not as powerful as the Lord Jesus.

Ali Corda said there was a spy in the midst. I could not be sure. But we were watchful.

Zorah Agabi Farshbat came to UK and was put in a dirty, crowded hostel in Kent. A Methodist man and wife were looking for holiday Bed and Breakfast and this was the only place available in town. So they stayed a night and met Zorah. They were drawn to this girl and her great need of friendship and they invited her to the Isle of Wight for a few days. She was then transferred to Doncaster, and was allocated a room in the same house as Bahman! There was also another young man in the a same house called Behnam. Behnam and Zorah were taken to church by Bahman and they were thrilled to hear the singing and praying, experience the friendliness and to feel the love amongst the believers. They very quickly came to trust in Jesus. They spent all their time reading the Bible. Zorah read the New Testament four times in three months. Behnam wanted to lead the Bible study and bravely stumbled through a passage on the second coming of Jesus, with Bahman helping him!

Before long these two - Behnam and Zorah were deeply in love, "like two pigeons," said Bahman - never apart." And then they wanted to get married. Zorah said, "I want to be pure for Jesus. I won't sleep with Behnam until we are married. Let's get married soon!" Their friends from Isle of Wight came up and stayed the night in our home and told me the night before the marriage that I was the best man! It was one of the happiest marriages I have attended. With no money, borrowed white dress and borrowed suit, food provided by the Iranian fellowship and flowers decorating the church by the English members, we had a wonderful celebration with dancing that lasted for hours.

After the honeymoon Zorah shared with the Bible study group how her mother and father were now believers in Iran because of her testimony to them on the telephone. Zorah has a beautiful voice and has composed Iranian gospel songs. She is also a gifted artist and painted a large oil picture on canvas of the Lord Jesus suffering on the cross. It is displayed at the front of the church.

Mikhlah is a cheerful young lady, rather diminutive, whose father lives in Doncaster with a lot of Muslims. Mikhlah had a room in Sheffield and travelled to Doncaster every Sunday for morning worship and twice a week for mid week Bible study. She was so faithful, and she studied the Bible and prayed for everyone. Often at the end of a morning service she would come up to me with an Iranian person and ask for prayer, and we would stand in a circle with arms over each other's shoulders and pray in English and Farsi. John and I went court to witness for her and she obtained asylum. There was much happiness and she came to the Doncaster meetings regularly since.

100. Witness to the courts

We spent many long hours in asylum hearings in local courts. Christine always came with us to court as a prayer supporter. 60% have been successful. It took a lot of time writing statements, visiting solicitors, praying with them, travelling to Leeds, Rotherham or Manchester. Four said that their statements to Home Office were false and now they were believers they cannot live with their consciences unless they put it right. The court believed two of them but decided Mehdi was using his Christian faith as a lever to get asylum. Kabir said it did not matter what the court says, he was now trusting the Lord and telling the truth and he would leave the decision to the greater judge of all men.

The courts needed to know (1) is the applicant a true and open believer - not a secret believer - otherwise they could be secret Christians in Iran? They also want to know (2) are they evangelical, because they cannot go back to Iran if they are telling others about Jesus? There is a death penalty for that. So the court was a platform for witnessing to the faith. Judge and barrister, solicitor and clerk all hear the true claims of the gospel. One solicitor said, "It makes you think again, when a young man changes his plea at some cost to himself, and says he has been telling lies. What is the power of this faith?" By contrast another solicitor said, "Here's God's army again!" It's like Paul's visit to Athens. Some mocked, others asked questions and a few believed. It's wonderful to know that "the few" really matter. If two are won for Christ and they in turn win another two, the fellowship grows exponentially to over a thousand with just ten reproductions. We were seeing something like that in the Iranian congregation. One is telling another and more and more come to hear about the gospel news.

197

101. Gifts emerge

Ali Corda is "intelligent" Ali. He told me very confidently that God was energy. "True," I said "but only partly true. He's more than energy Ali. He's intelligent and personal and has revealed Himself to us in Jesus." "No, He's just energy" he said. "Keep coming Ali and we'll talk more." And Ali kept coming week after week for a year before the Lord broke through into his life. It happened like this. I was preaching with a Farsi interpreter and Ali stood up and came to the front. "May I talk?" he said. "Sure Ali, the floor is yours." I was a bit apprehensive about what he might be saying. I asked Amin what it was about and he said, smiling - "tell you later." Everyone was listening to Ali with rapt attention and then there was a round of applause as he sat down. Amin told me that Ali had had a dream three nights before. He saw his mother in his dream. She had died some years ago, and was now saying to Ali. "You're wasting you life Ali. You're going nowhere. You've no purpose in life." Then she pointed with her finger to the wall where there was a cross. "That's the way Ali. That's the only way." And Ali said he was now going to follow Jesus.

This man Ali Corda (Alghassi) is a most remarkable Christian whom, I believed, would go all the way. He has such a heart for his brothers. He witnessed softly and powerfully to all Iranians, and then would gather them in his home for Bible Study where they devoured the Bible until the early hours of the morning. There must be 20-30 believers at church because of Ali's witness. Ali led the music group, which is something very different to an English church music group. We had drums and two keyboards, and the Iranians composed their own songs as well as trying to translate some of the English worship music. Like all music groups, this was a hot house for dissent and jealousies, but somehow it all held together.

They say that revival is messy. I now knew what that means. Christine and I stopped worrying about the many times people have come to our door with gossip. We listened and prayed, sometimes responding by giving sharp words at church, and we kept going in love. Our messages majored on God's love for us, the cross, Our love for God, Our love for our neighbour, Holiness of life, Prepared for persecution, Need for humility and evangelism.

There emerged a regular pattern of Christian activities. Sunday - worship 12.30 to 2.30pm. Monday - prayer meeting. Tuesday - bible study which Colin led, first at Sima's house, and then at the Riding Sun Pub that the church bought. Wednesday - prayer meeting. Thursday Bible Study which I led (first at our home and then later at church) 7pm - about 60 came each week. Friday - Bible Readings with Ali Boda. Saturday morning - English classes led by Nasser, and IT classes led by Shahram. Saturday evening - prayer meeting (Elizabeth and Ahmad). There were other meetings on and off. It was a moving feast.

Sima's family were a great blessing to us. She arrived in UK on Christmas day and was sure that God was saying to her that she was going to make a new start on the Birthday of Jesus. She came to Doncaster wanting to know about Jesus. After a few Sundays she had accepted Jesus as her Saviour, as well as her daughter Afsahni and son Mehdi. They became a tremendous strength to the church. When she got a positive at court she wondered whether she should leave Doncaster for the big city. We prayed a lot, and I said that she was a "mother in Israel". She decided that she and the family should stay here, and what a help they proved to be – opening their home for Colin's Tuesday evening Bible Study.

Going back to 2003, it was a great day and there were a lot of tears of joy when Ali Corda, Ali Boda, Reza, Kabir and Mohktar were baptised. John kindly invited me to share in the baptisms of these many Iranian converts - 27 baptisms by mid summer 2003. Christine and I were discovering that the Lord has given us a very special ministry in retirement.

Moj said to me that, when he first came to Hexthorpe, it was to look at my beautiful wife. "I wanted to see her and hear her sing, and slowly I began to hear about Jesus." Moj has a love for Jesus, but was not able to grasp the uniqueness of Christ. However he was irresistibly drawn to church and Bible studies. One day after we had prayed together, he threw his £20 drug purchase into the fire, but the addiction still has a hold on his life. His wife and son want to follow the Lord, but they are not yet able to say the Lord ONLY.

Moshsen is rather quiet and has a pony tail and a spotted face. He had been coming to church every Sunday for a year and asked why we had not invited him to be baptised. We found to our surprise that he had introduced several people to church and we agreed that he was ready for baptism. It was a great day for him.

Ali Zalbeigi is a clean hard working man who will always be found in the church kitchen washing up. He is the first to help whenever something needs to be done. He put tabs on his Bible so that he could quickly find his way around the scripture, and he would often be the first to read out a verse when I was preaching and asking for someone to read a text. His Bible was well thumbed and full of pencil marks. Ali became one of our right hand helpers.

Darwood came to our home one day with Syroos. He had been in Doncaster for two years and had been very depressed all that time. He would go to work, return home, and retire to his room and speak to no one. Syroos encouraged him to meet us and he came to share his story. He said he had had a vision of Jesus when he was 15 years of age in Iran, and Jesus said to him not to worry about his life, because it would all turn out well if he waited long enough. He came to UK. He now believed that the Lord had brought him to our home to learn about Jesus. We shared the good news with him and he started to weep for joy. "This is the happiest day of my life" he said. He attended church next Sunday and became a faithful attender ever since. He was baptised and then dropped again into deep depression. We explained how Jesus was immediately tempted after His baptism, and Darwood is progressing faithfully and with the occasional smile. I gave him my bicycle to help him get around and he was so thankful. He and Syroos formed the Hexthorpe Iranian Theatre group, to act out pieces of drama from the Bible. They began with the story of the beggar at the "Beautiful Gate" who was healed, and the Iranian congregation were spellbound.

Syroos has a tremendous gift in drama. The team of actors grew. They performed drama in church on the storm on Galilee, and Daniel. On Good Friday 2004 they dramatised the Trial of Jesus and the Crucifixion, which they performed in the Open air outside Priory. 200 gathered to watch this powerful message. There were two conversions out of this.

Syroos was walking down his street and saw a new Iranian sitting on the doorstep. "What are you so miserable about?" he asked. "You should be very happy to have arrived here in Doncaster." "Why?" "Because we have an Iranian church here." "I'm a Muslim." "That does not matter," he said. "I was Muslim. There are lots of people there who are Muslims, and we are all learning about Jesus." Of course, every Muslim wants to know about Jesus. He's mentioned in the Koran. That's always the starting point. Tell them about Jesus. Take time and then about the cross and the resurrection. That's totally new to a Muslim. It is shattering.

The Iranians have no difficulty believing in the miraculous, in dreams and visions. They do not question the accuracy and reliability and truth of the Bible. But we avoid talking about Christians, rather believers. We do not talk about the Bible but about the books of Moses, the prophets, the gospels and the letters. The former are etched on the memory from earlier Crusader days.

Anyway, the man sitting on the step was also called Syroos. He went with brother Syroos to our Circuit Meeting in Easter week. There were about 300 people there, and all who loved Jesus were invited to take communion. Syroos went up. At the end of the service when everyone was filing out for refreshments, this man was sitting alone. I went to sit beside him. He could not understand my English, but I prayed for him. He began to weep. This man was so thrilled to be able to take communion, that he became a believer there and then. I am not a theologian and don't know what to make of that, but I do know that this man is truly saved, and now baptised, and follows Jesus with a passionate heart. Every time he greeted Christine and me, it was with a bow and a profusion of kisses on the hand.

The Iranians looked to me for help and prayer. I keep telling them, don't look to me or to Christine, neither to Colin or Margaret or John, but look to Jesus. We are human and may fail you one day. Jesus will never let you down. He will always be there for you.

Ahmad came first to the Thursday Bible Study in our home. He had met a Christian in Iran but had decided not to become a Christian because he said his questions were not answered. After our Bible study he spoke up with a pertinent question. I told him "that's a great question" and did my best answer it. I learnt that the way of Jesus was to include everyone who wants to go His way. To be inclusive of everyone who is facing towards Jesus never mind what their beliefs are at the moment. Count them in. Include them. Ahmad said he felt that we cared about his questions and he kept coming. He is a gifted computer graphic designer and did a lovely logo for the Iranian

201

Summer Bible School we held in our home for a week in August 2003 - each morning with lunch. John and I shared the teaching - creation and the fall, the promise of a Saviour in the Old Testament, the life, death and resurrection of Jesus, the Holy Spirit and the Return of Jesus. Matthew came over to do the teaching on the Holy Spirit. Ahmad became a believer and is hungry for more, and many were deeply blessed through him.

Ahmad is an IT man. He used to do work for Iranian TV. One day Achram his wife received a phone call asking if she and her husband would like an air ticket to UK. She said they had no money. However, an unexplained miracle took place, they were given a low cost ticket and Ahmad and his wife and two lovely children arrived at Heathrow. He claimed asylum and was sent to Doncaster. His case was heard and not believed. However, in the meantime, Achram started to come to church. She is such a gentle gracious lady. She read her NT carefully and slowly, and prayed for many hours. Finally she accepted Jesus as her Saviour. This man and woman were baptised. She wanted to keep the veil on her head which I said was fine, and it took a whole year before she had the courage to occasionally remove the veil. Elizabeth got to know this family very well, and ministered to them in the Holy Spirit. One night they found themselves on the floor in the Spirit, and they have been deeply blessed ever since.

Ahmad programmed power point projection for me, which made a big difference to the Sunday morning services. After six months we were able to get funds to buy a church power point projector and lap top, and now it is in use each week. Another man Shahram is also an IT expert and he then operated the power point for us, because Ahmad became employed full time by Elam Ministries in London. He worked from home in Doncaster and produced all their Farsi literature. This was a tremendous answer to prayer for Ahmad.

102. Difficulties

There were difficult issues to deal with, as well as blessing, in this work of leading a new congregation. Chiefly our troubles began when in the autumn of 2002, Gorgin and Rashin said they were going to be divorced. Christine and I tried to listen and counsel as did John Wiltshire, but to no avail. A young student from Elam Bible College was coming to Doncaster regularly and we hoped he would become the Iranian pastor. John and I visited the Methodist District Finance Committee and were offered £9500 to start the work of an Iranian Pastor. Then we suspected that there was a mutual attraction between this man and Rashin. She believed God was telling her it was all right. Amazingly she fell to the floor during one of our prayer sessions and said she was "full of God". Then she fasted all the next day, and she still believed God was telling her to divorce Gorgin.

We went to court on behalf of Gorgin, and could honestly say he is an evangelical believer. The whole Iranian church is the result of his faithfulness. He was granted asylum. Rashin rode on the back of this, but since then left Doncaster and also left her husband and her small son Artin!

Naturally this divorce created heartache and big questions from the Iranian people. "How can this happen to Christians?" they said. About six of our key people, led by Bahman, met together and said they would form their own pure church. This included Reza and Zahri. Then to my surprise, Zahri left her husband Reza and took her children to live with Rashin for a few days.

One morning I woke up with a very stiff and painful neck. I sat in the kitchen with Christine, and as our habit is, we read our Bibles and prayed together before breakfast. I read Proverbs 29 verse 1. "A man who remains stiff necked after many rebukes will suddenly be destroyed without remedy." I could not understand what God was saying to me, but clearly he was trying to get me to understand something.

I read it again later in the day in The Message - a new translation. "For people who hate discipline and only get more stubborn, there'll come a day when life tumbles in and they break, but by then it's too late to help them. When good people run things, everyone is glad, but when the ruler is bad, everyone groans...... A leader of good judgement gives stability."

I asked the key people in the Iranian fellowship to come together, and told them that they must allow John and me to exercise discipline, and they must trust us to do what God expects. They went away and discussed it all again, and every one of them stayed at Church except Bahman. He never graced the doors of the church again, even for

203

Behnam's and Zorah's wedding. But the rest remained and we weathered the storm.

Bahman went to Southampton, joined a large House Church, and at Christmas 2004 I had a phone call from a Power Station asking for a reference, I think he probably now has a good job in UK.

I had to ask Gorgin to take a back seat in the services. He played his guitar and led the songs, but I had to keep a restraining hand on him for many months. It was hard for him to understand that he should not be up front in the worship and still be divorcing his wife. Rashin stopped coming to church and Bible Study and then left Doncaster.

I listened to Zahri and told her that she must return to her husband and say "sorry" even if she did not feel sorry. I told Reza he too must welcome his wife back with a request for forgiveness. There were many tears and, thankfully, a reconciliation for Reza and Zahri. However, they moved from Doncaster to Leeds, and then to London, joining the Iranian church there, and really the fellowship in Doncaster has been much sweeter since that time.

I had to preach for many Sundays about gossip, taming the tongue and living a life of love and holiness. I was seeing for the first time why so many of the New Testaments letters begin with doctrine and move on to practice. It is one thing to say, "I believe," and another to live a holy life.

I was told that a number of our fellowship were living bad lives during the week, visiting clubs and sex shops, and I had to speak clearly about this in the Sunday sermons - a bit unusual for me.

Thankfully we weathered the storm and came through to clear waters, but for the first time in my life I had to learn the hard practical lesson that discipline though painful, is necessary.

103. A separate service

In 2003 we found a good model for Sunday worship was for the Iranian people to join the whole English congregation for the first half of the service, and then when the children moved into their Sunday School session, the Iranians went into the Church lounge for half an hour Farsi meeting. The Church lounge however was soon too small. We had 20 meeting together in January 2003, but by August this was over 40 on two or three occasions. We then used the church hall with more comfort.

On Sunday 20th June 2003, we started a second Farsi speaking service at 12.30 to 1.45pm and I preached on "Choose yourselves today whom you will serve". I invited people to come up for prayer afterwards, and I was praying for one person after another for about 40 minutes. The power of God was very apparent. They often say "pray for me Richard." I say, "what about?" "No, Richard, just pray."

The numbers were on the 80 mark for several weeks in 2003, and the second service seemed the right way forward. We were anxious to keep in step with the Spirit.

104 More Afghan testimonies

In June 2003, Kabir came with Armhad (name changed) for the third Afghanistan Bible Study. It was wonderful to see their open eyes, full of wonder, especially Armhad, the Mullah who has come to believe in Jesus. He says he now knows that Jesus is the Son of God, but he fears to let it be known amongst his old friends. He used to preach in the local mosque and has not attended there since June 2003. We began to look at Mark's gospel yesterday and it was so exiting to see them absorbing the word of God for the very first time.

Armhad had been invited by Kabir to join our group to see the film "The Passion of Jesus." About 60 of us went together. However Armhad mistook the time and arrived at our house an hour early. So Kabir and Armhad and I read one of the gospel records of the trial and crucifixion of Jesus. We then went to see the film. Armhad spent the night talking to Kabir, and he came to believe in Jesus. He has now written a book in Urdu about the stories of Jesus and his face radiates to Lord.

Kabir phoned later in the day to say he had been witnessing to another Muslim called Arjgeebacka Ali (RG) for many days as he would come into the shop and talk to Kabir about his new faith in Jesus. Now RG is having many dreams about Jesus and he sees an enormous cross. We pray for him.

Kabir never stops talking about Jesus. He tells everyone who comes into the shop. Eventually the shopkeeper asked Kabir to leave, because the customers were complaining! Ten Muslims came to

Kabir's home and tried to enter. They broke his kitchen window and jumped into the house. The attacked him, cut his arm and broke his pictures of Jesus. Armhad fled up the road. I went to the police station with Kabir, but we pressed no charges. Both these men have come through this persecution much stronger. The came to our home at 7.30pm many Fridays for Bible study together. They have a deep concern for their people from Afghanistan and have told me many stories of their people coming to faith.

For example Christine prayed with an Afghanistan Muslim sitting in the court waiting room – Mr Khan. He then invited Kabir to Bradford. Kabir went but, when he got off the bus, a large black car was waiting for him. It was full of Muslims trying to convert him back to Islam. Finally, in Mr Khan's home, Kabir asked if he could show them a video. They thought that was polite when he had come so far, and they watched the "Jesus film" in their own tongue. There was not a dry eye.

Kabir worked in the black economy, packing potatoes in Boston. When going there on the bus one day, they were in a traffic jam. The driver decided to take a short cut. Then he got lost. Kabir said, "My God will show us the way and he directed them down the country lanes. A police car was blocking their way. "Look what your God has done" they cried at Kabir. "Never" he said, "My God will help us." And the police car drove ahead of them and led all these men, working in the black economy, to Boston, Lincolnshire!

Another time Kabir was in the factory, and they were all taken into the canteen. He found himself sitting in front of a plain clothed police man. "Papers!" "I don't have any." They were about to take his finger prints. He knew he would be put in detention, so he prayed. "Jesus, if ever I needed You, it is now." The policeman turned round to speak to someone, and Kabir quietly rose to his feet and crept out of the door into the dark night. Then he ran with a host of people trying to catch him. He found his way to a road, and then phoned me.

"Richard, please pray for me," and the phone went dead. He phoned a second, and then a third time. I heard him say, "It's all right Richard, I can see a signpost to Boston." He walked five miles into Boston wearing only a thin shirt, and sat in doorway until 2am. He was shivering with cold. A car stopped and a door opened, "What are you doing there? Get in." He sat next to a man who heard his story.

"Come home with me," he said, and he took Kabir home, gave him some fish to eat and then took him back to the factory where he crept quietly onto the bus. The driver told him to lie on the floor, because a lot of people were looking for him. And Kabir was then taken back to Doncaster. He has not been to Boston since.

Kabir told his brother Zahir on the phone, in Pakistan, about Jesus. His brother said he too would start to follow Jesus. He told Kabir he was on the road, walking to Lahore, to find someone who would tell him more. I made contact with OM, and when they were satisfied that this was genuine they agreed to help. We gave Zahir the phone number of OM. They linked up and OM provided accommodation for him for two weeks whilst they shared the gospel with him.

Zahir returned to his family a believer. His mother cried, "What shall I do now? Two sons who are Christian. No one will talk to me in village. I will not be able to go to the shops."

On the Sunday, Kabir came to church with a small shoulder bag – all he possessed in the world. He looked so sad. I asked what was the problem. "I'm going to Canada," he said. Then he told me that Zahir had been stabbed by his elder brother, and was probably dead. The whole church prayed. "Wait Kabir," I said. "If, in a week, you feel the same then go to Canada."

He phoned me at 2pm and said that Zahir was just alive in hospital. An old man had given him blood freely. As the days went by, Zahir recovered and Kabir became stronger than ever.

Abbas is a Muslim who came to court to support Ibrahim. Poor Ibrahim lost his case, but Abbas talked to Christine all day as they sat in the waiting area. He had been thinking hard. I have said to him many times, "stop thinking Abbas and believe". Two weeks ago in the Thursday night Bible Study in our home, the place was so full no more could get in. For the first time however we had no interpreter. I asked Abbas to interpret, but am not really happy with a non-believer interpreting, but there was no choice. He did really well. He then took me into the hall and said, "This morning I gave my life to Christ. Can I tell the people?" and he did.

We must have purchased 250 Farsi New Testaments and 40 in Pushtu for Kabir and Armhad.

Many asylum cases were getting positive results. The people at court were asking, "What is happening in Doncaster?" What indeed!

Baptisms continued, and by the end of 2004 we had been able to baptise over 90 believers. Some were family groups.

105. Joys and sorrows

Ali Raza Kahazi is a Kurdish speaking man from Northern Iran. He was being persecuted in Iran and fled to UK, seeking asylum because of the atrocities being conducted in Northern Iran and Northern Iraq upon the Kurdish people. Saddam Hussein had conducted genocide, destroying whole villages with poisoned gas, and in the confusion, Ali, who was a little boy at the time, fled into the country, leaving his mother behind him. He had lost his mother and had never seen her since he was a small boy. However, he believed that she was in a village in Northern Iraq and when he came to Doncaster he met some Kurdish people who lived in that village. He asked about his mother and they said they knew that she was alive. He persisted and eventually made contact and found that he had a mother who was alive in Northern Iraq. He was able to make personal contact and to his amazement, Ali, who was brought up a Muslim, found that his mother was now a Christian believer. Ali had been attending our church for some weeks and was totally overjoyed to have found his mother and that she is a Christian lady. We celebrated for days.

Ali Raza Kahazi had a friend who lived in the same house in Doncaster called Syed and Ali invited him to church. Syed was a food exporter from Iran to different countries, including the Philippines. This permitted him to travel and whilst in the Philippines he had met and married a Philippino girl who was a Methodist. That caused no trouble until one day at Christmas his wife and children attended the Iranian Embassy in one of the Gulf states and when they were asked questions the Iranian authorities found that Ali, who was a Muslim, had married a Christian girl from the Philippines. Ali was arrested and was in great danger because this is a capital offence. He managed to get some money together and come quickly to the UK in great fear. He was, of course, welcomed and found a family in our Iranian church.

On the day before Syed's full asylum hearing, he came to me and said that his little boy was in intensive care unit in Tehran and was unconscious. On the day of his hearing we were travelling back in the car from the court. He received a telephone call from the hospital in Tehran saying his little boy had died and they wanted to turn off the life support. Did they have permission? We pulled off the motorway and I spoke to the consultant, confirming the message, and we requested that they keep the life support going and give this boy another 24 hours and do their best for him. Treatment of course is very expensive in Tehran and they were questioning who was going to pay the hospital bill.

The next day Syed came to say that they had turned off the life support, his little boy had died and now the authorities would not release the body for burial until a lot of money was handed over. The poor man was totally distraught. We were able to support him with an interest free loan and he was able to send this to Tehran. The body was released. The Christian church in the Philippines gave him a burial but it took a long time to heal Syed's great sorrow. Finally however he came through with a wonderful testimony that God is with us, even in the darkest days. Syed is one of our keenest evangelists.

106. The truth
Reza met an Iranian girl in College. He told her about Jesus. She said she had studied the Koran in depth for seven years and knew all about Jesus. "But this is different," said Reza. So Zorah came two days later to our Thursday evening Bible Study. There were about 50 people there. She sat on the couch and cried all the time. That night she read the New Testament for herself. "It's so different to the Koran," she said, and in the early hours she accepted Jesus for herself.

About three months later, Zorah was baptised. She was radiant. Then on the Monday evening she came to our house in tears. Christine sat her down on the settee, and we listened to her story. "I woke this morning," she said, "so happy after my baptism, and yet so very sad." There was a long pause. "You see – I have lied to my solicitor. My statement is largely untrue."

Her full hearing at court was to be on the Thursday. She asked me what she should do. We looked at John 14, that Jesus is Truth, and the Holy Spirit is the Spirit of Truth. I explained that she was full of the Spirit at her baptism, and the Spirit of Truth was grieved by her lies to the solicitor. I asked her to go home and let me know if she wanted me to explain all this to her solicitor. A few hours later she phoned, and I then contacted her solicitor. I knew what would happen. The solicitor could no longer represent her. She received a phone call from the solicitor who was also a Christian lady, who told Zorah she had done the right thing, but she now had no one to represent her.

Colin and I went to court on the Thursday and asked for an adjournment. We were in front of an adjudicator who we believed was also a Christian. He granted an adjournment because Zorah had no solicitor and when we asked if he would hear the case personally next time, he agreed that, because he had spent a long time reading all her papers, that would be wise. Eight weeks later we were in court again with her. The adjudicator gave her a hard time, but in the end she got a positive. Elizabeth and her husband Nasser came to us in 2003. She is from South Africa and has been a Christian for many years with a lot of experience in a house church there. She has such a winsome way of speaking to the Iranians, and is a very spiritual lady, and is conscious of the power of the Holy Spirit. Clearly she has been sent to us to share in the teaching and pastoral ministry.

On 1 April 2005 Kabir attended Court in Newcastle for his full hearing, whether or not he should be sent back to Afghanistan. The Home Office representative began to weep when he heard Kabir's story. The adjudicator said to Kabir, "I am not a Christian, but tell me why I should become a Christian". Kabir then began to tell him the story of Jesus walking on the water and inviting Peter to come to Him. As Peter walked on the water he began to sink, but Jesus reached out His hand and lifted him up and helped him. Kabir said 'sometimes the water is very rough and very dangerous and we do know what to do. We look up and see Jesus and He holds his hands out to us when we attempt to move towards him. Sometimes we begin to sink but then we feel His strong hand lifting us up and we are safe. That is for everyone' said Kabir. The adjudicator gave him leave to stay in the UK as a genuine seeker of asylum.

107. The future
It feels like a mini revival situation, but what of the future? We do not know. Will many of them leave Doncaster for the big cities? Will

they maintain their first love? Will they want to form their own church? I guess those are questions we do not need to ask, but rather we should spend ourselves in sharing the good news of Jesus whilst Iranian people are so receptive. My dream is that there will be some genuine believers amongst them who will rise up as leaders and be willing to return to Iran when the revolution comes - return and evangelise their own people. From Iran to the neighbouring countries until the Muslim world hears and responds to the gospel.

It is ironic that after September 2001 I was compelled to write a paper called - a Christian perspective on 9/11. I asked what Christians were doing to share the faith with Muslim people. God graciously opened a door and gave Christine and myself an answer.

So the work goes on. As of the beginning of 2005, there are between 100 and 120 at the morning Farsi speaking service. Nearly 100 have been baptised. We are so thankful to have been able to play a small part in something which is quite unique in our experience.

FINAL DAYS

108. Lord, teach us to number our days
(From here Richard's style is more like an ongoing journal - Editor)

6th December 2004.
Since coming back from our cruise in the Mediterranean in November, I am increasingly struggling in health. My blood pressure has gone up to 230/160. I have started on Benzoflurazodine, then double beta blockers. The old heart is still thumping away. What will fail - stroke, retinal haemorrhage, kidneys? My only concern is for my love Christine, that she will be looked after and not be too bereft.

End of March 2005
Since about February 2005 I have found my feet unsteady, particularly the left side. I have dropped things with the left hand. Not only have I been clumsy but I have not been able to think as clearly as I would like. I saw a neurologist at the end of March 2005 who was sure clinically there was a space occupying lesion on the right side. I had a CT scan last week which confirmed this lesion in the thalamus and then saw Dr Jellynek last week, who confirmed the lesion and that there was some oedema which might respond to steroids, so I have started on steroids and feel a little improvement already. The plan is to see David Levy next week. It is wonderful that this radio-oncologist in Sheffield is a member of Matthew's church, a Jew who came to faith 2/3 years ago.

God has been very good in providing friends to help and support at every stage in this journey. Jean has been here at home every day offering to help practically in so many ways. Barbara came down from Edinburgh to spend a few days and help us. It was particularly valuable for Christine who carries the work load very bravely. The practical problems are transferring from bed to wheelchair and then to commode and trying to avoid falling over and bruising myself. The Iranians have been here every day offering support and Rod and Mary Potter have been marvellous. Rod has been in each evening to help get me to bed. One cannot say how valuable the help of Christian brothers and sisters has been. James and Katie and their little family are with us this weekend and again offering both practical help and it is lovely to see them all, and it lifts the heart to see a new generation beginning to pray and trust in the Lord.

At the present time my two eldest grandsons Benjamin and Joel, are in Scotland climbing the peaks of Ben Nevis with their Uncle Daniel and Auntie Barbara. We heard yesterday they caught some trout and discovered an owl pellet which they dissected and reconstructed the skeleton of a vole. I wish I was there to share their excitement with the wind blowing over the peaks and through the heather, and the sound of the rushing mountain stream. I remember as a youth climbing the strong hills of Scotland, particularly the Five Sisters of Kintail, and experiencing the presence of Jehovah, the great creator God in this wonderful landscape, and I know that my little grandsons will be capturing the same flavour of this wonderful experience at this present time.

I would challenge anyone who is uncertain of the reality and our need to fear Jehovah to climb the highlands of Scotland and look for the Creator God, the Great Jehovah, who understandably would be angry with our arrogance, our pride, our selfishness and our sin committed to one another, and then open the New Testament and see the cross of our Lord Jesus Christ where the wrath of God was satisfied. That would be a pilgrimage for any uncertain soul.

They travelled north by train a few days ago. I told them they would receive their tickets when they got onto the platform as a gift from their Uncle Daniel and Auntie Barbara. They were travelling first class, and they could be sure they would get to journey's end because they had the right ticket – a first class ticket. In life this ticket has been purchased for us at a great price, and it is free. It is God's gift of salvation, purchased at Calvary, at great price and is ours to receive and promises a safe journey and a confident arrival. This ticket is the assurance of the Holy Spirit in the heart when we give our hearts to Jesus. It is God's seal, which cannot be explained but can only be experienced. It is best received when young but is available at any age, if we will reach out and receive. I have discovered that here towards the end of the journey I do not have to look for Jesus, he is already there with a welcome, and with such joy and peace which is quite miraculous. I am sure that is a promise for any traveller and the mountain peaks of Jehovah the great creator God are there waiting for us.

Easter Saturday – 26th March
Yesterday was Good Friday 2005, when I had a telephone call from Raza John. Raza said, 'Richard, I had a very vivid dream last night which I must share with you. There was a man and a little boy walking down a road and the man was holding the hand of the little boy. I said, 'who is the little boy?' and the man said, 'It is Richard Porter' and I said 'who are you?' and he said, 'I am the Apostle Paul'. So perhaps my hand has been held by the Apostle Paul over these many years. I remember as a boy reading the book 'Paul the Dauntless' and it did influence my life a great deal.

11th April
Morning meditation – 'all things praise thee Lord most high, Heaven and earth and sea and sky.'

I sit in our lounge picture window drinking in the colourful delight of the spring garden. I see a regiment of scarlet tulips standing facing the sun to respect their commanding officer. To the right and left are waving yellow daffodils and white narcissi, sharing the praise of the spring morning creation. All things praise thee; Lord, may we.

12th April
Meditation for a fellow traveller. –

For someone at the end of the day who is a little anxious about the events of the day past or concerned about the night hours and the following day. Psalm 91 – 'He who dwells in the shelter of the most High will rest in the shadow of the Almighty'. I would say of the Lord, He is my refuge and my fortress, my God in whom I trust. Where is this shelter of the most High? It is sometimes called the secret place of the most High. It is not secret because it is difficult to find, but secret because it is a safe place. To be there in a secret place means to be resting in the shadow of the Almighty.

Jesus promised the secret place to his disciples. He said in John's Gospel, 'You are not servants but friends.' A master does not tell his servant what he is doing but he does tell his friends. He tells his friends all his secrets. That is what a friend is, someone who shares secrets. The secret things belong unto our God but the things that are revealed belong unto us and our children forever. God is a revealing

God and that becomes our experience. The secrets, however, are delightful, which Jesus shares with those He loves and who will follow. The Psalm continues 'there will be no fear for the one who dwells there. Whatever may happen round about, (verse 11) 'He will give His angels command concerning you, to guard you in all your ways'. Amazing that He commands angels to protect us. Who will guard us today? Angels – they will lift us up in their hands when my poor old feet wobble around and feel insecure. They are angels commanded to guard and bear me up so that my foot will not strike against a stone. That is a promise for us all, and what a comfort.

End April
Now I am not very well with this brain tumour.

I heard tonight that last Friday Raza's father, who is a Mullah in Tehran called together 120 Muslims to pray for me and for improvement in my health.

Dr Ku from China telephoned with encouragement, support and prayer. Our house is full of cards from China, Romania, Korea and around the world and many from Britain also. These friendships mean much and I am sure will be renewed one day in Heaven.

Early May - 4am
Short meditation –

Tonight I have been in the middle of Psalm 24, standing in wonder before the hill of the Lord. Someone is asking the question, who can climb the hill of the Lord, or stand in His holy place, and here am I this night with cautious steps, placing them on the path up the hill of the Lord. This is the creator God who has made the Earth. It is His. He has established it and here is a rising path inviting this simple sinner to hide himself in the mercy of God. Here on the hill is a cross, a simple wood, a bowed head covered with a crown of thorns, blood to wash the guilty clean. Here is one, the King of Glory, my Jesus, my Lord. But the waver of my hands can fulfil the Lord's demands, could my zeal no respite know, could my tears forever flow, that I see Him on his azure throne, He must save and you alone. Welcome, welcome King of Glory, open our gates, come in, come in. There was no other good enough to pay the price of sin, only you can unlock the gate of

Heaven and let us in. Come on my brothers and sisters up this hill to see and kneel before this Lord of Glory. On his merits alone we are offered clean hands and a pure heart, and dare I say with confidence, to receive grace to help in time of need.

Psalm 125, verses 1 and 2
Those who trust in the Lord are like Mount Zion,
which cannot be shaken but endures forever.
As the mountains surround Jerusalem,
so the Lord surrounds His people, both
now and forevermore.
Underneath and round about are the
Everlasting arms.

Mid May

I was lying in bed last night and had a strange feeling that I was floating in a sea of love, of kindness and prayer of many friends across the world and here in my home town. How can you put a measure on that? I would encourage any who read this to remember the words of Jesus, 'Do to other people as you would like them to do to you' and there is another word; 'Cast your bread on the waters and it will return to you after many days'. Indeed that is true. Don't be afraid to share the good things you have received with a waiting, needy, hurting world.

I have decided that there is only one thing that matters in this world, and that is love. There is enough to go round if people are generous enough. And love is of God - 1 Corinthians 13 is the key chapter. 'If we don't have love we have nothing'. It has taken me a long time to learn the depths of that in an everyday experience.

It seems to me that at the beginning of the 21st century there is a movement of God's spirit across the world, converting, renewing, reviving, from China through Central Europe, across the Islamic countries. I was able to share with the Iranian church two Sundays ago, a word that I believe was prophetic in Isaiah, about God's servant Syrus, anointed and chosen, and I thought the Persian Church from Afghanistan through to Iran, Iraq, is a chosen instrument to share the good news of Jesus with the Muslim people across that part of the world. This may well be the hope for the future, when there is so much terror and fear in the world today.

I would say to you young people, identify where God is at work if you can, and share in that Ministry. The world and all Heaven is waiting. The key words, I think, are love, forgiveness, confidence, commitment.

I was reminded of the need we had for a ladder to gain entrance into the loft of our house. I did have a ladder that went up, but my good friend Rod Potter said that is not the way. You need a ladder that comes down, and he constructed a ladder in the loft which pulls down, so that we could climb up into the loft.

When Jacob had his dream and Daniel was promised a vision of Heaven, there was a ladder of angels coming down and going up. First we need a ladder that comes down, and Jesus is that ladder. That will provide a staircase to Heaven. I am on my way upstairs with this secure ladder from Heaven. I don't have to establish my own ladder but I have to have confidence to step onto the ladder already provided by God's grace and love. There is no other way but the cross of Jesus. It says clearly, there is no other way for a man or a woman or a child to be saved. No other name under Heaven, given amongst men whereby we must be saved, but Christ Jesus. If there was another way God would have used it, rather than allow His only Son to suffer so much for us.

I apologise if this paragraph has turned into a sermon. It is meant to be a testimony.

So Lord, teach me to number my days. Would I do anything different? Not at all.

> *"Let me labour for the Master from the dawn to setting sun,*
> *let me tell of all His wondrous love and care,*
> *then when all of life is over and my work on earth is done,*
> *when the roll is called up yonder I'll be there"*
> ....by the grace and love of my Saviour.

Editor
Richard passed away at home peacefully at 2.30pm on 20th July 2005. He was bed ridden for the last month, rational but increasingly sleepy. He was not in any great pain, and received the most loving care by Christine at home, supported by family, friends and nursing care. Apart from the odd days of discomfort, worry and confusion, he remained calm in himself and so aware of the reality of heaven. His very last words, the day before he died, to Christine were: 'I love you, precious', followed by 'I love you, Jesus'.

Glory to God!